HOLY WAR

HOLY WAR

COWBOYS, INDIANS, AND 9/11s

MARK CRONLUND ANDERSON

 University of Regina Press

Printed and bound in Canada at Friesens

Cover design: Duncan Campbell, University of Regina Press
Text design: John van der Woude Designs
Copy editor: Dallas Harrison
Index: Patricia Furdek
Proofreader: Kristine Douaud
Cover art: "Army action figures" by Kitch /Veer

Library and Archives Canada Cataloguing in Publication
Anderson, Mark Cronlund, 1960-, author
Holy war : cowboys, Indians, and 911s / Mark Cronlund Anderson.

Includes bibliographical references and index. Issued in print and electronic formats. ISBN 978-0-88977-414-8 (paperback).—ISBN 978-0-88977-416-2 (html).—ISBN 978-0-88977-415-5 (pdf)

1. Mass media and war—United States—History. 2. War and society—United States—History. 3. Imperialism—History. 4. Popular culture—United States—History. 5. Indians in popular culture—United States—History. 6. War—Religious aspects—History. 7. September 11 Terrorist Attacks, 2001. I. Title.

P96.W352U55 2016   303.6'60973   C2016-900752-9   C2016-900753-7

We acknowledge the support of the Canada Council for the Arts for our publishing program. We acknowledge the financial support of the Government of Canada. / Nous reconnaissons l'appui financier du gouvernement du Canada. This publication was made possible through Creative Saskatchewan's Creative Industries Production Grant Program.

CONTENTS

ACKNOWLEDGEMENTS

Adapted sections of Chapter 1 and Chapter 8 first appeared in "The U.S. Frontier Myth, American Identity, and 9/11," *Journal of Psychohistory* 38, 4 (2011): 314–27, and "Intercultural Communication, the American Frontier Myth, and Several 9-11s," in *From Here to Diversity: Globalization and Intercultural Dialogues*, ed. Clara Sarmento (Newcastle upon Tyne: Cambridge Scholars Publishing, 2010), 75–86. Sections of Chapter 4 previously appeared in "The Mythical Frontier, the Mexican Revolution, and the Press: An Imperial Subplot," *Canadian Review of American Studies* 37, 1 (2007): 1–22.

Many thanks to my terrific research assistants for their invaluable help—Jessica Brown, Melissa Lalonde, Aaron Muir, Melissa Munro, and Anna Weber. I am also grateful for grant support from the Social Sciences and Humanities Research Council of Canada and the President's Research Fund at Luther College, University of Regina. Big thanks also to Duncan Campbell, Karen Clark, Donna Grant, and Bruce Walsh at the University of Regina Press. Finally, and most importantly, my family has endured a lot of shenanigans as well as inspired my best efforts, such as they are. Thanks and much love to Madelaine, Dagmar, and Carmen. It is no exaggeration to say that I would be fairly lost without them.

CHAPTER 1

INTRODUCTION: "A MISSION FROM GOD"

Long ago he formed an ideal conception of omnipotence
and omniscience which he embodied in his gods. Whatever
seemed unattainable to his desires—or forbidden
to him—he attributed to these gods. One may say,
therefore, that these gods were the ideals of his culture.
—Sigmund Freud[1]

I am persuaded no constitution was ever before
as well crafted as ours for extensive empire.
—Thomas Jefferson[2]

Noam Chomsky and George W. Bush seldom find reason to agree, but they both argued that 9/11 stood alone in United States history. Nothing like it had happened before, they said. And to be sure, nobody had earlier crashed planes into the World Trade Center towers. That was new. Both men, deeply committed and well-intentioned ideologues, heroes to their adoring fans, stressed the point. "For the first time, the guns have been trained the other way," Chomsky said as a part of a series of interviews that were published as a book. He noted emphatically that the continental United States had not been attacked directly on its home turf since the War of 1812.[3]

Both men also agreed that the United States had been attacked by savages. In his nationally televised address to the nation on September 11, 2001, Bush noted, "thousands of lives [were] ended by evil, despicable acts of terror....[T]oday our nation saw evil, the very worst of human nature."[4] It is hard to argue with such sentiments.

Yet it lies precisely here that Bush and Chomsky neglected something intrinsic to 9/11 because once the United States launched the two ill-fated wars in Afghanistan and Iraq the story no longer seems unique. The reason is simple. The 9/11 event and the response to it, collectively the "9/11 story," are as old as the nation that was born fighting Native Americans. In other words, considered as simulacra, as mythopoesis, such 9/11-like stories have played out again and again in American history. If you consider the 9/11 story from the way the news media cast it,[5] you find that it not merely mirrors America's violent and nurturing mythical frontier conflict, it is the frontier conflict. As John Mead has argued, the cultural response to 9/11 symbolized "the reopening of the American frontier and the collective reinvestment in our Manifest Destiny."[6] In other words, the 9/11 story reprises an old-fashioned, updated Indian[7] war.

And so 9/11 was not, and is not, new. Instead, it spins a primal American yarn dating to the earliest days of settlement in the seventeenth century. It is America's own creation story. In its initial expression, it found Americans or, more accurately, proto-Americans forced to defend themselves against perceived Indian savagery. Early on such sentiments became well established in American popular culture in the form of captivity narratives, which focused imaginatively on the kidnapping of "white" females by "red" savages and the heroic manner in which the white women resisted their captors and were predictably "redeemed" by heroic white males.[8] In its infancy, the myth operated on a series of simple binaries. For example, the white Protestant settlers who laid the groundwork for inchoate American core culture were goodness itself, chosen by God, virtuous, decent, abstemious, hard-working, whereas the Indians were bad, Satan's minions, barbaric, out of control, profligate, and lazy. Interpretation of scripture not merely shaped this construction but breathed life into it. In today's parlance, we might call those Indians "terrorists," but initially, and then especially in the centuries that followed (because the Indian wars lasted with few interruptions for nearly 300 years), we have come to know them better as the Sioux, Pawnee, Apache, and so on. In particular, for more than a century, Hollywood westerns have served up a smorgasbord of Indians cast as veritable monsters.

The early Indian wars set the stage and provided a kind of necessary cohesive impetus for early settlement and subsequent expansion across the continent generation by generation. It is difficult to overstress the importance of the early conflicts because they established a cultural framework, a community, an emerging nation, in which America organically embraced its self-sense of divine mission, better known to us nowadays as American exceptionalism. One consequence of the long Indian wars is that those proleptical Indian savages became archetypal. One outcome is that, as portrayed in popular culture, Mexicans, Nicaraguan revolutionary Augusto Sandino, Saddam Hussein, former Panamanian leader Manuel Noriega, and so many Central Americans, Vietcong, conflated Arabs/Muslims, and countless other "Others" have subsequently played the role of Indian stand-in(s) in later American conflicts that popular culture presented as structural, spiritual, and emotional heirs of the early Indian wars. Mythical, in other words. These are the subject of this book.

The perpetrators of 9/11 may be considered Indian stand-ins, conveniently cast in the role of "imaginary" Indians, adhering to a settler nation's shared illusions.[9] Americans have also imagined that they are a chosen people, thus exceptional, special, almost virginal. God—the one with the long white beard and the one whom George W. Bush identified as having chosen him to rule—loves America most, after all. God chose America and blessed it. God chose Bush, according to him, to lead in the war on terror that erupted after 9/11. "I am driven with a mission from God," he said.[10] Americans have claimed divine succor and sanction for 400 years. Accordingly, the nation assumes the right to strike at its enemies with extreme force because the right of self-defense is embraced as timeless and universal. By the nineteenth century, writes Anders Stephanson, "Peace and annihilation were seemingly two sides of the same coin."[11] Also, crucially, America draws its right to exist as having been granted to it by God. Righteous payback thus punctuates American history from centuries-long war against Aboriginals, to the Mexican War, war with Spain, interventions in Central America, war against Vietnam, to note just a few examples.

Despite the obvious horrors of 9/11, by engaging and defeating the "new Indians," the nation thereby affirms its core character as an exceptional people, a freedom-and-democracy-loving-mom-and-apple-pie utopia that, as it happens, also symbolically rebirths itself violently because the nation was born in violence fighting Indians. Herein abides a lusty, onanistic impulse busy at work in the circular and redemptive frontier narrative. As Stacy Takacs has observed about the response to 9/11, "Politicians and pundits alike depicted Americans as innocents besieged by wild savages and desperate for strong men with guns to rescue them. President George W. Bush, in particular, laced his public performances with frontier 'folkisms' calculated to reassure the public that he was a strong, capable leader.... [T]he U.S. could do no wrong because its mission was 'defensive.'"[12] So the 9/11 story is not simply about payback for 9/11 but also about payback as a gesture to a life-affirming ritual that birthed the nation in war against Indians. One result is that one might expect to find evidence of such in popular culture.

"IMAGE OF THEIR COMMUNION"

The 9/11 story, then, is not simply as old as the American nation; in a "thick" way,[13] it *is* the nation in its most elemental form: rebirthed and bathed in violence against symbolic Indians. The key idea is that nations constitute "imagined communities," Benedict Anderson has argued in a widely influential book. The nation, Anderson argues, "is *imagined* because even the members of the smallest nation will never know most of their fellow-members, meet them, or even hear of them, yet in the minds of each lives the image of their communion."[14] "Nations, like narratives," writes Homi Bhabha, "lose their origins in the myths of time, and only fully realize their horizons in the mind's eye."[15] The stories they share, we share, and constitute our national communities, bound by deep feeling, commitment, common purpose, and comity. Anderson shows that the press of necessity plays a key role in promulgating such communities,[16] in part functioning as a kind of synecdoche, where the part stands in for the whole. If Anderson and Bhabha are correct, you can anticipate that a nation's popular culture will express and champion its myths.

The press also importantly wired the nation, drawing together disparate groups and peoples separated by geography and local custom. Additionally, the press provided and maintains a common national language and in this way is traditionally understood as preparing the "rough draft" of history.[17] Myth is central, according to Bhabha, because myth provides a warm and reassuring cloak, a gooey, self-fulfilling substance that naturalizes all it touches, the current that runs through media content to grant meaning to the bits of information conveyed (and chosen to convey). Myth offers the narrative shell and the adhesive that gums American culture together. In this way, members of a nation all are culpable for the promulgation of the stories we share about what we believe and share—including "scholarship, religion, science, politics, mass media, the workplace, theology, and recreation," notes Beverly J. Stoeltje.[18] Myth provides the stories as well as the language that render the nation intelligible to itself.

The media's 9/11 story also derives from a deep mythical precedent: America's frontier narrative. Its creation story. It serves up a contemporary retelling of America's creation myth and serves the invaluable and necessary function of ritual symbolic rebirth. So, yes, war may in fact be hell, as Civil War General William Tecumseh Sherman quipped, but it also can be life-affirming because it may symbolically retrace the nation's founding conflict. This is precisely the argument of two of the more influential historical studies published in the twentieth century: Henry Nash Smith's *Virgin Land: The American West as Symbol and Myth* and Richard Slotkin's *Regeneration through Violence: The Mythology of the American Frontier, 1600–1860.*[19]

Recognizing a pattern of ongoing symbolic rebirth is critical to understanding the 9/11 story because the frontier tale expresses what scholar Eldon Kenworthy has aptly called America's "founding myth."[20] It is the mythical tale of America's birth. An article in *Newsweek* discussing oil development in Alaska put it this way: "America's founding myths are largely about taming wild places. The frontier shaped the

American character even as we shaped it, moving from the Allegheny Mountains to the Mississippi, and onward to the Missouri, the Rocky Mountains and the Pacific. But the frontier is all but gone now [in 2001], and what remains occupies a unique place in the American psyche."[21] The author here romanticizes the frontier and conflates historical reality with the imagination but does so appropriately, that is, mythically. Again, myths are the stories we tell ourselves about ourselves to give meaning to our collective existence. "Mere frequency of repetition appears to confirm their authenticity," observes Ray Raphael.[22] Like religion, myth explains where we came from, how we should behave, where we are going, and why.

Myth operates as a fusion, to quote Smith, of "concept and emotion into an image."[23] Myths serve as the glue that binds a nation together, Joseph Campbell has widely and influentially argued.[24] They are "Born of the womb of cultural necessity," as Gregory M. Pfitzer puts it.[25] "A mythology is a complex of narratives that dramatizes the world vision and historical sense of a people or culture, reducing centuries of experience into a constellation of compelling metaphors," adds Slotkin.[26] In short, "A people cannot coherently function without myth," observes John Hellman.[27]

Mythical space is almost perfectly fungible, and linear time, which usually dictates the academic telling of history, must take a back seat to the mythical tale. "Myths are descriptions of processes, accounts not merely of what has taken place, but of what now takes place and of what will take place in the future: the process is assumed to be timeless."[28] As "story" the myth "repeats itself as if it were the 'beginning.'... [It] is repeated over and over for each new generation as myth, epic, history, war, art, novel, and film retell the story."[29] In this way, as I will endeavor to illustrate, many 9/11s preface our current 9/11 story. In other words, the frontier myth erases linear time while simultaneously employing it as evidence of its own truth, as in the 9/11 story.

But let me pause before going any further because you might by now reasonably object and point out that 9/11 was situated clearly in space and time. Real planes hurtled into real buildings, and these real buildings burned and fell down, and thousands of real people died, real wars ensued, and then more real people died. And I would agree.

Yet the story reaches much deeper. The American frontier myth does not merely sanction American conflict but indeed insists on it, in what Slotkin has identified as a process of "regeneration through violence."[30] At a basic level, the results of such conflict—which begins with an unprovoked attack by one's enemies and is followed by vigorous and justifiable counterattack—provide the nation with potentially limitless bounty of continual rebirth since conflict serves the purpose of symbolically reenacting the nation's own founding war. "Others," in this mythopoeic yarn, so reek of treachery, Godlessness, and darkness as to invite conquest, effortlessly playing the role imaginary Indians had centuries ago.[31] Indeed, it surfaces widely in American literature and film, studies have shown, from the novels of James Fenimore Cooper to the *Rambo* movies, *Avatar*, the hit TV zombie series *The Walking Dead*, and the 9/11 story.

"TRAUMA DEMANDS REPETITION"

Like a child birthed in violence, a nation born in war may become hard-wired to repeat the behavior, suggests a generation of psychohistorical research.[32] "Trauma demands repetition" and will thus replay over a lifetime when it becomes fixed in the character during the formative stages of development.[33] The result is that "re-enactment of victimization is a major cause of violence."[34] In this way, the trauma of being born in war becomes neatly and self-fulfillingly circular because it is compulsively revisited and serves the useful purpose of mythical rebirth. It is like, to paraphrase baseball legend Yogi Berra, déjà vu all over again. In a sense, then, early trauma plays out like a broken record over the course of a life. In this way, a nation born in war may become destined to reexperience the trauma/narrative in such a way that war becomes revivifying.

It is a well-established phenomenon. For example, one widely cited study notes that "victims of trauma respond to contemporary stimuli as if the trauma had returned, without conscious awareness that past injury rather than current stress is the basis of their psychologic emergency responses."[35] Hence the knee-jerk obligation in America to consider perceived attacks upon it by employing aspects of the frontier narrative in whole or in part. Freud called it the "repetition compulsion."[36] Although his reputation has long since fallen into disrepair, the phenomenon he tagged endures. Even the popular journal *Psychology Today* cites it as a "common problem" that plagues human relationships.[37] As philosopher Mary Midgley observes in her book *The Myths We Live By*, "[O]ur imaginative visions are central to our understanding of the world...but are really fed by fantasy."[38] And so my point is just this: a nation born in the trauma of war will invariably and necessarily relive the trauma when threatened. If Anderson's observation about the key role played by the press in the creation and promulgation of nationalism is correct, then one might expect to find evidence, narrative strands and traces of the founding traumatic conflict, in the press and in popular culture more generally. I explore this idea by examining a variety of popular culture depictions of American conflict since the Mexican War, 1846–48. The dates are important because the Associated Press, which effectively inaugurated the birth of the wired nation, had just been created, in 1845.

Of course, the idea that "trauma demands repetition" also begs the questions of whether nations have explicable psychological makeups and, if they do, whether those collective psyches bear resemblance to the individual. The answers are yes and yes. It is pretty straightforward. Just think for a moment how we understand the nation as a kind of kinship, what Richard Grossman identifies as a "discursive overlap between the family and the nation." You have got the fatherland, the motherland, the founding fathers, mother earth, nations coming of age, the birth of a nation, nuns are your sisters, priests are your fathers, God is your father, Sam is your uncle, then God has a son, friends become brothers or sisters, and so on. The nation is all about family values. Again, Grossman writes, "The notion of an extended family also invokes authority based on a hierarchy that is deemed 'natural.'"[39] Further, adds David Leverenz, "Like any conception of manhood, an emphasis on honor functions ideologically, which is to say, as a social fiction constructed by empowered constituencies to further their power, yet felt as natural and universal law."[40] Thus, patriarchal familial organization engenders political and economic systems dominated by males, what Pfitzer terms a "national expression of 'self.'"[41]

North American culture is suffused with nationalist images that conjure up the gestation and maturation of its nation-states that parallel a human life cycle. And they constitute a kind of mythic civil religion where you pay your dues every time you get down on bended knee to pray to your flag or the queen or fallen soldiers who sacrificed and possibly died for you in distant lands. Rituals abound. The holiest of these, for America, is war, specifically frontier war, because the nation was born on the (socially constructed) frontier fighting (socially constructed) Indians. And it has never stopped fighting Indians. Trauma demands repetition.

Long after the nation was born, as a political entity the United States was birthed, bathed, and ushered forth from a maelstrom of conflict with England. So the country, too, was begat by war in its revolutionary period, "born and bred," as William Appleman Williams argued in his seminal study *Empire as a Way of Life*.[42] And this provides a well-deserved source for its famous opposition to imperialism. Let's face it: America hates imperialism because the country was born fighting imperialism.

But more than that, colonists-cum-Americans had been at war with Indians since the arrival of the first settlers, and, after the war of independence, newly minted Americans continued to war upon Indigenous peoples through the nineteenth century. These two conflicts—the short war with England and the long war against Indians—effectively fuse to fashion a mythical one-two punch in which the media play a vital role. Thus, if the country was born in war against England, then the nation—the primal entity upon which nationhood rests and around which the country coalesces (if unevenly)—was birthed fighting Indians. In short, what you get is a country that abhors imperialism (because it fought English imperialism) and a nation born in and to imperialism (because it fought to take Aboriginal and, before the Indians were finished off militarily, "half-breed" Mexican lands). Erik H. Erikson explains how this can happen in the most banal of ways: an "individual unconsciously arranges for variations of an original theme which he has not learned either to overcome or to live with."[43] It is what Bhabha refers to as "splitting."[44]

Don't believe it?

The United States, between 1798 and 1945, engaged in no fewer than 169 "uses of armed forces abroad."[45] Yet the United States, not unlike ancient Rome or seventeenth-century Spain or nineteenth-century Great Britain, has remained preoccupied with the idea that it offers a kind of salvation to the world. In other words, America casting its behavior as some variety of "humanitarian intervention" is nothing new. For that matter, Chomsky observes that this "was a standard description of European imperialist ventures in the nineteenth century."[46] America's unique contribution has been its homegrown frontier myth, employed to deride European imperialism in particular at the same time as rationalize its own imperial behavior. In circular fashion, the myth champions and rationalizes American expansionism as unavoidably good because it produces and promotes Americanization, a self-evident good, according to mythical Americana.[47] A Marine general in director Stanley Kubrick's film *Full Metal Jacket* puts it this way while explaining why the United States is involved in the Vietnam War in the first place: "Inside every gook, there is an American trying to get out."[48] Regarding genocidal American attempts to educate Indians, the nineteenth-century version of this was "kill the Indian to save the man."[49]

From its birth, through a decisive period of maturation in the nineteenth century, and up to today, like an unruly adolescent (it makes me think of Tom Sawyer) the United States fought and fought and fought—and still fights. These sometimes traumatizing and always conditioning actions imprinted upon the psychological makeup of the nation. And a pattern emerges. Despite hollow and frequently bellicose rhetoric that proclaims four-square in favor of peace and freedom and things such as isolationism or so-called "good neighbor" policy, the United States has been at war more or less every year since its inception.[50] "By 1930," writes Greg Grandin, "Washington had sent gunboats into Latin American ports over six thousand times."[51] E. Bradford Burns counts more than 150 interventions in the Caribbean Basin from the latter nineteenth century to the early 1980s.[52]

Since the Civil War, the more well-known hostilities include those waged against Indians, Spain (over Cuba), two invasions of Mexico, occupations of Costa Rica, Cuba, the Dominican Republic, Haiti,

Honduras, Nicaragua, and Panama, undeclared actions in Guatemala and El Salvador, contributions to toppling governments in Chile and Argentina, the First and Second World Wars, war in Korea, war in Vietnam, the first Gulf War, and wars in Iraq and Afghanistan. There were many more, of course, but these in particular were framed in popular culture and political discourse as frontier wars. The actual conditions for war are, of course, always different. New leaders, new fighters, new technologies, new enemies, arise. New issues surface that may prompt war that in turn may have little or nothing to do with the frontier myth. Yet frontier conflicts remain consistent across time.

To think about this in another way, consider the most popular American literary and film genre, the western, which draws its semiotic power from the frontier myth.[53] Violence resides lustily at its core. Without violence, the western is nothing.[54] And, like the western, popular sports—football, boxing, hockey, professional wrestling—glamorize and valorize violence as inherently heterosexually manly.[55] Americans outshoot, outrape, and outmurder other industrialized countries by wide margins. They are comparatively armed to the teeth. The national anthem promotes and champions violent behavior. Above it all soars the beloved bald eagle—understood inaccurately as the ultimate bird of prey. America's founding document, the Declaration of Independence, embraces aggressive self-defense as a central principle to incite and justify bloody revolution; it is in effect a call to arms. So, yes, the country has fought, likes to fight, is good at fighting, and champions particular forms of scripted violence, in the case of the frontier myth, that reenact symbolically the nation's birth in violence. Nothing is more American than regenerative imperial war,[56] if newspapers, magazines, movies, TV shows, and presidents tell us anything.

"A LONG TRAIN OF ABUSES"

The American penchant for war is often attributed to the Monroe Doctrine. Named for President James Monroe, the creed, issued in 1823 in response to the collapse of Spain's empire in the Americas (though Spain held on to Cuba and Puerto Rico till they were lost to the United States in the 1890s), famously warned European countries not to attempt to gain by Spain's loss. As such, it affirmed American commitment to oppose further European imperialism in the Americas. Nevertheless, the United States reserved for itself the right to intervene when and where it saw the need and was able to do so (it is worth remembering that the United States wasn't even a regional power in 1823). This was reified further with the Roosevelt Corollary issued by President Theodore Roosevelt in 1904.[57] That said, the importance of the corollary is often exaggerated because unilateralism has always defined America's behavior in the world, since George Washington's presidency. The doctrine was itself simply a more famous invocation of the "more generic" no-transfer policy.[58]

In other words, the desire for empire has never actually been disguised, though it generally has not been discussed in polite company. Yet all of the lower forty-eight states were forcibly taken either by the United States directly (growth to the Mississippi after 1783), or taken by others and then purchased (Louisiana Territory), or taken by the United States from peoples who had lived on that land for more than 10,000 years (the American southwest, from Texas to California). "Indians, maybe," John Wayne drawls in the classic western *Red River*, which with artful condensation retells the Mexican War.[59] This is a great movie line because it simultaneously collapses and deflects the ambiguity as it denies the ethical contradiction of American behavior. Wayne delivers it perfectly, half-cocked, bemused, as he prepares to take Texas for America by shooting a Mexican hired gun from his horse. There is no "maybe" about it.[60] Again, the proposition is simple: a nation born in violence is apt to repeat the behavior, like the proverbial gosling that trailed after the farmer who slew its mother.

Thus, for the United States, continuous warfare reaffirms the right to life. In fact, it celebrates birth by reenacting it or by interpreting events so as to wring symbolic rebirth from them. In this way, the 9/11 story is not at all unique; it merely adds another link in the chain of a long-established cultural pattern.[61] Consequently, when arch-foes Chomsky and Bush agreed that 9/11 stands alone, they were, at least mythically, quite mistaken. An analysis of the pattern reveals a close structural congruence among America's major conflicts, 9/11 and the reaction to it, and the frontier myth—its creation story. In common parlance, such conflicts, despite the very real horrors inflicted on various Americans and despite the ever-changing scenes and characters, civilian and military, refresh the nation.

The revolutionary struggle lasted till 1783, and hostilities were taken up again with Britain in 1812. The subsequent American victory effectively secured independence for the country, though it was small by today's standard. Yet its martial instincts were not tamed. In fact, just the opposite, for not only were Americans cut from imperial English cloth,[62] but also they had been forged more deeply and irritably by several decades of war against what came to be perceived and portrayed as an abusive parent, as in the Declaration of Independence:

> But when a long train of abuses and usurpations, pursuing invariably the same Object evinces a design to reduce them under absolute Despotism, it is their right, it is their duty, to throw off such Government, and to provide new Guards for their future security. Such has been the patient sufferance of these Colonies; and such is now the necessity which constrains them to alter their former Systems of Government. The history of the present King of Great Britain is a history of repeated injuries and usurpations, all having in direct object the establishment of an absolute Tyranny over these States.

The nineteenth century also witnessed ongoing and determined war against the Indigenous population—really, from day one of the colonies until the early 1890s, when the U.S. Army effectively ended it at Wounded Knee, South Dakota. This epochal engagement featured war with Mexico, 1846–48, from which the United States harvested California, New Mexico, Arizona, Texas, and morsels of Nevada and Colorado. It gathered new steam after the Civil War ended in 1865 and reached a point of near-national hysteria eleven years later upon the death of Colonel George Armstrong Custer. Later came war with Spain in the 1890s that wrested control of the Philippines from Spain, which the United States then held in various states of dependence till the 1980s, and Cuba, which remained bottled up until Fidel Castro took it back for Cubans in 1959, and Puerto Rico.

The twentieth century proved to be much the same. The United States turned inward slightly prior to the First World War—the period of so-called isolationism. But somebody forgot to tell Latin America, which saw its share of outright invasions, occupations, undeclared not-so-secret wars, and general meddling with murderous outcomes. Plus, the United States maintained its assault on Native Americans via administrative instruments,[63] set the domestic authorities loose on suspected "red" communists after 1918, and once again took after them, with a sustained determination that would last decades, beginning in the 1930s.[64] Then later came the Vietnam War, set against the backdrop of the cold war ("During the cold war Americans hated communism so much that they thought every Russian was a threat," writes Garry Wills[65]), and the two wars against Iraq, especially the latter, preposterously billed as payback for 9/11. And there were various engagements in Latin America, against Argentina (1970s), Brazil (1960s), Chile (1970s), Colombia (1990s–2010s), Cuba (1960s), El Salvador (1920s–90s), Grenada (1980s), Guatemala (1940s–90s), Nicaragua (1910s–80s), and Panama (1890s–1980s). I draw two conclusions from this overview—one, the pattern of continual, compulsive war is rather obvious; and, two, isolationism never happened.[66] U.S. foreign policy is instead better understood, from Washington's presidency to today, as unilateralist and meddlesome.[67] None of this is obscure academic knowledge; it might be considered common knowledge to those who simply read newspapers, because all of it was widely reported in the American press.[68] It is in this context that Grandin has aptly termed Latin America the "empire's workshop."[69]

By now you might have taken offense and want to rejoin that things are more complicated, not so reductive. For example, all countries engage in war from time to time. After all, nations, like people, one can argue, have a universal right to self-defense. Agreed. Every conflict has its own particular context and history; they can't all be reduced to one mythical explanation. The causes of, say, the Mexican War were particular to it, as were the causes of the first Gulf War, and this holds for all conflicts. True. I agree.

Yet still there remains a pattern of continuous warfare over the past two centuries that is unmatched in the Western world. Was it all self-defense? No, not really. It is clearly not the case that the United States can play the self-defense card with any consistency because, to begin with, it does not exist on a hostile continent—apart from its own aggressive behavior toward Indians and Mexicans and nonwhites within its domestic population. Europe, for example, beats North America hands down on this count over the past two centuries. Or take Mexico, America's southern neighbor, pilloried in American popular and political culture as preternaturally violent and exemplifying innate inferiority,[70] three decades younger than the United States, yet it has fought only when attacked directly (in turn, by France, Spain, the United States, France, the United States, and the United States). On the whole, Mexico has been, apart from having to repel foreign invaders, a more peaceful country than the United States (though it too waged war on its Aboriginal population).

Nonetheless, it lies here in America's posture as an innocent crying out in the name of self-defense that we must look for answers, because the United States has framed all of its conflicts as proper on the ground of self-defense. Without exception, its hundreds of conflicts have been justified this way. Countries, of course, invariably portray themselves this way during times of war. What makes the American case distinctive is its own specific cultural explanation, writ in frontier mythology and oozing from popular culture. More to the point, the pattern or framing of the initial conditioning wars has provided a narrative shell into which America's key conflicts fit neatly, affording self-defense a well-worn and comfortable trail, the frontier myth, a distinctive American genre, as the chapters in this book detail by tracing the frontier myth in various forms of popular cultural expression since 1846. The conditioning effects of centuries-long warfare against Indians, much of which was informal and unofficial (think Natty Bumppo or John Rambo or Arnold Schwarzenegger versus savage hordes), constitute a key strand, perhaps *the* key strand, of America's national DNA. To reiterate, "the relative permanence of early trauma" requires "its inevitable restaging in war, social violence, and economic injustice."[71] Again, trauma demands repetition.[72]

"ENCHANTED GARDEN"

The regenerative process at the heart of the frontier myth is best and most famously explicated in the "frontier thesis" or, as it is sometimes known, the "Turner thesis." Written in 1893 by Frederick Jackson Turner, a young professor at the University of Wisconsin, "The Significance of the Frontier in American History" would become the most important piece ever written by a historian in the United States. The roughly 10,000-word essay,[73] available on Google, offers a glorious and heroic endorsement of manifest destiny,[74] the idea that the United States had a divine sanction to expand ever westward and deliver the good news of capitalism, Protestantism, and democracy to those who might stand in the way.

Turner didn't invent anything. Instead, with rhetorical flair he articulated a long-standing American cultural vision. Thus, "the great frontier myth...could have been written virtually any time between the 1620s and 1880s," according to historian Fredrick Pike.[75] It appears like this. The United States was born of its frontier experience, necessarily violent because the frontier was overrun with wild animals and savage peoples. These savages (i.e., Indians) were in themselves the embodiment of untamed nature. Lone white male immigrants, laden with and tainted by so much sissified, urban, eastern, or effete European cultural ephemera (febrile aristocratic tendencies and all the immorality that they entail), ended up ineluctably on the frontier. Henry Nash Smith famously termed it an "enchanted garden." President Andrew Jackson raved that it was "free from the influence of European ideas and institutions."[76]

The mythical frontier proffers that meeting point of refinement—that is, cultural baggage that corrupted the easterner/European—and barbarism, a role conveniently played in the first case by Indians but later by any espied paganesque, nonwhite Other, Indian stand-in (e.g., Mexicans, Spaniards, Vietnamese, Iraqis). Turner simply called it the "meeting point between savagery and civilization."[77] He was a man of his age, Patricia Nelson Limerick notes, so "English-speaking white men were the stars of his story."[78] Turner referred to the process of white males going to the frontier over several centuries as a "perennial rebirth" of and for the nation.[79] "From east to west," he observed, "we find the record of social evolution."[80] He observed that

The frontier is the line of most rapid and effective Americanization. The wilderness masters the colonist. It finds him a European in dress, industries, tools, modes of travel, and thought. It takes him from the railroad car and puts him in the birch canoe. It strips off the garments of civilization and arrays him in the hunting shirt and the moccasin....In short, at the frontier the environment is at first too strong for the man. He must accept the conditions which it furnishes, or perish....The fact is, that here is a new product that is American.[81]

Conflict and conquest naturally ensued because, sooner or later, savages attack. That's what savages do. And when they do, says Turner, something special happens to those white male immigrants. Something magical. The trials and tribulations of the frontier, because of its dangers (which, by the way, elicited the abilities to prosper, to hunt, and to kill), strip the man (not the woman, for she stays indoors where she belongs or, more typically, back east) of his cultural freight. The alternative is death. The true frontiersman, once stripped down, *qua* the prototypical American Adam (think Edgar Rice Burroughs's *Tarzan of the Apes* or Owen Wister's titular *The Virginian*), or sometimes Jesus Christ[82] (think *Dances with Wolves* [1990] or *The Man Who Shot Liberty Valance* [1962]), not only survives but also prospers. He models America. He personifies America. Turner found that the process was both inevitable and universal wherever frontier conditions arose. (This would therefore include Argentina, Australia, Brazil, Canada, Chile, New Zealand, Russia, and Venezuela, because in each case one finds a settler nation pitted against Aboriginal peoples).

The personal characteristics required for American-style success on the frontier—honesty, hard-work ethic, rugged individualism, cleverness, Protestant virtue, mental and physical toughness, and so on—emerged spontaneously after the frontier worked its deterministic magic. According to Turner,

to the frontier the American intellect owes its striking characteristics. That coarseness of strength combined with acuteness and inquisitiveness; that practical, inventive turn of mind, quick to find expedients; that masterful grasp of material things, lacking in the artistic but powerful to effect great ends; that restless, nervous energy; that dominant individualism working for good and for evil, and withal that buoyancy and exuberance which comes from freedom—these are traits of the frontier, or traits called out elsewhere because of the frontier.[83]

Here in this American Eden, once the process of stripping down has been completed, the man reemerges as something entirely new. And as he does so he personifies the all-American archetype we know so well: white, male, strong, individualistic, clever, democratic, handsome, deeply suspicious of government, taciturn, honest, heterosexually decent, Protestant, a master of self-control, and, well, sexy in a meat-and-potatoes way. And notice, by the way, how the various elements of this list juxtapose neatly in binary fashion with the espied characteristics of the Other: nonwhite versus white, feminine versus masculine, weak versus strong, herd instinct versus individualism, stupidity versus cleverness, and so on—in short, and in sum, Indian versus frontiersman.

But more than that, the Turner essay presciently articulates America's creation story. So powerful has been the sway of its line of argument that it dominated the academy for decades, and "its importance as the canonical text of the frontier myth has never been surpassed."[84] This has been the case even after historians began, especially after the 1960s, to systematically demonstrate that on all of his major assertions Turner was flatly mistaken.[85] When "individual historians simply set aside the thesis and studied particular Western places, people and events," it led to "exploding the model," writes Limerick.[86]

And you might fairly expect as much. Stripped of culture, isn't the would-be American Adam/Moses/Jesus nothing more than a naked mammal without any operating software? Not according to the myth. Instead, once stripped down, the American Adam is reborn and reequipped with readily identifiable mythical characteristics. To picture them, think of the most popular actor in Hollywood history,

John Wayne,[87] whom historian Garry Wills cleverly termed "Manifest Destiny on a horse."[88] Or consider John Dunbar from *Dances with Wolves* or Jake Sully from *Avatar* (2009). Think Hollywood western or action star.

Those for whom the process did not occur, those who could not hack it, expired. Wave after wave of this mechanical process of stripping and rebirth populated the United States, the story continues, leaving in their wake a vigorous nation born specifically of this (inexorably violent) process. It is easy enough to conjure up images here of John Wayne, a younger Clint Eastwood, his hero Gary Cooper, even Ronald Reagan (to his admirers), or countless other western stars. But you might also consider *Alien*'s Ripley, Schwarzenegger's action heroes, Han Solo from *Star Wars*, Walter the Vietnam veteran from *The Big Lebowski* (1998), Rick the cop and his son Carl from *The Walking Dead* (2010–), and, insofar as he is a mediated construction, George W. Bush posturing in the weeks immediately following September 11.[89]

The frontier myth also identifies sacred American democracy as having been born on the frontier. Turner writes,

> But the most important effect of the frontier has been in the promotion of democracy....As has been indicated, the frontier is productive of individualism. Complex society is precipitated by the wilderness into a kind of primitive organization based on the family. The tendency is anti-social. It produces antipathy to control. The tax-gatherer is viewed as a representative of oppression....The frontier individualism has from the beginning promoted democracy.[90]

But here again Turner errs. White males did not flock to and populate the frontier as if it were some kind of safety valve. Instead, people pushed west in groups, usually organized around family units. Turner fixates on the individual male because he was a product of his times, a racist, male-centric, misogynistic world. Further, European immigrants did not pour onto the frontier. Although technically the land, in some cases, was free, travel to it was not. Nor were draft animals, farm equipment, seed, food, housing, and such.[91] And, in fact, it was easterners, seasoned Americans and not raw immigrants, who gave rise to democracy in the west and modified it to fit local needs. In other words, internal migrants to the west brought democracy and other WASP trappings with them.[92] Turner had the process of democratization backward. Democracy in the west really grew from eastern seeds.

Additionally, there exists no evidence that stripping down occurred, let alone mythical rebirth. When you think about it, it really makes no sense. But it makes cultural sense, even if Turner wasn't able to articulate precisely why. The reason is that the myth owes its gestation to the Puritans, religious outcasts whose views imprinted upon the emerging nation in the seventeenth century.[93] The frontier myth "had at its heart a Judeo-Christian rejection of Nature and Nature's God. Our national myths require too many concessions to primitive accumulation, ownership, and control," writes Pfitzer. As a result, wild nature, the land, "must be metaphorically cast as an obstacle to be overcome, as a stream to be forded, a prairie to be fenced, a path to be forged, and a native people to be annihilated."[94]

But what of the Indian? If the process was universal, as Turner claimed, then why were Indians not stripped and reborn? Because they were Indians and Indians did not really count. Turner was a paragon of social Darwinist times and the heir to English tradition that, in its earliest Puritan guise, saw Indians as agents of the Devil, meaning that they didn't register fully either as human beings or as owners of the land on which they had lived for thousands of years. Early New Englanders gained spiritual sustenance from the notion that they were much like the ancient Israelites and as such saw American Indians in the same way that those Israelites had imagined "heathens." To make matters worse, "Puritans believed that Satan ruled the wilderness areas of the world and its inhabitants."[95] Turner also drew from a long tradition that identified a range of cultural markers as signs of land ownership—the erection of permanent settlements, bridges, fences, gardens, roads, and such, that led to the obvious conclusion that Indians required no consideration.[96] Paradoxically, then, the frontier thesis argues that the land both was and was not—at once—occupied. Devoid of civilized beings is what you are meant to understand.[97] But more than that, Indians, like the wilderness, presented obstacles to be overcome in the desire to achieve God's grace by conquering the frontier as a sign that they had received God's grace. Circular logic, of course, but the long and short of it meant that the land was there for the taking.[98]

The myth is also, to put it in contemporary terms, unapologetically racist. No surprise here that Turner was both a product and an echo of his times. And such thinking was always commensurate with the blossoming of American expansion, imperialism. America began as an imperial iteration of British empire building and continued afterward even as it denounced imperialism as an expression of its own imperialism. Racist attitudes suffused the corresponding diplomatic behaviors. Notions about the alleged inferiority of Latin Americans, for example, "set us off on the path we still follow," Lars Schoultz writes in the preface to his influential 1998 study *Beneath the United States: A History of U.S. Policy toward Latin America.*[99] "This is a mindset that led President Monroe to announce his Doctrine, that pushed President Polk to declare war against Mexico, that inspired President Roosevelt to wield a Big Stick, that induced President Taft to implement Dollar Diplomacy, that encouraged President Wilson to teach the Latin Americans to elect good leaders."[100] It has surfaced in recent years, Schoultz finds, for example where George W. Bush employed a well-trod cliché and portrayed Latin Americans as children in comparison with Americans,[101] echoing a pathbreaking study, *Latin America in Caricature*, by John J. Johnson, that explores similar depictions across a century of editorial cartoons.[102]

As a consequence, it did not matter that the frontier was already occupied. It did not matter that it belonged either to American Indians or, in the second greatest land grab in the history of the Americas (after initial European invasions), to Mexico (i.e., the Mexican War of 1846–48). This point is crucial because the key foreign policy undercurrent of the frontier thesis is its concurrent apology for and practice of American expansionism, that is, imperialism. Turner missed the mark when he argued that the frontier was settled by waves of white males, frontiersmen-to-be, because it was in reality settled by waves of migrants who, fighting hungrily for new lands and fresh opportunities, were invariably supported by the government, including the U.S. military.

"IT WAS ANYTHING BUT NEW"

So Turner was wrong.[103] Yet it turns out that popular culture and political discourse couldn't care less.[104] Academics, on the other hand, came slowly though widely to disregard Turner's model. For example, in the late nineteenth and early twentieth centuries, Presidents Woodrow Wilson and Theodore Roosevelt, also noted and influential historians, both heartily validated Turner's model.[105] More recently, historians such as Patricia Nelson Limerick and Richard White have demonstrated a variety of ways in which Turner's essay amounts more to wish fulfillment than to rigorous scholarship.[106] Still others, such as Richard Slotkin, have traced the etiology of the frontier myth in popular culture and found that it has continued to thrive.[107]

Limerick has observed the myth's resemblance to the Pillsbury Doughboy: poke it all you want, but it always bounces back to resume its jolly, pliant, yet durable form.[108] This points us to the beauty and power of myth, its unerring, dependable, and sometimes maddening (for academics) plasticity. The outcome is nearly breathtaking in its reach and scope because the mythical frontier remains at work seemingly everywhere in American mass culture. "Myths are sacred to the people who hold them," Denise M. Bostdorff reminds us.[109] Just for a moment, consider how many ads you have seen that are set somewhere in the mythical west—for cigarettes, SUVs, beer, mountain bikes, shampoo, cell phones, pizza, fried chicken, movies, you name it. Presidents invoke it routinely for political purposes.[110] Even Pierre Trudeau, longtime Liberal Canadian prime minister, famously employed what became known as his "gunslinger pose" in an effort to appeal to Canadian voters.[111]

By reducing the frontier plotline to a heroic white man struggling for freedom and democracy against a savage horde and wild nature, the thesis sugars manifest destiny, the nineteenth-century idea that the United States had a divinely sanctioned mission to expand its continental borders and to assimilate or, if necessary, crush other cultures in its wake, all draped in a syrupy cloak of academic, intellectual legitimacy.[112] In short, manifest destiny and the premise upon which the frontier thesis is based—that is, imagined American exceptionalism and virtuosity—are joined at the hip. And while this destiny is typically dated to a report made in 1845 by journalist John L. O'Sullivan—who championed its characteristics of "unpausing struggle and excitement"—manifest destiny was already by then a long-held American precept.[113] As Stephanson, among others, has argued, "It was anything but new."[114] In fact, it ultimately became experienced as nostalgia, again as evidenced by the wide popularity of the western, because "agents of colonialism long for the very forms of life they intentionally altered or destroyed."[115]

Stephanson has pithily charted manifest destiny from the Puritan theology that imprinted itself onto the colonies and the nation as a whole:

> Its origins lay directly in the old biblical notions, recharged through the Reformation, of the predestined redemptive role of God's chosen people in the Promised Land: providential destiny revealed. The world as God's "manifestation" and history as predetermined "destiny" had been ideological staples of the strongly providentialist period in England between 1620 and 1660, during which, of course, the initial migration to New England took place.[116]

Richard T. Hughes dates the widespread feeling among the English that they were God's chosen people, which later took root in New England, to the 1540s.[117] In short, God chose the people, and God chose the land. Continental expansion, in this light, fulfilled a divine plan "to realize God's will on earth."[118] And the untamed land, including the Indians who dwelled upon it, served as the darkness that had to be subdued, overcome, tamed, and settled.

It is important to keep in mind that the whole mythical enterprise is premised on real-world and real-time imperial land seizure and a fight to the death to get it. Indians fought back but ultimately were defeated militarily. Yet the frontier myth elides and recasts this winner-take-all imperial gambit, recasting it as defensive and, as noted, regenerative because it symbolically reenacted the founding birth trauma. "The idea of nature suggested to Turner a poetic account of the influence of free land as a rebirth, a regeneration, a rejuvenation of man and society constantly recurring where civilization came into contact with wilderness along the frontier," Smith writes.[119] And the ongoing struggle against Indians, as the nation was being born under the weighty influence of Puritan-inspired thinking, fashioned "an identity overdetermined by outward violence against Indians and internal oppression of blacks."[120]

"RASH PROPHET"

Meanwhile, if Turner was mostly wrong, in an important way he was richly farsighted. Near the close of his essay, he asserts that the process of Americanization—that is, birth and rebirth gained by civilization conquering espied savagery—would continue indefinitely and beyond the borders of the continental United States. He saw the future abundantly well: "He would be a rash prophet who should assert that the expansive character of American life has now entirely ceased. Movement has been its dominant fact, and, unless this training has no effect upon a people, the American energy will continually demand a wider field for its exercise."[121] It is interesting that he should use the term "prophet" because Turner was, of course, a kind of American seer in his own right. He was "Prophesying," in the words of Steven Ponker in the *London Review of Books*, "in the sense that it tends to institute or inaugurate religions or systems of belief."[122] As noted, it wasn't so much that Turner invented anything new—he did not—but what became significant for the emerging world of modern academia is that he wrote it down. He codified what is essentially a civil religious text. In this way, the Turner thesis serves as a kind of American bible. Now, you might say, "Well, I have never read Turner's thesis, so it can't be all that important." But when was the last time you read the Christian Bible? North America is chock full of both Christians who never read the Bible and atheists who pooh-pooh religion but have ethical outlooks that derive more or less directly from religious contexts. My point is that you do not have to read the Bible to be influenced by it or, without knowing why, abide by its values. Same goes for the frontier myth.

America's creation story, admixed with the narcissistic charisma of the frontiersman, provides the reflexive position of the rationale for war, bottled explosively and chillingly in the parlance of American "cowboy" diplomacy. For example, Ronald Reagan referred to nuclear weapons as "peacekeepers" and the illegally funded Contras, who sought to disestablish the democratically elected government of Nicaragua, as the "moral equivalent of the founding fathers." Similarly, George W. Bush sought at first to portray payback for 9/11 as a religious "crusade" and applied tough cowboy talk about how "we're gonna smoke 'em out" as he sought to emulate and supplicate Reagan by playing the cowboy, donning the cowboy hat and the boots and having his picture taken at his ranch in Texas, driving around in his pickup. David Leverenz shows how the stripping down and rebirthing process in American literature and film effectively fashions a "mythic transformation" that

> relieves white readers of guilt for the pleasures of Indian killing. While a red man threatens, the narrative depicts him as a snaky beast. After he ceases to be dangerous, he becomes a man so that he can bless the suitably empathetic killer with a new identity: Deerslayer becomes Manslayer....Here is a new myth of American manhood in the making: to be civilized and savage in one composite, self-divided transformation.[123]

But this is also pure manifest destiny, embodied in the Monroe Doctrine.

The frontier myth ultimately prospers and relies on a misapprehension of reality. Take your pick: that Puritans were chosen by God, that God chose America on their behalf, that American expansion revealed part of God's plan, that Indians were devils (also in God's scheme), that devils must be crushed, that the frontier stripped men down, that those men were reborn as frontiersmen à la John Wayne, that the process was universal, et cetera, et cetera. America's various frontier wars then become, in turn, premised on a legacy of fantasy yet imaginatively bolstered by actual historical contexts.

Considering the frontier wars individually, one notices too how each is built more proximately upon a grand smoking-gun prevarication. Perhaps this is to be expected. The moral legitimacy of the frontier myth in the first instance, for example, rests upon the assertion that

Americans were fighting a defensive war against Indians. Obviously, they were not. Indians didn't invade England or New England, New York, or Philadelphia. Each historical frontier war coughs up a comparable mendacity. Like the fixation with weapons of mass destruction (WMD) after 9/11, frontier conflicts are also built upon foundational untruths specific to the historical contexts in which they occur. Further, as I will argue, because these ensuing conflicts recapitulate the frontier myth and because the myth has become tangled up with western iconography, it is perfectly accurate to aver that the United States really is a cowboy nation.[124]

It begins like this. Various American frontier wars prefigure 9/11. They are different yet symbolically cut from the same cloth. They include, but are not limited to, the Mexican War of 1846–48—and the invention of alleged Mexican invasion; Indian wars, especially the end of Custer in 1876—and the ridiculous allegation that Indians had started the wars, forcing Americans to fight defensively; U.S. intervention (twice) in Mexico during its revolution, 1914 and 1916—and the assertion that civilization compelled armed intrusion; U.S. interference in Nicaragua from 1926 to 1933, nominally to punish Augusto Sandino, labeled just another half-breed—and again the notion that inferior people necessitated and invited U.S. tutelage; the Vietnam War—justified by the perjury of the Gulf of Tonkin; Ronald Reagan's frontier rhetoric in the 1980s—and the wild exaggerations about communism and the "evil empire," in particular as it related to Nicaragua; all the way to 9/11—and WMD. This study explores how the frontier myth figured prominently in how popular culture portrayed these conflicts. They share a basic storyline because they riff upon the same imperial tune. But if the music remains the same, the instruments change, and new band members replace old ones.

The concluding chapter considers Bush's attempt to depict himself as a frontiersman and explores *Avatar* and *The Walking Dead* as examples of the myth in contemporary popular culture. I have chosen these cases in part from expediency, calculation, and happenstance. For example, my first book explored propaganda operations in the Mexican Revolution, so I was already somewhat familiar with the attendant primary sources. My familiarity with Reagan's America, which in turn piqued my interest in Sandino, reflects my living and studying in Oregon in my twenties. Whereas by accident, on a suggestion from my daughter, I began watching *The Walking Dead* and became immediately hooked. This book is naturally imperfect, but I offer it to suggest that the myth leaves tracks across a wide variety of popular expressions over the past 170 years or so.

I want to stress that I am not saying the frontier myth directly caused any war, but I am saying and will endeavor to show the frontier myth has been routinely, reflexively, organically employed in popular culture as a way to contextualize and rationalize aggressive America's role in numerous conflicts. I rely on an extensive secondary literature as well as voluminous primary sources. Early chapters plumb print media sources, whereas later chapters assess Hollywood films, presidential speeches, and a television show. I aim to test the assertion that, if the frontier myth remains operative, naturalized across American history since the point at which media began to become the mass media, then you should find ample evidence of it in popular discourse. And we do.

CONCLUSION

We cannot live without myth. Myth becomes us. "Whenever reality reinforces a child's fantasied dangers, the child will have more difficulty in overcoming them," notes Selma Fraiberg.[125] Consider this case in point. Because America was born fighting Indians, perhaps it comes as little surprise that troops imagined Vietnam as "Indian country" or saw themselves during the Gulf Wars as "cowboys." And so such conflicts recapitulate America's creation story, that is, its frontier myth, and thus bear striking resemblance to one another, despite the particular empirical qualities and eccentricities of each war. Where the study of history seeks to differentiate, myth abides its own internal logic. The result is that the United States has not merely been at war for two centuries but has also been fighting the same war for two centuries. Naturally, the two wars that erupted after 9/11 are obviously discrete from each other and differ from, say, the Indian wars or the U.S. occupation of Nicaragua in the 1920s. Yet the framing and rationalization of the context of each conflict within political and public discourse relate a tale drawn from the same well. It is always an inaccurate story when juxtaposed with the work of historians and other scholars committed to empirical study,[126] yet it is perfectly accurate when assessed culturally. Like religious belief, then, the frontier myth is profoundly real and deeply moving to its congregation, yet fundamentally nonrational. Or, to put it less dramatically, in Benedict Anderson's phrasing, nationalism is "imaginary." Iga Progoff suggests that we think about myth as an animate, waking dream, drawn from the depths of collective imagination and at the same time delimited by it.[127]

CHAPTER 2

POLK'S WAR: "BLESSINGS OF HEAVEN"

Multiply and replenish the earth, and subdue it.
—Genesis 1: 28

*"Well, then, says I, what's the use of you learning to
do right, when it's troublesome to do right and ain't no
trouble to do wrong, and the wages is just the same?"*
—Huck Finn[1]

The nineteenth century served as a kind of adolescence for the United States. Like a pimply, rangy, teenage boy, the country was exuberantly restless, violently expressive, hormonically incurious, kind yet irritable, generous yet self-centered, and often at war with itself. And it grew in spurts like a teenager. Like any juvenile, alternately respectful and unpredictably thoughtless, its growth was both steady, as explorers, trappers, prospectors, ranchers, and settlers in turn poured ever westward, and it was bold, as witnessed by the massive Louisiana Territory purchase from France by President Thomas Jefferson in 1803 and in 1846–48 when the United States wrestled nearly half of Mexico away in the name of racial superiority, divine sanction, and limited democracy—that is, manifest destiny.[2]

"Manifest destiny," a term coined by newspaperman John L. O'Sullivan in 1845, nearly perfectly expresses the workings of a juvenile mind, replete with joyful, boisterous optimism and pushy self-confidence, yet tinged by nagging self-doubt and, when reality clouds the dream of easy gratification, outright denial. O'Sullivan may have invented the term, but he didn't invent the sentiments it expressed, even then well established. As was customary in the mass media of the day, he waxed poetic:

> Texas is now ours....[T]he sweep of our eagle's wing already includes within its circuit the wide extent of her fair and fertile land....She comes within the dear and sacred design of our country....Let their reception into "the family" be frank, kindly, and cheerful....[O]ther nations have undertaken to intrude themselves...between us and the proper parties to the case, in a spirit of hostile interference against us, for the avowed object of thwarting our policy and hampering our power, limiting our greatness and checking the fulfilment of our manifest destiny to overspread the continent allotted by Providence for the free development of our yearly multiplying millions.[3]

O'Sullivan wrote in the heady wake of Texas's independence from Mexico, earned in 1836 (but not recognized by Mexico), and its desire to become part of the United States (the feeling was mutual). The president, Jacksonian Democrat James Polk, had been elected in 1844 on an expansionist platform—he wanted Texas, of course, but he also wanted more, as had Presidents Thomas Jefferson and Andrew Jackson before him, all the way to California. But simply gobbling up Texas was resisted by the Whig Party (the Republican Party did not yet exist) and others who opposed the expansion of slavery, as would automatically occur (that the peculiar institution had been outlawed in Mexico in 1829 no longer mattered). This was crucial because pro- and anti-slavery factions were locked in a dance in which both sides agreed that neither would lead (for the time being). The delicate embrace required maintaining an increasingly vexing political balance and, as northern free state populations burgeoned, calculated fiction. Thus, Texas, where slavery thrived and was entrenched, by its very existence as a potential new state, threatened the carefully constructed peace between North and South. Further complicating this picture, Americans widely supported expansion. As William Appleman Williams notes, "expansion had become the lowest common denominator of American laissez-faire politics."[4] Some recoiled at the potential expansion of slavery, while others argued that expansion at the expense of a neighboring republic roughly equated to imperialism, which violated a core American founding principle (Indians did not factor into the conversation). So these, then, were some of the muddy dynamics that would climax later in the Civil War. Yet the year was 1846, and Polk wanted what he wanted, and most Americans, at the very least, didn't mind.

Manifest destiny rested on three basic ideas. First, the United States was chosen by God. Favored by "Providence," as O'Sullivan explained, continental imperialism was actually part of God's "dear and sacred design" for America. And it was. K. Jack Bauer notes that America's "mission was to carry the gospel to the rest of the world,"[5] which of course began with Indians. O'Sullivan was referring to a Protestant God, not articulated as such because it would have been widely understood by readers, in the same way that the Declaration of Independence meant property-holding white men when it averred that "all men are created equal"—not blacks, not Indians, not Latinos, and certainly not women. Protestants—and most Americans were proudly, assertively Protestant—tended to abhor Catholicism in the nineteenth century. "They viewed the pope as antichrist and Catholic clerics as vermin from the bottomless pit," observes Richard T. Hughes.[6]

Second, expansion was inevitable because it reflected nothing less than the perfect expression of unfettered freedom. On this point, O'Sullivan is simply blunt: "Texas is now ours." Then he applies a heart-warming symbol appealing both to martial impulses and soaring freedom, the eagle: "[T]the sweep of our eagle's wing already includes within its circuit the wide extent of her fair and fertile land." (Perhaps things might have turned out differently had Benjamin Franklin's idea prevailed and the turkey had become the national bird.)

Third, expansion was good, O'Sullivan claims, because it brought more American-style democracy and burgeoning capitalism into the world, bonding, bursting growth for the "multiplying millions." His words, like the Monroe Doctrine of 1823, also issue a threat to those entities, in this case Mexico, that would "thwart...our great-ness[,]...checking the fulfilment of our manifest destiny to overspread the continent." The point is clear: do not mess with the eagle. As the *Detroit Democratic Free Press* phrased it, "We do not desire a war with England, but if she meddles with our affairs, we would prefer it to submission."[7] The *New York Herald*, meanwhile, spoke for the press when it provocatively argued that the Mexican War was actually sponsored by "European despotism."[8]

"FORGOTTEN WAR"

Two dominant and inconsistently interwoven narratives coexist to tell the story of the Mexican War. The first and vastly less popular is the academic version. Scholars often call the conflict America's "forgotten war" in part because it pales in comparison with and was soon overshadowed by the Civil War, launched fifteen years later in 1861. The war also remains best forgotten because it picks at the scab of expansionism to reveal a blatant imperial lust for territorial conquest. And Americans hate imperialism. They have always hated it, public discourse has argued, from the Declaration of Independence to Ronald Reagan's famous "evil empire" speech and beyond. Yet the country has also practiced imperialism, and this creates a nearly impossible situation for the national psyche. And therein lies a central conflict at the heart of the frontier wars: with deep emotion, America commits itself to opposing imperialism as it engages in imperialism.

America's frontier wars wed these two unlikely suitors by burying the hatchet, artfully reconciling opposites at odds in the juxtaposition of a national dream and national behavior. In this way, frontier wars are selectively remembered, in effect, as their own opposites. Imperial aggression may become a compelling romp in the name of freedom (e.g., Spain-Cuba, Vietnam, Afghanistan) or selectively forgotten when reality is simply too big to deny (e.g., Indian wars, Mexican War, Contra war). Terry Eagleton, among others, has observed that a nation always engages in selectively remembering its past.[9] For example, three-quarters of American college graduates are today ignorant of the Bill of Rights, and 73 percent "are unable to identify America's antagonist during four decades of the cold war."[10] Some news stories evoke comparable responses. Consider a contemporary example, the American atrocities (e.g., rape, torture, sodomy) at Abu Ghraib prison in Iraq in the early 2000s. Legendary CBS newsman Dan Rather simply put it this way: "This was a story nobody wanted to be true: the story of how some American military personnel were humiliating, abusing and torturing Iraqi detainees."[11] The reality of war with Mexico also served up a heaping of unpalatable truth about the nature of American expansionism. Best to forget it or, better yet, pretend it was something else. Indeed, it is perhaps understandable why nobody wants to be reminded of a narrative centered four-square on American racism against Mexican "greasers," striking religious intolerance, giddy and self-congratulatory violent onslaught, punctuated by behavior fairly characterized as barely containable id run amok. Who on earth would want to be reminded of that? Far better to focus on the gallant fighting heroes and imagined benefits of manifest destiny. Better to forget or to pretend. Or, best of all, reinvent.

Thus, the second and dominant narrative of the Mexican War has been conjured up in popular culture and offers near-perfect mythical pitch and cadence. It posits the conflict with Mexico unambiguously as a frontier war. This requires that (a) America was innocent; (b) Mexico initiated hostilities; (c) America was compelled to fight a defensive war; (d) Mexicans were savages; (e) the American response to the conflict was morally justified and even necessary; and (f) the icing on this imperial cake tastes of symbolic rebirth won by frontiersmen. That is, expansion via this war regenerated the United States.

"AN UNNECESSSARY WAR"

Academic historians are a peculiar bunch, alternately snooty, vain, and pretentious, yet also open-minded, flexible, and intuitive. In other words, for the most part they are just like everybody else—with a couple of unusual exceptions. To begin with, there is the requirement that historical analyses be built, in the first case, upon primary sources. This represents an attempt to ground understanding and interpretation empirically, beyond the allure of the flavor of the moment.

And it rightly grants the profession a certain respectability and veri-fiable heft, especially when combined, second, with grueling gradu-ate training that imparts the wisdom of tried and true methods and approaches to getting it just right. The training aims to reward those who research carefully and properly and to weed out those who are not clever enough, do not work hard enough, and/or insist upon not following the established rules.[12] That said, there is no accounting for taste, and normally nerdy historians are famous for donnybrooks over how best to interpret things historical.[13] And, equally problematic, the rules keep changing. For example, scant decades ago the profession widely insisted that primary sources consisted exclusively of written documents—no exceptions. Yet today those studying, say, Native American history routinely employ oral testimony.[14] Or, in another case, until recently the study of film was simply not taken seriously, whereas now it has earned its rightful place in the academy.[15] As evi-dence, consider that the mother of all historical journals, the *American Historical Review*, for some years now has published film reviews, that is, assessments of films informed by scholarship.

Further, those who specialize in the study of the study of history (historiography) identify a range of issues that suggests strongly that historians are not immune to the same cultural influences that affect everybody else.[16] How could they be exempt? Let's be honest, academic history is basically a literary discipline.[17] And this poses difficulties because it implies that historians channel culture even as they seek to reveal culture to itself. Think of it as an updated version of *know thy-self*—or at least keep trying. Nothing wrong with that. In other words, the study of history is also necessarily interpretive rather than objec-tive. Why? Because culture bounds the sorts of questions—and thereby shades the sorts of answers—that said historians may seek and find.[18]

Consider Woodrow Wilson. Before becoming president of the United States, he was governor of New Jersey and before that presi-dent of Princeton University and before that president of the American Historical Association and before that an academic trained in political science and history. And he excelled as a scholar.[19] Yet, for all that, it may come as a surprise to discover that one of the principal guiding forces of his study of American history was his deep and heartfelt racism.

To cite just one example, when the pathbreaking racist film *Birth of a Nation* was aired at the White House, Wilson cheered at the point in the film when the Ku Klux Klan, during the period of postbellum Reconstruction, ride to the rescue of the South. He later commented that the film was "like writing history with lightning." Couple such a worldview with the arrogance that often accompanies power, and his infamous slur that he was "going to teach Latin America how to elect a few good men" makes a lot more sense. I use Wilson as an example not to pillory him but to show how academics, both the famous few (e.g., Wilson, Stephen Hawking, Noam Chomsky) and the rest of us, invariably and necessarily reflect the culture from which they emerge. Just think about it. America's revered founding fathers were almost to a man slave owners. At the same time, women were legally considered wards of their husbands and denied the right to vote or, informally, smoke cigarettes in public, let alone get tattooed or body-pierced. And yet we revere (for good reason) those founders and their wise thoughts about freedom and democracy. One sure result is that history changes constantly. The stuffing of history—the names, dates, what people actually did—of course, remains the same, but history rests upon interpretation, and how history is remembered adjusts to fit the times in which it is remembered. Thus, Wilson's views and indeed the views more generally held by academics of Reconstruction—the period of rebuilding the South in the decades after the Civil War—have been discarded and recast and reinterpreted to keep pace with ever-chang-ing worldviews.[20]

Such influences have steered how academics have interpreted the Mexican War. The early and widely considered definitive book on the war was published by Justin H. Smith in two volumes in 1919.[21] The fact that the war had been over already for seventy years when this book was published, oddly, seems about right to this historian's ears. There usually exists a predictable lag between events and the initial set-tling of their academic interpretation. Of course, books fly off the shelf often before important events fully unfold, but there remains a sense in academia that the best historical interpretations tend to emerge after the dust settles, which tends to take decades at least (and many reason-ably argue that the dust never really or fully settles). And so it was, at least by the consensus of experts in the field today, about the Mexican War. Plus keep in mind that modern academia was in its infancy in the middle of the nineteenth century. What we might understand or identify as the modern university really came into being later in the century, at about the time that Frederick Jackson Turner's epochal essay first aired in Chicago.

Fast-forward to today (and by today I mean the past thirty-five years or so, roughly the term of a historical generation), and interpretation of the Mexican War takes on a shape that sits comfortably on the left side of America's ongoing culture wars. The contemporary academic view of the war—"Polk's War" remains a common handle for it—is naturally tangled up in how Polk's tenure as president is assessed. This work builds upon the accomplishments of earlier scholars. A recent and sympathetic study of Polk by Robert W. Merry captures it well:

> [H]e is seen today by many as an imperialist manipulator who bent the truth and the nation's will to his questionable objectives. The Whig attacks on the man back in the 1840s continue to stalk his reputation some 160 years after his death—that he usurped illegitimate power to manufacture an unnecessary war; that he lied to the American people about the actual events that generated hostilities with Mexican troops; that he stole territory from a weaker nation lacking the resources to fight back; that he cast his nation into the role of international aggressor.[22]

Fair enough. Elsewhere, in a terrific short book, Ernesto Chávez effectively expresses the gist of the war and its importance:

> The U.S. War with Mexico was a pivotal event in American history. Not only did it set a precedent for the acquisition of foreign territory through war, but it also proved to be one of the causes of the American Civil War. As an expansionist war, it enabled the United States to incorporate a "conquered" population.... The war was also significant because of an increasing centrality of race both in defining Mexicans

as the enemy and in debates about annexing Mexican land. Labeling Mexicans as "nonwhite" ensured that Americans would view them as the enemy both during the war and after. This in turn set a pattern for how the United States would regard its "enemies" in future military clashes.[23]

By the time the war broke out, "The notion that white Anglo-Saxons represented civilization while other races were its foes was already a staple of U.S. discourse," notes Timothy J. Henderson.[24]

In fact, scholars agree, President Polk was, like many Americans of the 1840s, a racist imperialist. Like most presidents before him, he was a slave owner and considered people of color inferior to whites. A similar view prevailed across the nation with respect to Mexicans, mostly considered to be lowly half-breeds. Polk also thought that the United States should and must expand all the way to California. And he coveted Texas. In short, he fully endorsed manifest destiny and eagerly sought a pretext to war with Mexico. Nonetheless, it remained unclear how far south into Mexico territorial expansion might extend.[25]

Mexico found itself in a political quagmire in the 1840s. Nominally, the country was a democracy, but in fact the conditioning effects of several centuries of top-down rule by the Spanish monarchy and the Roman Catholic Church rendered Mexico's early experiment in democracy a sham, at least by today's standards (and it is worth remembering that until well into the nineteenth century some 85 percent of Americans couldn't vote, including blacks, Latinos, Indians, women, and white men who did not meet property-holding requirements). This accounts, in part, for Mexico's weak response to the challenges posed by the United States on its northern shore.[26] One astute observer recorded, "All is decaying and growing fainter. Men seem trusting to some unknown future that they will never see.,...Still, they dream on."[27]

Additionally, Mexico's attempt via immigration to gird Texas from U.S. encroachment backfired spectacularly. Mexicans themselves had proved unwilling to relocate to Texas. So in the early 1820s Mexico opened Texas to Anglo settlers such as Sam Houston, who were allowed to purchase large tracts of land for pennies on the dollar compared to the cost of American agricultural land. They were also granted exemptions from taxes for five years. In return, the settlers agreed to learn Spanish, turn to Roman Catholicism, and embrace and abide by Mexican laws and customs. By the early 1830s, when Mexico chose to officially close the door on this immigration policy, it was clear that it had not only failed but also achieved the opposite effect. Instead of creating a bulwark against Yankee expansion, the policy fueled it. By and large, the new settlers didn't learn Spanish, didn't become Roman Catholic, and didn't embrace or adopt Mexican laws and culture. Instead, they were American through and through. And this meant that they harbored negative views about Catholics and tended to perceive Mexicans as a mongrel race. To make matters worse for Mexico, by 1835 and the eve of the Texan war of independence, Anglos vastly outnumbered Mexicans. Demographically and culturally, Texas had become lost to Mexico.[28] The war that ensued, among other things, highlighted Mexico's political turmoil and further contributed to American notions about the alleged racial inferiority of Mexicans.[29] As Fredrick Pike notes,

> Anglo Americans who crossed the border and viewed Mexico either before or, as soldiers, during the war had little doubt that Mexicans and Indians were pretty much one and the same.... To Native Americans and to the large Hispanic population incorporated into the United States in consequence of the Mexican war, Anglos soon applied the term greaser. In Anglo perceptions greasers were part Negro, part Indian, filthy and greasy in appearance.[30]

Anglo-Americans "lumped Mexicans together with Indians who lacked valid claim to full-fledged human rights."[31] To put it more directly, "American supporters of the Mexican war wished to see the Mexicans as inherently flawed, their society as sliding toward dissolution, thus creating an opening for American control," observes Paul Foos.[32] In this way, racism and stereotypical thinking contributed to a denial of imperialism and instead focused on the good stuff, the narrowly defined democracy, the triumphal Protestantism, and the presumed economic opportunities—manifest destiny, in short, in gilded splendor.

Yet, while Americans in the 1840s widely endorsed expansion, sharp disagreement existed about the value of accumulating Texas. "One of the great American political battles was on," writes Walter Nugent.[33] The problems were basically three. First, with a rising tide of abolitionist sentiment brewing in the North, a region that grew at a rate faster than the South, the issue of slavery had begun to strain the fabric of national political life. Texas complicated the picture because slavery thrived there, and, if Texas were to be absorbed into the body politic, slavery would come with it, automatically earning resistance not only from those who opposed slavery but also from those who thought that it shouldn't be allowed to expand (e.g., the young congressman from Illinois, Abraham Lincoln). This, in part, was why Texas remained independent as late as 1846, having won its freedom ten years earlier. Second, some Americans opposed the prospect of inevitable war with Mexico following absorption of Texas into the United States. And third, adding Texas (and any other territory that would accrue to the United States as a result of war with Mexico) would amount to the practice of naked imperialism and thus stand for precisely what the United States had fought against in its revolutionary war, thereby making a mockery of America's founding principles.

All that said, Polk took full advantage of a concocted border dispute to force war on Mexico. When peace was effected in 1836 to end the war for Texan independence, the defeated Mexican general (and frequent Mexican president) Antonio López de Santa Anna signed a treaty that recognized Texas's right to independence. The problem with this was simple: it was not legal. Santa Anna had no authority to sign such a treaty and, further, he was a prisoner of war when he signed it. Certainly, he had been defeated, but as a general he had no more authority to sign a peace treaty than, say, any U.S. general today. None of this mattered to Polk and his admirers.

While part of Mexico, because of its small population Texas had been administered from its neighboring southern state, Coahuila. This relationship offered Texas limited political voice in the state legislature, which engendered growing bitterness among its citizens. Meanwhile, the border between the states, acknowledged by both countries, lay at the Nueces River, about 160 miles southeast of the Rio Grande, the present border between Mexico and Texas.[34] "[I]t had never been disputed until Texans, newly independent in 1836, started claiming it," Nugent notes.[35] Fast-forward ten years, and now Polk alleged, contrary to all sound evidence, that the border lay at the Rio Grande. He had wide support too. "The thing is too preposterous for argument," the *Baltimore Sun* trumpeted in support of the president. "All the territory east of that river was included in the United States."[36] Assiduously saber-rattling—after all, for political reasons, he needed a pretext for war—Polk dispatched troops to the northern shore of the Rio Grande to support his claim. This aggressive and purposefully provocative gambit effectively constituted an invasion of Mexico, which Mexicans had every legal and moral right to resist by force.[37] And when Mexican forces did resist—and shortly after when hostilities erupted at the Rio Grande—Polk declared that Mexico had invaded the United States. And so the war was on because it finally had become "unavoidable," according to Patricia Nelson Limerick.[38]

It was a war that the United States won easily, mostly because of Mexico's political confusion and comparative poverty. Nonetheless, the victory was generally interpreted in the United States as a ringing endorsement of manifest destiny and the view that Mexico, indeed Latin America more generally, constituted a motley collection of racialized degenerates.[39]

"MEXICO...HAS INVADED"

The frontier myth, like all myths, grafts itself onto the material world, which often includes specific historical events. This grafting lends credibility to the myth, but also simply reflects the fact that people live in the real world, so it is from this world that myth and its conventions inescapably emerge. Witness the fiction that the United States had fallen under attack by a savage horde, a key mythical frontier plank, conjured and delivered up effectively to willing audiences by President Polk. Yes, wrote Polk to Congress on May 11, 1846, Mexico invaded the United States, and consequently the United States had the right—nay, the duty—to respond with extreme prejudice. Polk understood the region separating the United States from Mexico as the "frontier defined...

not as a boundary but as an area to enter and occupy." Williams here employs sexual and gender overtones, reflecting "America's steadily growing conviction that it could not live with any other nation occupying any significant part of the North American continent."[40] In short, Polk, like most Americans, fully understood the frontier *qua* ineluctably violent by definition. In a pithy preamble to his war message, he noted the "existing state of relations between the United States and Mexico," by which he meant "the suspension of diplomatic intercourse" eight months prior, engendered by "the long-continued and unredressed wrongs committed by the Mexican government on citizens of the United States." Then came an obligatory passage, a bona fide American political rite: Polk touted America's "strong desire" for "peace" and "friendly" relations as he prepared to launch war.[41] But more than that, alas, this is a morality tale that requires an ethical hook, say, civilization versus savagery. So Mexico would dutifully have to play its role too. And it did, said Polk, for it had rebuffed and "refused" American overtures for twenty years! Enough had become enough.

Then in April, Polk continued, "Mexican forces…assumed a belligerent attitude" and perpetrated "grievous wrongs." In sum,

> [W]e have tried every effort at reconciliation. The cup of forbearance had been exhausted even before the recent information from the frontier of the Del Norte. But now, after reiterated menaces, Mexico has passed the boundary of the United States, has invaded our territory and shed American blood upon American soil. She has proclaimed that hostilities have commenced, and that the two nations are now at war.[42]

In short, America had no choice. Mexico had forced its hand. Mexico had invited war. Mexico had initiated war.

In truth, the news was hardly unexpected, given that Polk had promised expansion. It's what got him elected. Yet he had to tease the message, as best he could, to deflect political opposition to the war, famously opposed by Abraham Lincoln, Ralph Waldo Emerson, Henry David Thoreau, Henry Clay, and Mark Twain. But Polk also had wide support. The *Detroit Democratic Free Press*, for example, labeled opposition thinking as "reason of the heart...poison in the breath...against their own country...when forced to take up arms in self defense, to repel invasion."[43] Yet despite the opposition, the war was on, and tens of thousands of unruly, poorly trained, Mexican-hating, and often vicious volunteers swelled the ranks and took the war finally to Texas, California, and at length Mexico City.[44] It is a curious thing to launch a defensive war, as Polk framed it, yet set out to gain enormous territorial advantage. Mexico lost 49 percent of itself, and the United States gained its southwest, fulfilling Jacksonian and Jeffersonian dreams of expansion all the way to the west coast.

But do simply lying about a war and declaring it defensive, when in fact it was driven by a lust for territory at any cost, make it a frontier war? In this case, according to the popular culture of the day, yes. Turner sketched expansion as violent and inexorable—and we get that here in spades—but isn't this a feature common to all imperial ventures? Again, yes, as in the *New York Sun*'s bizarre claim: "We have not attacked a single Mexican, except in self-defence."[45] Turner also premised inevitable conflict on an understanding of the frontier existing (as noun) and operating romantically (as verb) as that ever-shifting line that separated "civilization" from "savagery" (his words) on America's western shores, from a "semi-savage horde," the *New Orleans Picayune* put it in mid-May.[46] Polk hinted as much by identifying America's innocence, Mexico's aggressive and abhorrent behavior (e.g., "outrage and extortion"), and the region as the "frontier." But how was the term "frontier" understood in the popular culture of the 1840s? O'Sullivan, for example, characterized bloodless growth as "frank, kindly, and cheerful."

Newspapers more generally provide a rich source of popular thinking. This is so, as noted in the introduction, because traditionally they have served as the mother of all mass media and have been crucial in telling audiences what to think about (known as framing) as well as what to think (known as agenda-setting[47]). Reminding us of the centrality of popular culture, David Altheide avers that "We learn about the world and how the world is run through the mass media and popular culture. Indeed, the state of a citizen's worldview can be gleaned by its dominant news sources."[48] The press has also functioned to establish and reinforce national myths, which provide the cultural glue that holds a country together as an "imagined community." Especially in the nineteenth century newspapers effectively shrank and consolidated the nation and provided it with a ready lingua franca, so they played a key role in creating and preserving the national imagination and, in particular, the frontier myth.

The Mexican War additionally provided a watershed moment for the press. Dailies back then bore scant resemblance to those of today. For example, much of a given paper's front page was devoted to ads, and the length of the paper tended to be a mere fraction of the typical length of one today. Moreover, the news stories were mostly narrative in style and simply stacked one upon the other without much apparent or, at least, consistent regard for priority. The inverted pyramid style of hard news writing, an industry standard for many decades now, wherein a story leads with its most important information, had yet to be invented. Meanwhile, the Associated Press had been formed from five New York newspapers just the year before, though sharing and borrowing news items was common, especially as northern newspapers borrowed from southern, given the region's proximity to Mexico.[49] Also for the first time, newspapers dispatched correspondents into the field of operations, though they still relied heavily on reports from travelers of various sorts (e.g., those on holiday or business) and letters from a wide variety of sources (e.g., politicians, would-be pundits, clergy, interested citizens, and anonymous informants). In the field, reporters frequently needed interpreters to translate Spanish into English. Further, it is important to remember that publications tended toward the deeply partisan—that is, in a sense they were all like Fox News but perhaps more so—and thus typically tied ideologically to the Democratic or Whig Party of the day. Little distinction existed between hard news and editorial comment, as in the widespread practice exemplified by the *New York Sun* referring to U.S. troops as "Our boys."[50] Finally, communication was slow, and thus it sometimes took weeks for news to reach audiences.[51] Even dispatches from the field of operations at the Rio Grande took days to get to Washington, so when Polk delivered his war message he was quite right to state that hostilities were already well under way.

The press was divided in its support for the war, though most major papers favored it. And even those publications that opposed Polk, such as the *New York Herald* or Horace Greeley's *New York Tribune*, nevertheless presented the conflict as a mythical frontier war, expressed deep antipathy for all things Mexican, and supported expansion, as in Greeley's famous invocation "Go west, young man." In fact, the *Tribune*, exalting agenda-setting, argued that the "war cry of the press" had helped to fuel "blind popular enthusiasm" for it.[52] The pro-war press, in particular, toed a line closely supportive of Polk and abounded with mythical frontierisms and, indeed, a larger narrative that characterized the more general conflict as a frontier war. From among dozens of possibilities, I have chosen seven newspapers that offer a fair representation of the coverage both in terms of content and geography. These include the *Baltimore Sun, Charleston Courier, Detroit Democratic Free Press, New Orleans Picayune, New York Herald, New York Sun,* and *New York Tribune.*

"ON THE FRONTIER"

The *New Orleans Picayune* declared war fully eight days before the president. "The war has begun in earnest! The enemy is upon our soil!! Louisiana volunteers, the hour has arrived!!!…Mexicans crossed the Rio Grande," it recorded enthusiastically on May 3, 1846. To add insult to injury and heighten the drama, it noted that General Zachary Taylor's forces were "completely surrounded." The paper bore the news grimly:

> It is a mortifying reflection that an American army should be so beleaguered, on our own soil, by a Mexican force. The bare announcement of such a fact ought to arouse a spirit that nothing could appease but a thorough and withering chastisement of the invaders …upon the frontier… [to avoid an outcome] disastrous and humiliating to the national pride.…[T]he blood of brave men has been shed.[53]

Tapping a Jacksonian vein, on May 9 the *Charleston Courier* and on May 12 the *Baltimore Sun* agreed:

We have borne with Mexico until patience ceased to be a virtue. She has refused to fulfill her solemn treaty...to indemnify our citizens for injuries inflicted and treated our remonstrances with contempt and disdain. She imprisoned Americans in loathsome dungeons...and even inflicted disgusting corporeal punishments on them....[And she has] waylaid and murdered our officers and men.[54]

And earlier, on May 1, the *New York Sun* cited an April 12 dispatch indicating that "On the frontier...the Mexicans had formally declared war."[55]

Although slower to boil because of the sluggish quality of 1840s communications technology, the *Detroit Democratic Free Press* concurred, lamenting "the invasion of the territory of the United States by the Mexican troops....[T]he territory of the United States had been invaded, and with an armed force....Texas had been annexed to the United States, and the Rio Grande had been recognized as her boundary by the United States," all in a single paragraph.[56] In other words, à la Turner and Polk, America had fallen under siege to a barbarous horde not merely at the gates but spilling over them. All this inflicted upon a virtuous and entirely innocent republic chosen by God as a beacon of freedom, democracy, and so on. Righteousness demanded payback. And this was not simply "blowback," a term popularized by American diplomatic historian Chalmers Johnson, where a pattern of American behavior erupted, ironically, in its face and then came back to haunt it.[57] No, the press made it clear: Mexico started it; America was innocent; and America had a manly duty to defend all things associated with the imagined ideal feminine. "We received her [Texas]. We protected her. While guarding her soil from the ravages of a tyrant....The despots of Mexico have thus provoked us to war...on the frontiers of Mexico. But we war not for conquest. It is a war of principle," growled the *New York Sun*.[58]

The *Free Press* took up the story with no less gusto, but at a pace that reflected its greater distance from the fighting. To begin with, the paper also swallowed a hoax that war had begun and then outed that hoax on May 5.[59] But war had in fact begun by then and was followed days later by Polk's war address, which the *Free Press* published on May 18 and 19. Like the *Picayune* and *Courier*, the *Free Press* laid the blame for war squarely at Mexico's feet. For two days, May 15 and 16, it hammered away at the story, packaged in moral outrage and saber rattling, that "American blood has been shed,"[60] a phrase also printed in the *New York Herald*.[61] In their own right, Mexican "outrages" constituted grounds for American resistance to espied Mexican aggressions, the *New York Sun* said, expressing a common press sentiment.[62] The matter of the border dispute was in this fashion mostly overwhelmed by bellicose posturing. Capturing the essence of the matter quite brilliantly, sans the martial rhetoric, the *New York Tribune*, which opposed the war, put it that "A Mexican will never consider himself at home on the right bank [north shore] of the Rio Grande."[63]

Days later the news that Mexico had started the war became a dominant thread in the *Free Press* coverage.[64] But, the coverage sought to make clear, the alleged invasion of American soil occurred in the context of long-standing Mexican aggression toward the United States. In this and at every step, America was entirely chaste and thoroughly wronged. "The grievous wrongs perpetrated by Mexico upon our citizens throughout a long period of years," began the simultaneous rhetorical assault and defensive maneuvering.[65] "The Mexicans, in strong force, assemble and order us to quit our own territory on pain of attack. They cross the river, attack out outposts, kill our officers and men, and finally surround the whole camp of Gen [Zachary] Taylor...in order to starve them."[66] Another day: "Mexico commenced the war without any sufficient cause."[67] Given the rhetoric, the *New York Herald*'s warning, "A terrible retribution awaits the Mexicans," seemed well placed.[68]

The *Picayune* also noted the "excitement" in New Orleans for war, an understatement if one accepts the paper's own coverage. On the milder side of the reportage, as people gathered and men clambered in public to volunteer to fight, solemn rites were enacted, including "a national salute fired, while the Stars and Stripes was planted a few feet" away. All that "now remains," the paper announced, was "for the patriotic among our citizens to discharge their duty,"[69] a common nationalistic appeal for volunteers.[70] A letter printed from "old rough and ready"[71] Taylor himself called on the "gallant state of Louisiana" to "respond with alacrity to this call upon the patriotism of her sons."[72] The less mild coverage, on the same page, called for volunteers to "defend their soil and revenge their butchered countrymen....The first blow has been stricken. The war has begun. The country is invaded. A field is open in which valor may reap laurels, and courage achieve glory....The time is come for action! action!! action!!!"[73]

In short, the papers left little doubt that America had been attacked by a vicious and unsavory foe, a savage. As the *New York Herald* put it, feminizing Mexico, "She has struck the first blow, but ours will be the second."[74] It was time for Americans to parade their "sacred love of country."[75] Indeed, the war afforded a chance for all men of "true grit" and "clear grit" to prove it.[76] Similarly, the *Free Press* employed the symbol of the flag to sharpen its promotion of nationalism. "Our flag waves over the Rio Grande," it quoted an officer to bolster claims of general American superiority and greater bravery.[77]

This tack increased in intensity in a matter of hours in the *Picayune* and was matched in the *Free Press*. Two days later the former, after first reiterating its cant about Mexico's aggression, highlighted American forbearance and, like Polk, stressed that the time for manly action was at hand. Now Mexico deserved a "sound drubbing....National character demands that the scathe of battle be felt near the vitals of Mexico." Or, from the *Free Press*: "Our forbearance has gone to such an extreme as to be mistaken in character."[78] In sum, the press was unequivocal. America was engaged on its western shore in a "frontier" war that pitted civilization against savagery, initiated by half-breeds.

"WE MUST NOT BE DISGRACED"

The *New Orleans Picayune* drew a bead on the "imbecility" of Mexico: "Mexico has made the perfidy of the United States a theme of constant and bitter denunciation...with galling repetition [and additional] offensive tirades...barbarous onslaughts...insolence and defiance...insult in every form." All this contrasted sharply with the American desire "to renew friendly intercourse." Indeed, "In all these transactions Mexico has been the assailant, the United States the sufferer."[79] Again, the *Free Press*: "We have tried every effort at reconciliation...from the frontier," but "Mexico has passed the boundary of the United States, has invaded our territory, and [has] shed American blood upon American soil."[80] In this way, the paper built a case for Mexico's frontier savagery.

Lest there be any doubt, the *Picayune* intoned, "We are speaking now of historical facts." These facts included "murder," "treachery," "bullying,"[81] "evil,"[82] sneaky loquaciousness,[83] and a history of depredations on "helpless women and children"[84] by Mexico, rounding out a context for the paper's oratorical defense of frontier war—that Mexico had attacked, that Mexico was debased, that America was entirely innocent in the affair. The *New York Herald* meanwhile identified "[t]he stupidity and weakness of the people" as a principal problem with Mexico. "Mexico," it continued, "is now the meanest and lowest in the category of nations. Her peoples are ruled with a rod of iron, and are sunk in imbecility and infamy....[T]he only principle that guides them is self-aggrandizement."[85]

Other dailies concurred. Chief among Mexico's many innate problems was its addiction to "despotism" and "murder," the *New York Sun* explained,[86] whereas for the United States "Our people, when once settled, are the last in the world to submit to a despotic government, and the first to raise the standard of Independence."[87] Again, the *Free Press* agreed. Even before it adopted the hoax about war, it characterized Mexico as "belligerent," guilty of an "invasion," and "eager to attack and conquer 'Anglo Americans,'" thus racializing the sides.[88] Two days later it referred to Mexican behavior as a "shameful...outrage."[89] Then Mexico became a "wily beast" on May 19.[90] With understated finesse the *New York Herald* expressed the prevailing view well: "The Mexicans are a peculiar race."[91]

Mexicans appeared in the *Free Press* as debased, wild, and of little worth—"perfidious,"[92] to the *Baltimore Sun*. On May 5, they were "supercilious" and "vain."[93] A May 12 report described their homes: "The dwellings...are constructed of canes, brush, mud...essentially Mexican." It chastised their "growing indolence," the pernicious effects of corrupted rule ("the military is supreme"), and "their attitude is decidedly hostile."[94] On May 13, readers could learn that the other side of the "Mexican Frontier" was a place where "murderers" roamed freely.[95] "Assassination," too, was common enough.[96] "Murder by banditti," was reported on May 15.[97]

Meanwhile, in the days and weeks after the war began, the *Picayune* sharpened its rhetorical talons. In one case, for example, the "Mexican horde beleaguered" American troops. Worse, they "dealt barbarously upon those Americans who fell in action....[T]hose killed were hideously mutilated."[98] The *New York Herald* warned that Mexico was "infested with hordes of the most desperate banditti...constantly lying in wait."[99] In late May, the *Free Press* summarized its views this way: "The United States is strong and Mexico is weak....[O]ne is enlightened, the other ignorant; the generosity of the United States should win the gratitude of Mexico...even now, poor, feeble, ignorant, despised and distracted."[100] Americans should stand on guard against "true Mexican duplicity," the *Baltimore Sun* chimed,[101] "indolence and rapacity," the *New York Sun* contributed.[102] Even the *New York Tribune*, which opposed the war, heaped scorn upon and belittled Mexicans as "meek" and "cowards" yet claimed that they were unduly aggressive—for example, the land was frequented by murder[103]—a classic construction in which the feeble Other nonetheless represents a clear and present danger.[104]

Mexico's savage status was further supported by news that drew attention to the country's political turmoil, which in turn augmented that strand of frontier myth/manifest destiny arguing that Mexicans would stand to learn a thing or two about democracy as the lucky beneficiaries of American conquest. For the *New York Herald*, the war "appears to be the natural course of events; and it is only fulfilling the destiny which we were appointed to carry out."[105] It wrote of "the foundation of a new age, a new destiny, affecting both this continent and the old continent of Europe....It is our duty not only to repel the Mexicans, but to take possession of the northern departments of Mexico."[106] And why not? Mexicans were "petulant and pugnacious neighbors."[107]

While scholars agree that Mexico's political condition was, at best, fluid and disorganized and, at worst, permeated by ineptitude borne of competing cultural imperatives, the press framed Mexico's political jumble as signifying its inherent backwardness and racial and cultural inferiority. For example, a typical missive written in mid-April and printed on May 2 in the *Picayune* cast Mexico's key political players as greedy, sneaky, warrish, violent, deserving of mockery, and decidedly undemocratic. No reader would have been surprised to learn that

Mexico had been at war with itself for twenty-five years, as reported in the *Picayune*.[108] Such political machinations were likened to cock fighting. The army, it seemed, would prevail in Mexico's nominal democracy. "Both parties agreed that war with somebody was the only means of getting money for the army."[109] Mexico's political system earned damnation as corrupt, tyrannical, and ham-fisted.[110] The pejorative tag "greaser" also surfaced widely. For example, in an attempt at humor, the *Picayune* referred to Mexican General Pedro de Ampudia "of fried oil memory," that is, greased.[111]

Importantly, Americans had in the meantime merited divine support. The *Baltimore Sun* stated that "Our enemies will lick the dust; God, to whom belongeth the victor, has blessed us with its triumph."[112] The *New York Herald* offered, "This war is a holy war. It is a war of freedom."[113] The results tapped into not-so-latent espied Mexican cowardice. "The enemy threw down their arms and fled in every direction, leaving behind them everything they possessed."[114]

The *New York Sun* painted the war, at least in part, as an attempt to avoid shame: "Our national reputation—ever dear to each individual citizen, because it is intimately connected with our independence as one of the nations of the earth, demands the immediate abandonment of all half-way measures in our dealing with the military despots of Mexico....Let that blow be immediate." The daily captured the prevailing press sentiment accurately: "We must not be disgraced by allowing a cowardly race of robbers to strike a successful blow against" America. There was to be "No trifling with these enemies of civilization."[115]

"THIS BATTLE WAS SOUGHT BY THE INDIANS"

The flip side to the largely faceless Mexican savage was the American frontiersman, best expressed in the espied conduct of its military heroes, according to the press. Zachary Taylor, in particular, drew unbounded praise as a natural leader of men (a popularity he would employ to win the White House in 1848). The *Baltimore Sun* characterized Taylor in legendary terms: "He is a citizen of Kentucky, as brave as a lion, whilst his cool and intrepid conduct on former occasions gives assurance that the honor of his country must always be safe in his hands."[116] The *New York Herald* simply observed that "The old general is as cool as a cucumber."[117] The *New Orleans Picayune* extolled his "gallantry and determination,"[118] while the *Detroit Democratic Free Press* tagged him "defender of a frontier post."[119]

Missing from these sketches are a distrust of government and a loathing of the "tax collector," as Turner presented long-standing American visions. Yet two things. First, even in the nineteenth century, a war required some semblance of a professional army—or at least professional officer corps—which mildly lessened the reflex attack on government. Yet the coverage finessed the point by consistently heaping praise on the volunteers. The *Picayune*, for example, took to calling them "Avengers" and "Guards"[120] while downplaying the role of the professional soldier. However, it frequently singled out the conduct of key officers, such as Taylor[121] ("Old Zack—God bless him!"[122]), who had a frontier-like penchant for playing by his own rules rather than Polk's. In fact, Polk sought to reduce, marginalize, and punish Taylor for his independent behavior, for his going *rogue* and acting the *maverick*, to put it in contemporary terms. Yet this very behavior won such widespread adoration that Polk's hands effectively became tied.[123] Again, the anti-war *New York Tribune*, which called the outbreak of war "a dark day for our Nation"[124] and "a flagrant outrage,"[125] and even went so far as to note that "our troops and not the Mexicans, are the actual and wrongful invaders,"[126] lauded Taylor (partly to use the praise as a cudgel to attack Polk[127]): "It is said that a more gallant officer than Gen. Taylor never lived."[128] Such was the "sturdy pride which characterizes the Anglo Saxon race...and our country."[129] Indeed, said the *Free Press*, America was constructed of "That which levels mountains, builds cities, establishes empires, extends republics, industry, indomitable courage."[130]

The *Baltimore Sun* ran a mythical biography of Taylor, a kind of short journalistic backgrounder, to explain his "gallant" character. The story explained how he had cut his frontier teeth fighting Indians on the frontier. The year was 1836, and predictably the Indians had struck first:

> This battle was sought by the Indians....Col. Taylor received
> a challenge from Alligator, telling him where to find him
> and bantering him to come on. Col. Taylor desiring nothing

better, immediately pushed on…fearful that the wily Indian might change his purpose.…The Indians yielded ground inch by inch, and then only at the point of the bayonet. After three hours of bloody contest, the Indians were routed and pursued with great slaughter.…This was the last stand the Indians [in Florida] ever made…and the only instance in which they voluntarily gave battle.…Col. Taylor won the day.[131]

"Wild" Indians also plagued supply lines in northern Mexico, news reports confirmed. Travel had become "dangerous," the *New York Sun* fretted, "Indians with their arrows having shot several people."[132] On another day, it feared that Indians "might unite" and "destroy all the whites" on the Mexican frontier.[133] A visual depiction, rare in 1846 war news apart from the occasional map, "Specimen of the Mexican Soldier," appeared on the front page of the *New York Herald* on May 26.[134] The "specimen," the caption reads, "is half Indian and half Negro." Five days later the paper proclaimed that Taylor's early military success "equals that of any campaign in the history of the Anglo-Saxon race," and it labeled those who opposed the war "traitors to their country and their race."[135]

That the war should, must, and would be fought with zest and enthusiasm was underscored in nearly all war reportage in the *Picayune*.[136] Such attributes abounded in frontiersmen such as Taylor. But the *Picayune* made it clear that the war itself also engendered such behavior:

> The Mexican War has already furnished instances of the generosity which makes courage an attribute divine.…The enthusiasm of duty dulls the sting of death and cheats it of its terror.…It is the conduct of war like this that teaches us that the moloch of war is not wholly a devil. Glory is not always arrayed in garments of crimson.

Indeed, a "war conducted upon the precepts of an exalted civilization will leave none of the bitterness of barbarous strife behind it. Victories achieved in the name of patriotism, unmixed with baser impulses, will not be sullied by cruelties."[137] L.L. Allen, a chaplain to the Louisiana volunteers, identified the "blessings of Heaven upon their acts,"[138] though he could not have known that of the 100,000 or so Americans who volunteered 1,700 would die fighting, 11,000 would die from disease, and an "astonishingly high" number would desert, including some who "switched sides."[139] Sacrifice, then, was essential since it helped to fulfill the Christian context in which the myth is so clearly located, as in the conflation of sacrifice with patriotism and pecuniary interests, what the *Picayune* termed "the blood tax of liberty."[140] The *New York Herald* made the espied inevitable American victory read like garish pornography: "Grim visage war is upon us, the excitement deep and intense. The rattling of the drums—the shrill notes of the fife—the waving of plumes—the gleaming of steel added to the deep toned thunder belching from the cannon's mouth."[141] No surprise, then, that "the eyes of the civilized world are upon us."[142]

"A CHRISTIAN AND ENLIGHTENED AGE"

And what of the regenerative properties of the conflagration? To begin with, it invited a diminution of rational faculties, the *New Orleans Picayune* asserted: "War should be like a fever—an acute, burning fever....Its ravages should be terrible and of short duration."[143] Further, "If the United States do[es] not have recourse to blood-letting upon a large scale, the effect will be deplorable in every respect."[144]

But could it really have been so? Shouldn't it have been obvious that this was a war fought principally for territorial gain? The answer is a resounding no. Europeans fought such wars, the press averred, but not Americans. "The French in Africa, and the English in India, are pushing their conquests over massacred natives, and both of these are crushing the Republic of La Plata [Argentina] with the iron heel of war. Smoking hamlets yet blaze...in Poland and Switzerland...king-ridden subjects of darkest despotisms." Counter that with the way America prosecuted a war: "Should the only republic on earth, capable of sustaining the cause of popular sovereignty or of exciting envy in the hearts of monarchies, exhibit meekness in the prosecution of a war, forced upon her by insult and aggression, it will be an invitation to the enemies of liberty to fall upon and overwhelm us." In other words, a failure to wage war on Mexico risked American annihilation. To put it another way, war with Mexico would breathe new life into the nation.[145] And why not, after all? "This Union is recognized as among the greatest powers in christendom," the *Picayune* exaggerated wildly. "We have taken rank by the side of those empires which have required centuries to build up and consolidate."[146]

Greeley's *New York Tribune* opposed the war, to begin with, because Greeley despised Polk at every turn. Nevertheless, the paper endorsed and promoted the creation story in its depiction of the arena of war as a mythical frontier zone, of Mexico as a half-breed Other, of Mexicans as natally aggressive, and of America as a virtuous, innocent land (except for Polk and his ilk). Yet, at the same time, it accurately portrayed the war as the "frontier" conflict it was,[147] a war of "plunder of a large portion of Mexico."[148] Likewise, the *New York Herald*, pro-expansion but anti-Polk, cited Mexico's aggression as the principal reason: "It then became necessary to plunder Mexico of a large portion" of its territory.[149] This is the very point that Williams made, that the myth candies the imperial gambit, not just making it easier to swallow but also making it delicious, irresistible, even compulsive.

The Treaty of Guadalupe Hidalgo formally ended the war on February 2, 1848, though it took weeks before news of the signing was published in the press. During that time, newspapers continued their support for and opposition to the war along the same lines as they had in 1846. By month's end, it had also become clear that Taylor would stand for the Whig nomination for president that fall. (He did and won handily over two-time bridesmaid Henry Clay.)

If anything, the two years that passed after Mexico allegedly invaded the United States hardened the views the press expressed on Mexico and Mexicans, and remained what the *Picayune* aptly called "the all-encompassing topic of the day."[150] One might be tempted to conclude that this was a case where familiarity bred contempt, but the contempt was already well established in 1846. Moreover, the press in 1848 continued to frame the war in mythical frontier terms, even those dailies that opposed the war and what they perceived as Polk's improper imperialist gambit, built upon a provocative untruth.

The frontier still pit civilization against savagery, as the myth demanded. The *New York Herald* heaped scorn upon Mexico's Catholicism, terming it "narrow minded and shallow."[151] Keep in mind that it also considered Virginia slaves "[a]s contented as a race of mortals can be found on this earth."[152] Plus, the outcome of the war, it alleged, had led to a startling leap forward for the United States: "We are much of the opinion that, during the past four years, the progress of new thoughts, feelings, and purposes, in the United States, has been almost equal to what it would be in half a century of normal existence."[153] The *Picayune*, with volatile and artful compression, tangling up Turner and O'Sullivan, summed up the press sentiment nearly perfectly in four words: "Our superiority is manifest."[154] Indeed, as George Washington's birthday was lovingly celebrated, and sounding much like Ronald Reagan in the 1980s, "A shout went out—the children of American soil were the same as of old."[155]

The *New York Sun* explained the source and nature of American superiority in a manner that presaged Turner:

> Led by no thirst for golden plunder, they landed on the continent of North America, trusting to a supreme guidance for shelter and abode. They found an inhospitable soil and a strange savage race to oppose them, but they were men of resolution and endurance, prayerful and hopeful men—and making signs of peace to the savages of the forest, they were permitted to erect their rude cabins....Slowly but steadily, the pilgrim seed took root and produced harvests, and rude cabins became cottages scattered far and wide as the wilderness receded....[M]ost of the conflicts were excited by the cupidity of the Indian....The American seeks no land over which his liberty, enterprise and prosperity cannot be spread for the exaltation of the human race...wherever they come into conflict with inferior conditions of human existence, until they absorb continents and hemispheres.[156]

Juxtapose this with *Free Press* David-versus-Goliath sentiments and the assertions collectively, if taken at face value, surely tug at the heart strings: "We are in the middle of a war with a powerful and warlike nation. The eyes of the world are upon us. Our brave little army has covered itself with immortal glory. The enemy...have been overawed at the invincibility of our troops [and] astonished at their humanity."[157]

Inevitably, the *New York Herald* called for the annexation of all of Mexico, the end result of which would "create a new national code of morality for all nations to follow hereafter, thus still more to astonish the people of Europe with our magnanimity, our national victories, and moral self-denial."[158] In short, frontier rebirth had been fully, boastfully effected. Violently gendering the matter, the *Picayune* crowed that "we have an iron grip upon her which she cannot relax."[159] Mexico was a whore, the *New York Herald* spat, but "She Will Learn to Love Her Ravishers."[160] Mexico, in the absence of American tutelage such as would come from annexation, the paper said, was

> showing nothing but symptoms of returning to barbarism, anarchy, and a gross savage state. The American conquest, with all the lights and improvements, both religious and scientific...will communicate to the Mexican people a new energy and new life, which in twenty years will change the nature of the country and assimilate its people to a Christian and enlightened age. They are called Catholics but they are not much removed in their religious notions from what they were in the time of the Montezumas...which would really be a benefit to the whole of that half-civilized and semi-christian people. Even the Catholic priests there are sort of semi-savages.[161]

Another day Catholicism was termed a "sort of semi-christianity."[162] That the Catholic faith was weak and misguided was evidenced by the fact that "At no time in this country has any distinguished individual risen from among the Catholics."[163] The key to rebirthing Mexico, the *Herald* explained, is "that we must toil...like the pioneers of civilization on our western borders" so as to effect the necessary change, improvement, that is, regeneration.[164]

The task of civilizing Mexico would be steep, the paper argued, expressing the common press sentiment, because the population was largely "Indian" and

> more debased than our own slaves....[T]heir clothing [is] scant, their food coarse but abundant....Ignorant and superstitious...pretending to civilization...mixed up with that mongrel breed, half negro and part Spanish are the class from [which] the bands of robbers and guerrillas are formed. Fierce, cruel, vindictive and cowardly, they are implacable in their enmities and treacherous in their friendships.[165]

The *Picayune* agreed and added, "If there be a Mexican nation it is a nation of Indians and Mestizoes [sic]...essentially Chinese,"[166] whereas the *Baltimore Sun* employed the terms "greasers"[167] and "swarthy"[168] to refer to Mexicans. Alas, Mexico simply did not "possess masculine vigor."[169] Its people did, moreover, according to the *Detroit Free Press*, from time to time "broil" enemies on "a gridiron," or "cut off heads" so as to "stew" them "in oil." On other occasions, they "cut Texan ears off and pickled them."[170]

When news finally arrived that the United States would take roughly half of Mexico's territory as booty of war rather than the whole country, the *New York Herald* accepted the outcome but prophesied that the United States would "steal away the remainder at the first opportunity," no more than twenty-five years hence.[171] Even the *New York Tribune*, which considered the war nothing more than naked, immoral conquest ("was there ever a war so steeped in hypocrisy and villainy as this?"[172]), identified the frontier lands of the southwest as the line between civilization and barbarism. For example, as one inexorable result of the conquest, it argued, "We shall now doubtless have hostilities, actual or threatened, with the Comanches and other savages."[173]

Taylor meanwhile continued to garner wide support from the press. The volunteer troops drew special commendation from the *New York Herald*: "For the defence of the country we only require a militia well organized, who feel that the presence of an enemy on the soil of the country is a national disaster."[174] Indeed, the "boys" of war proved themselves worthy of the mythical roles in which newspapers cast them. Consider "HOW THEY DIED IN BATTLE," a typical story from the Picayune. "As his last breath flowed, he whispered to me," the story intoned, "'Do the boys say I behaved well? If I have, write home to my people.'" Another case, this of an amputee: "Die he must, it was thought. 'I know better than they do,' he said. 'I'll try another [amputation]; and when they cut it again I hope they will cut it so that it will stay cut.' A third amputation was performed and he lived." Or, to conclude a story, "and as he fell upon the ground, said, 'Forward, my men!—my word is always Forward!' And so saying, he died."[175]

"TO ME!"

On the 100th anniversary of the end of the conflict, 1948, John Wayne fought and won the Mexican War on film. He plays Thomas Dunson in Howard Hawks's *Red River*, considered widely by critics to be a cinematic masterwork.[176] The film closely recapitulates the war with effective, dream-like condensation. It opens with a well-provisioned and -organized wagon train heading inexorably westward, off to California. Viewers through the 1960s, when the western dominated Hollywood and television, would have understood right away that Dunson has already experienced rebirth as a frontiersman. You gather this information from the broad shoulders bearing his easy and confident athleticism but also tearing a page from Turner in his buckskins and swagger. Naturally laconic, he possesses an iron will. Dunson, in short, is America in the making: a frontiersman striking out boldly away from the herd, because that is how men do it. And he is strong, a natural leader, virile yet ultimately self-controlled, savvy, dangerous, focused, capitalist, and fatherly.

Leaving his love interest behind for his masculine job of work, Dunson breaks off from the wagon train with his trusty sidekick, Nadine Groot, who had begun as a partner but who conveniently morphs into the role of significant other (played by the reliable Walter Brennan). They head south into Texas. But Texas belonged to Mexico, right? Not so much. Texas was as Mexican in 1845 as some of it is

American today: filling up fast with neighbors, as Americans poured into Texas in the 1820s and 1830s or as Mexicans have poured into it in recent decades.

At any rate, Dunson and Groot veer toward Mexico and decide to stake Dunson's claim south of the Red River. Throughout, the movie draws special attention to river crossings, which of course figured as the central trope in justification for the war. Then three things happen in quick succession. First, they see smoke in the distance and understand that the wagon train has been massacred by Indians. Groot grouses, "Why do Indians always want to go burning up good wagons?" Dunson mourns for his dead lover for as long as it takes him to turn his head and say, with abbreviated remorse, "Yeah," and then they strike camp. We know now that Dunson has fate on his side, otherwise he might have been felled by the hostile Indians, and we are reminded that Indians are savages who attack for no reason whatsoever.

Second, Indians, without subtlety whispering bird sounds (a skill at which Groot excels), strike that night and are easily dispatched. In these scenes, we learn to appreciate that Dunson is one hell of a man and are reminded that Indians are basically barbaric and stupid. However, they must be overcome to signify the grace in which our frontiersman stands.

Third, a boy with a cow (get it—Dunson's got the bull!) appears. The lad, Matthew Garth, is feisty and already handy with a pistol/phallus. Dunson smacks him down, takes his, er, smaller pistol away, showing that it is now his to command, and promptly adopts the boy. "He'll do," he says with a smirk. The scene reinforces that Dunson is a commanding, benevolent, and natural father figure.

Next thing, they brand the cattle, over which Dunson patriarchally and paternalistically claims full ownership. And of the land? "Who does it belong to, Tom?" Groot asks in a leading way. "To me," Dunson barks. The camera angle, reflecting the point of view of a child, heightens the effect, in what is sometimes crudely referred to as a "crotch shot," drawing the viewer's eye up through Dunson's groin. Dunson stands with his legs spread wide.

Then two Mexicans appear, one a gunslinger. They indicate that Dunson, Groot, and Matt "are welcome" to stay on Don Diego's land "for a time," but they must recognize that it belongs to another. Dunson counters—no, he interrupts the Mexicans consistently, showing them no respect—and asserts that the land had been "taken" from Indians and that now he is taking it for himself. The gunslinger objects, and Dunson kills him. And that is that.

Set against an epic cattle drive, the film chronicles a father-versus-son/passing-of-the-torch/coming-of-age struggle. The Mexican War, that is, the presenting of positions, actual conflict, and fight to the death, takes less than two minutes. And this is appropriate for the frontier myth. The myth, after all, is not really *conflict in itself* but conflict as the means to an end of rebirthing the nation. Violence abets the process and gets tangled up in the promotion of white heterosexual American masculinity or, at least, a fetishized mythical version of it. It is precisely for these reasons that Wayne's victory in 1948 is every bit as epochal as the original war, insofar as it represents the tip of a larger popular culture iceberg. The war is over, long live the war.

CONCLUSION

American newspapers, even those that opposed President James Polk and/or the Mexican War, cast the conflict as a mythical frontier serial installment. It featured plucky American innocence on the verge of defilement by contemptible half-breed Mexico, regeneration through violence, God's blessing, and the centrality of the frontiersman (e.g., old "rough and ready" himself) to the sine qua non of expansion. But it is the conventions that make a genre, not the other way around. Competing sides in any war are apt to see themselves as the aggrieved party, not uncommonly favored by the gods, and convinced, at least with a favorable outcome, that the effort reaffirmed them. In this way, the United States is hardly unique. What makes it different are the details of otherwise fairly quotidian imperial behavior. For example, note how the newspaper narrative parallels Turner: we espy that settlers went not just westward but also into a specific imaginary American west, engaged and defeated imaginary savages in that west, and thereby contributed importantly to growing the imagined United States to the west. The frontier myth did not give rise to the war, fight it, or win it, but it did provide a kind of nationalism from which newspapers narrated it in American mythical terms.

The Mexican War is often referred to as America's "forgotten war" by scholars. Forgotten mostly because it so openly flouted American anti-imperial self-perceptions when the conflict was so obviously an imperial gambit. Forgotten because the United States trampled on Mexico's rights and freedoms as surely as it averred that the same rights and freedoms were universal. Forgotten as a form of denial, then. Forgotten amid the celebration of its own adolescent growth spurt. Of course, the facts remain clear and largely undisputed by scholars, as any survey history textbook will tell you: Polk was elected president on an expansionist platform, and he delivered on his promise, despite heated and uproarious partisan opposition. Meanwhile, the country grew and prospered. A gold rush quickly captured the nation's fancy in 1849, and the lure of California, and the Pacific Ocean, and the burgeoning confidence and the optimism all contributed to a kind of cultural amnesia. The inherent hypocrisy upon which the war was constructed and fought was thus understandably best forgotten. Henderson observes,

> It is quite possible that the U.S.–Mexican War had the pernicious effect of helping to instill in Americans the notion that the world's peoples are a compliant mass and that invading and incorporating foreign lands is an easy and painless undertaking. Subsequent U.S. experiences in the Philippines, Cuba, Vietnam, and Iraq have abundantly belied this notion but the lesson, it seems, never quite gets learned.[177]

CHAPTER 3

JESUS CUSTER: "THE BULLIEST DAY SINCE CHRIST WAS BORN"

"Sometimes there's a man."
—*The Big Lebowski*[1]

"The only good Indians I ever saw were dead."
—*General Philip Henry Sheridan*[2]

Sometimes there is a man, the Coen brothers' classic film *The Big Lebowski* slyly and ironically asserts. "He fits right in there," the voice-over narrator, actor Sam Elliott, affirms with a laconic gravelly drawl. A man for his times. The film playfully and with nuance throws down a challenge to the idea of the frontiersman as well as to 100 years of Hollywood westerns, at least in part by suggesting that these historically grounded cultural fixations, like John Wayne's filmic ego and handle, the "Duke,"[3] need a do-over to keep up with changing times.

The film tracks a few weeks in the life of the Dude, a pot-smoking leftie slacker (played to near perfection by Jeff Bridges). And indeed the Dude proves to be a kind of man for his times and still surrounded on all fronts by mythical characters and frontier conventions. They range from his best friend, Walter, the conflicted Vietnam vet haunted by frontier-style notions of honor and payback (acted with explosive charm by John Goodman), to his eponymous rival, the other "Big" Lebowski, a conniving, underachieving, aging blowhard (David

Huddleston) who falsely claims to have won his manhood fighting in Korea; from the punctuated appearances of the sarsparilla-sipping cowboy Stranger (Sam Elliott), who narrates the story, to a minor incident in which a mild-mannered bowling opponent named Smoky, who happens to be Native American, allegedly steps over the toe line, provoking Walter to draw a pistol on him.

But ultimately this film is the Dude's story. In this sense, the voice-over is right on: "Sometimes there's a man." That's the Dude. The frontier myth, however, in part because myth elides linear time, promises something more. We might put it this way, from the movie: "Sometimes there's a man," and "He fits right in there." And let's add this: "A man for his time but also a man for *all* times." George Armstrong Custer, the Civil War hero who died famously and ingloriously at the hands of those Indians whom he had hitherto excelled at massacring, was likewise such a man, a man for his times. But precisely unlike the Dude, Custer played the role of American frontiersman with such aplomb and to such effect as to rustle up for himself mythical status, especially in death.

Custer's métier built upon and reflected a childhood disposition for mercurial, wanton behavior. Writes Jerry Keenan:

> Custer's Civil War career was marked by conspicuous gallantry in action, and his flamboyant behavior made it impossible not to notice. His fair, handsome features with long, reddish-gold hair and colorful uniform made him one of the war's most striking figures. His skill and boldness as a natural leader of mounted men won the respect of friend and foe alike. By war's end [at age twenty-six] he was a brevet major general of volunteers.[4]

Yet Custer could be impetuous, disobedient, and cruel. Crucially, though, he was a winner in war, and this tended to disguise his less admirable traits. His was a classic American rise from obscurity to iconicity. He finished dead last in his class at West Point but distinguished himself during the Civil War and soared, as a result, to national acclaim. Later he was handpicked to play a key role in the political decision to conquer, once and for all, the last remaining "wild Indians" on the Plains in the 1870s.

In this effort, Custer earned a then-approbatory label as a "squaw killer." He specialized in the sneak attack against noncombatants—that is, women, children, and elders—though this wasn't widely reported, of course, by the media of the day. And he played his part to near precision. With relish and much success, he led poorly trained troops again and again as the advance guard for manifest destiny: frontiersmen like Custer, already forged in the crucible of war, violently lay the groundwork for settlers to follow in the west (actually, one of the problems politicians faced was that many civilians had already gone there). In death, Custer won lasting, mythical fame, according to the most popular college history survey textbooks, as captured in the old saw "Custer's Last Stand."[5] And he became "styled in myth," according to the most popular history survey textbook at use today in the United States.[6]

In a story that stunned the nation, Custer and his immediate company of 208 men were killed on June 25, 1876, in the Dakota territory (present-day southeastern Montana). News of his death didn't appear in eastern papers until July 6.[7] The first impulse was to doubt the reports, or put them down as some "heartless hoax," the *New York Times* explained,[8] probably the work of those who resented the "boy General"[9] for his many victories.[10] Custer, despite great popularity, also had determined enemies, which became known publicly only after he died. Yet the framing of Custer as he has come down to us owes much to the tireless efforts of his widow, Elizabeth ("Libby" to Custer), to promote him as a mythical hero, a kind of American semidivine.[11]

"AROUSED TO WAR"

As was the case during the Mexican War, in 1876 newspapers still relied heavily on reports from nonprofessional news staff—letter writers, self-identified observers and experts, travelers, military officials, and unnamed sources of unknown credential, all of whom were sometimes inaccurate and often had axes to grind. Moreover, papers remained deeply partisan, a practice that held up until well into the twentieth century. Yet it was more than that. Custer's fame, after 1865 and his daring feats in the Civil War, was erected upon his impressive ability to kill Indians. His successes, deeply nestled in the comforting embrace of the frontier story, made his death at the hands of Indians simply unthinkable. Nonetheless, it happened.

In fact, Custer and his entire company were wiped out while attempting to do what they were famous (and popular) for—terrorizing and annihilating Natives. The irony of his death was mostly lost on a press that, if considered fairly reflective of the country's thinking, displayed a remarkable lack of curiosity about the larger context into which his death fit as well as a gaping absence of reflexivity for a story that shook the nation to its core. Instead, his death was quickly framed as part of a set-piece iteration of the frontier narrative. The barbarians had broken through the gates. Again! As America grieved and uttered oaths of disbelief and then outrage, the press began to call for righteous payback. And, in time, these prayers were answered. A war against Indians that had raged off and on since the arrival of settlers at Jamestown in 1607 was effectively terminated less than fifteen years after Custer died, with the massacre of Lakota Sioux, America's last "wild Indians," at Wounded Knee, South Dakota. After 1876, the army got serious.

As with Polk's war, the period known as the "Indian Wars" after 1865 (part of but not to be confused with the broader term "Indian wars," which date to 1607) evoked strong sentiments in the press. The reason is obvious: in mythical terms, everything once more lay at stake. America meant growth, and such increase symbolically rehashed its "perennial" (Turner's word) rebirth, echoing the lines of the anonymous fireman, in the much lauded documentary film *9/11*, who observed that every American "generation" meets with a "disaster" that it must confront, endure, conquer, and grow to manhood from.[12]

Long predating the war for independence, the existence of the settler nation was predicated on two core behaviors: inexorable physical increase blessed by God, and war against Aboriginals who dared stand in the way of God's plan. Four days before Custer died, the *San Francisco Daily Bulletin* updated this hoary American tale and put it in then-contemporary terms with quotidian candor: "The Indians are aroused to war by the presence of whites in the Black Hills."[13] Yet no newspaper on any occasion noted that settlement by whites on Native lands was, in itself, an act of war, an invasion, imperialism in action. Instead, the newspapers stressed that the federal government had faithfully undertaken the forced purchase of the Dakota territory via the Fort Laramie Treaty of 1868 (the questionable legitimacy of such documents and the U.S. willingness to abandon them at a moment's notice notwithstanding), which the Sioux rejected (and continue to reject down to this day). Further, once settlers and miners poured into the region, and in the absence of any concord between settler and Aboriginal nations, the Indians lost control of their destinies. A standard press interpretation suggested that they wore themselves out and exhausted American goodwill via "the scalping process." Ergo, the *San Francisco Daily Bulletin* argued, "The outcome must be the same as in all former Indian wars—the redskins will have to give way before the onward march of civilization."[14] In other words, before Custer's death the press sketched a context for his death in sharp mythical terms, inevitable and desirable advance steered by the blessings of God's grace.

That is not to say that consumers of the creation narrative agree precisely on how to interpret the past (any more than Christians do) but, rather, simply that myth necessarily draws from the well of historical experience to dehistoricize the past. The examples are legion. Consider the bootstraps myth, popularized by novelist Horatio Alger, which wildly exaggerates the probability of being born poor and becoming wealthy in America.[15] Or the improbability of some of America's most cherished myths—the Chosen Nation, Nature's Nation, Christian Nation, Millennial Nation, and Innocent Nation.[16] Or the related myths of American exceptionalism[17] or "democratic egalitarianism."[18] Or the various Christian myths built around the personage of Jesus Christ. And so it was with Custer, who in death became a kind of American Christ, a messiah who in death rebirthed the nation. Vine Deloria Jr. hit the mark in one of his thoughtful books, *Custer Died for Your Sins*,[19] when he said that Custer sacrificed his life so that the country might live without remorse. Indeed, after one unnamed battle on the "frontier," Custer was reported to have told a fellow officer, "MAJOR, THIS IS THE BULLIEST DAY SINCE CHRIST WAS BORN."[20] As Stephen Prothero writes, "Though Americans have hailed Jesus as a personality who stood out from the madding crowd, they have applauded him loudest when he has walked and talked like them."[21] And so it was with Custer.

As a result, press framing of his demise was probably the most seemingly natural of all frontier conflicts in that it appeared to correspond more comfortably to perceived reality. But I don't want to overstate the point. The frontier myth adjusts to suit the times so long as the believers believe, in much the same way that Christianity endures because it abides and fluctuates to keep pace with changing times.

Custer's demise throws up a classic case of blowback with an unusually extensive provenance. Custer died as a casualty of long war initiated by England centuries before and carried on with no lack of relish and preoccupation by the United States through the end of the nineteenth century. But it wasn't just Custer. Many Americans lost their lives to Indians. So why does his memory haunt us still? Answers to this question abound. One thing that commentators tend to agree on is that his death remains the most famous moment of the Indian wars because it speaks to his great personal hubris. Others have argued that his death symbolically represented the beginning of the truly modern age since it effectively closed the door on the nineteenth century and the last of the great Indian battles (though the carnage continued until the massacre at Wounded Knee in 1890[22]). Yet others argue that it struck a chord because it just seemed impossible, like the *Titanic* sinking. Some also note that Custer's determined and devoted widow succeeded in fashioning Custer as a fallen martyr in the many years she devoted to this cause after his death. All of these ideas hold merit, yet something deeper was also at work, as press depictions illustrate clearly. Reportage of his death and the response it evoked in the short term simply confirmed what Americans had always believed about Indians and about their own destiny. In this light, Custer's so-called "last stand"[23] becomes a significant flashpoint of mythical frontier war.

"SO FAR FROM CIVILIZATION"

The Mexican War for some was an obvious imperial land grab, but not so with Custer's efforts. His tireless work as a crusader for American expansionism and Indian killing, after centuries of such conditioning behavior, meant the idea that American continental growth equated with imperialism was simply not a matter up for discussion. In a way, growth was not territorial expansion at all because there was no disputing that America owned the land (whereas in 1846 this issue had been hotly debated). Meanwhile, as ever, Americans rhetorically opposed imperialism as sincerely and vehemently and seriously as they enthusiastically engaged in it. What could be more American? After all, they had been suckled on both teats.

Fortunately, the myth provides a mechanism for reconciling these opposites. Nevertheless, seizing half of Mexico in a naked land grab dressed up in the silly allegation that Mexico had invaded the United States generated opposition despite the fact that the majority of Americans wildly supported expansion and the war. This suggests that the fabric of myth can only be stretched so far before empirical reality intrudes and the myth either goes bust or adjusts, however awkwardly. Ultimately, though, it comfortably survived the Mexican War. Indeed, it prospered as a result of it.

Custer's death presented little opportunity for ambivalence. America was born in war against Aboriginals, and every square inch of the nation was built upon Native lands. Nothing is more American than this simple fact. And this work had not yet been completed in 1876. Further, and to its credit, Mexico had been viewed as sort of partially European as well as kind of Christian. Indians were neither.

Interpretations of Custer's place in American history have been tainted by an academic tendency to skirt the issue by ignoring the central fact that the United States was and always has been an imperial power. How else can one possibly explain the growth from thirteen to fifty states? The land was never given away; it was taken away directly or purchased from someone else who had taken it. Instead, though, we get watery explanations suggesting that most settlers, for example, were not imperialists but merely acting from self-interest. The federal government, likewise, was not imperialist but simply acting to protect settlers. Besides, the argument runs, don't forget that all Western countries were basically racist in the nineteenth century, so it is not fair to judge them by today's standards.

The details of Custer's demise are well known and have been examined with tenacity since 1876, when Custer died in southeastern Montana at the hands of Lakota, Cheyenne, and Arapaho warriors. What went wrong? This question has absorbed Custerologists, a collection of fervent types from a wide variety of backgrounds, including academic historians.[24] It is a valid question, of course, but one that might well never be answered to the satisfaction of the cottage industry feeding on the story. Yet one might also respond that the law of averages is what went wrong. Indians had beaten Americans in battle lots of times before. Nevertheless, what made Custer's end so spectacular was the overwhelming sense of its improbability. This derives, as most historians point out, from the timing. The Civil War was over, and the country lay on the verge of Reconstruction. More to the point, western settlement was inevitable and frankly unstoppable, despite hollow promises by the outgoing Ulysses S. Grant administration. The only question that remained, in the day, was whether Indians would simply die off in the face of civilization (a widely held view) or whether it would be necessary to further hasten their demise by killing them. Enter the boy General.

Custer, a lithe sartorial wonder who bore resemblance, with his flowing locks and facial hair, to a 1970s rocker, starred in a national production of a mythical morality play that would continue to lead America to the promised land, to regenerate the nation in manly fashion, wash itself clean in its own Eden. Newspapers of the day spoke the mythical frontier parlance that Turner later channeled so ably. Denver's *Rocky Mountain News* simply termed the mythical frontier "[s]o far from civilization."[25] It was often referred to simply as "Indian country"[26] and in the spring and summer of 1876 teemed with news from the "Indian frontier" or of "frontier warfare."[27]

The frontier was then a kind of shifting geographical zone, but also a site identified as representing the cultural gulf that separated white from red. A typical report appeared in the *Chicago Tribune* in early June: "Well authenticated reports from the frontier declare a party was massacred." As ever, "The attack was a surprise."[28] Newspaper reports always evinced disbelief when Indians fought to defend the lands upon which they had lived for hundreds and thousands of years. In such ways, then, as with the Mexican War, the frontier still served as the meeting place, as Turner had it, between "savagery" and "civilization," conflated by the *Chicago Tribune* on July 8: "The Texas people are constantly begging for more troops to protect them and their property from the raids of Indians and Mexican greasers."[29]

A headline in the *New York Times* expressed the commonplace idea well: "THE NEW BASE FOR THE EXPEDITION AGAINST THE INDIANS—ON THE YELLOWSTONE RIVER—A PICTURESQUE COUNTRY—A CAMP IN A HOSTILE COUNTRY."[30] In general, the papers I considered in their entirety for the summer of 1876—the *Rocky Mountain News, New York Times, New York Tribune, Chicago Tribune,* and *San Francisco Daily Bulletin*—cast Indians as mythical "savages," generally without much explication because the phrase was well known to readers. Readers, for example, would have thoroughly understood the implications, as the *New York Times* cast them: "Peaceful removal or war will be the result."[31] Thus, too, in the apt headline of the *Rocky Mountain News*, Indians, though cast as craven and inferior, presented "A Formidable Foe."[32] In a way, the portrayal is ironic. After all, how can hapless, child-like creatures of the forest so easily and automatically menace a vastly superior foe? Well, remember, a seasoned reader would have already known that Indians were also cunning and slippery and vicious. In this clumsy way, newspapers were able to reconcile the imagined simple, defanged creature with a monstrous savage. To do less would have been to insult the manly men who fought and killed them. The maintenance of Custer's dignity required having a worthy adversary. The flip-side of this, according to Reilly, led, for example, to stories "portraying Sitting Bull as a military genius."[33] He had to be. Anything less would have dishonored the army.

"A CROW WILL HUNT A SIOUX AS A FERRET WOULD A RAT"

The press sometimes drew distinctions among Indians, the general rule being that those who aided the U.S. effort were better, "friendly" in a way, than those who resisted American invasion. But they were no less savage, as evidenced by a *Rocky Mountain News* depiction: "A Crow will hunt a Sioux as a ferret would a rat, and beside this commendable quality, he is always a true friend of the white man." On the same day, the paper drew attention to "OUR ENEMY...the cutthroat Arapahoes, Cheyennes, and Mandans."[34] Custer's own "ferret" scouts also died at the Little Bighorn. The *Rocky Mountain News* explained the logic of employing Crow scouts this way: "It takes a thief to catch a thief."[35] Blending culture and race without distinction, the press cast Indians as savages in a variety of ways, then. Such portrayals presented themselves with regularity in these newspapers, frequently overlapping and crosscutting, providing evidence always to support the larger cultural drama in which they performed.

Indians were animal-like. Like so many rodents, "Indians were swarming in the Platte valley."[36] Another day Indian warriors "swarmed in numbers."[37] Thus, soldiers hunted them, as in the case of General George Crook, who had "a simple opportunity to hunt" Sitting Bull.[38] Or, to be beaten in war, sometimes Natives "had to be corralled" like so many horses.[39] Synonyms for "savage" included "Redskins" and "Red Rascals" who required "Running Down,"[40] "red devils,"[41] "Sioux scalp-lifters,"[42] and, most simply and commonly, "Indians." The term "Indian" equaled the term "savage." Run-of-the-mill reports routinely employed phrases such as "scalped and mutilated," "were on the war-path," and "savage menace." Indians, said these reports, engaged reflexively in bestial behavior, such as would invite war, as in "white men's scalps reeking yet with fresh blood are brandished" as trophies.[43]

Indians were heathen. In this way, a sweat lodge ceremony became a "séance."[44] And Christianity just would not stick, even when Indians had been tutored in Catholicism: "However many, children or adults, may have been baptized by the faithful Jessuit [sic] itinerant missionaries, the Indians still remain blanketed savages."[45] The *New York Tribune* observed that "No efforts at civilizing and Christianizing the Indian can succeed as long as these people are permitted to roam at large over half a continent."[46] The solution was obvious, the *Chicago Tribune* averred: "Nothing less than extermination will prevent the Indians from claiming victory."[47]

Of course, Christianity provided the bedrock upon which notions of civilization rested. This was problematic because "The American continent was not designed for the exclusive use of a few millions of breech-clouted vermin and cowardly savages. The Indians never had been and NEVER WOULD BE CIVILIZED. When he becomes civilized he is an Indian no more."[48] The *Chicago Tribune*, as if offended, concluded that "The establishment of schools…only tended to make them worse than they were before."[49] One solution proffered by the Chicago daily was intermarriage: "The pure-blood Indian could not be controlled or civilized, but the race was elevated by inter-marriage. It would be economic and in the interest of peace to make an appropriation to send able-bodied men among the Indians and encourage them to inter-marriage."[50] In a related exchange, the *Chicago Tribune* reported that one solution was to free the military from the mundane task of protecting immigrants so that it might concentrate on "punishing the savages and assisting miners."[51] This story drew an angry letter in retort. The author, the letter writer complained, "must have considerable Indian blood in his veins to advocate the union of ignorance and miscegenation as a means of elevating the Indian. No full-blooded white man would do it."[52]

Indians were heinous murderers. They pined for the "warpath,"[53] an unconscionable drag on progress. Thus, it followed that "if the present terror continues the settlement of the valley will be set back for years."[54] Such passages pointed to the inevitability of conquest and presented Indians as a horrible yet temporary obstacle in the march of progress. Other days: "The attack was a surprise….[T]hey [Americans] were cut and murdered";[55] "Stragglers are constantly being murdered by the Indians";[56] "massacre by Indians";[57] "The murders on the Plains are committed by the Indians from the agencies."[58] Such everyday news reinforced notions about Indian savagery as well as served as a warning to whites to stay the course.

Indians were erratic, of the body, and not trustworthy. "We had barely stretched out for a little rest before brisk firing was heard on our left and the friendly Indians came dashing in with wild whoops," a story in the *Rocky Mountain News* recorded.[59] Or, in a report from the *Minneapolis Tribune* printed in the *Chicago Tribune*, of several men who had been murdered, the first met his end after "Indians gained his confidence and shot him." The next was "killed while cutting logs." Then Chris Nordstrom was "shot at a campfire at night" and George War "killed in a fight for stock."[60] Or, in a "Special Dispatch" from Leavenworth, the *Chicago Tribune* explained that "He was drinking from a spring when shot by the Indians."[61] Sioux fighting amounted to "Little less than savage frenzy or the fighting of demons."[62] The term "friendly Indians" was really an oxymoron. "They certainly manifested such carelessness and apathy to the fight, having their war dances and infernal noises around camp at night."[63]

Indians were cunning, thieving, and sneaky. For example, according to the *Rocky Mountain News*, Indians violently harassed the gold miners who had poured into the Black Hills in violation of a treaty (that the U.S. government had broken). "The Indians seriously molest the miners without exposing themselves to danger."[64] In another case, the *Chicago Tribune* explained, "it is supposed they had a large reserve massed in the ravine, and expected to entice the small party [of whites] into a pursuit so as to surround and annihilate them."[65] The passage is revealing in that it presents the statement as hypothetical or simply probable—"it is supposed."

Again and again the papers hammered away at this storyline.[66] Indians would steal anything, including gold, but they preferred to pilfer horses. As the *New York Tribune* reported, "A dispatch from San Diego said, 'Indians and Mexicans are plundering houses and running off stock in the vicinity of Campo, where the families are collecting for protection. The prospects are good for a general outbreak on the border.'"[67]

The Indians were stupid, haughty, and cowardly. "The Indian chiefs, notably Lone Wolf, expressed great contempt for the fighting qualities of the soldiers and spoke of them in derision as squaws," noted the *San Francisco Examiner*. "It is the Indian's nature to mistake toleration and forbearance for cowardice, and doubtless they attributed the caution of Custer's troops to avoid the unnecessary massacre of Indians to fear, and hence called the soldiers 'squaws.'"[68] Meanwhile, the *New York Times* reported on a battle that took place roughly a week before Custer died: "The enemy, who had begun the attack, and showing thereby their confidence in their ability to whip the command [under General Crook], retired.…[T]he Sioux were prodigal in their use of ammunition."[69] In short, we learn that the Sioux were poor at calculation, given to cowardly retreat, wasteful, and lousy shots. Overconfidence was not uncommon among them: "Unless fighting Indians are tremendously whipped in their first encounter with an armed force, they are fortified in their own lofty opinion of their prowess, and so prolong the subsequent contest until utterly dispersed."[70] Here the *New York Times*, as with all the newspapers consulted, casts the armed struggle as emanating from the essentially aggressive and violent character of Indians rather than as a defensive struggle to retain their homelands and remain physically and culturally viable. Elliott puts it in a larger context: "The iconography of Custer at the Battle of the Little Bighorn derives from a collective desire on the part of Americans to see their historical conquest of North America as a defensive, rather than offensive, history."[71] Moreover, Indians were stubborn and seemed to learn nothing in the face of the inevitability of their coming annihilation. It would have come as little surprise to readers to learn that "Dodging, and skulking, and scattering out, as the savages always do,"[72] were normal and to be expected.

"Injun country" was empty. The frontier narrative has always wanted to have it both ways. On the one hand, the western land lay vacant, hence was there for the taking; on the other, the land was occupied by savages (it being clearly understood that savages could not *own* land), thus allowing exceptional whites, as good Protestants, the chance to earn their right to the land. One might assume that empty was better—but not necessarily. By fighting Indians to gain the land that God promised them if they fought the Indians, they were still fighting bad old Satan and fulfilling their manifest destiny. They were still, two and a half centuries later, attempting to walk in Puritan shoes.

Of course, things had also changed. After the Civil War, there were renewed attempts by some whites to engage in sanctimonious good works to "civilize" the Indians, which in turn supplied a handy justification for the ongoing invasions. Yet the problem with Indians, the *New York Times* reported, was that "they did not cultivate" the land, so it "was of no use to them."[73] This widespread allegation was popular both in Canada and the United States in the latter nineteenth century. It derives from a centuries-old English custom, based on English Protestant understandings of God's will, which holds that ownership of land can be obtained through domestication of said land—that is, by erecting fences, planting gardens, creating permanent structures such as barns, and otherwise taming the land.[74] "[I]t can hardly be in question," the *New York Times* said, "whether it is not better to educate the Indian, to build houses, and schools and churches for them, to teach them to cultivate the soil, and acquire useful trades, to civilize them."[75]

In sum, the press cast the frontier myth as a given and Indians as savage antagonists compelling regenerative defensive war. There was no particular need to explain to readers that the very idea of Indian land was a contradiction in terms—even though the government paid for it and struck treaties, which clearly acknowledged that Indians had some rights to it. But not quite. The press held that in fact it was white land; it simply had yet to be redeemed. And the government was then compelled by force of law to break the Black Hills treaty legally, simply by decreeing the land white land and unsuccessfully trying to pay off the Sioux to whom the land had otherwise belonged. The fact that "[t]hey invited war," as the *New York Times* pithily summarized press sentiment, lent the narrative a kind of teleological inevitability.[76] The *San Francisco Daily Bulletin* explained matter-of-factly, "The territory…commonly known as the Black Hills country is to be open to exploration and settlement."[77] No questions asked, no recriminations expressed.

On the whole, news reportage normally contained no particular lines of attribution. It occasionally cited a given source as the author or speaker, but there was no attempt made to achieve journalistic balance or verify the authenticity of behavior that no person from any paper had actually witnessed. In other words, the press rated dismally in reliability and accountability.[78] But it simply did not matter. The press sympathized utterly with the reports of Indian savagery and fully endorsed the frontier myth as a way to understand the Indian wars.

"THE ENEMY HAD BEGUN THE ATTACK"

Headlines aim to set the stage for the stories they introduce, and in so doing they attempt to tell, to summarize, and to frame stories, space permitting. Consider this chronological range of headlines from June 1876:[79] "A BLOODY BUTCHERY, News from an Expedition to the Black Hills,"[80] "MASSACRE IN THE BLACK HILLS, A COMPANY OF FORTY-NINE MEN FROM CINCINNATI KILLED BY INDIANS,"[81] "A MASSA-CRE BY THE INDIANS…MURDERED—FORTY-NINE MEN CUT DOWN,"[82] "MURDERS COMMITTED BY INDIANS FROM THE AGENCIES,"[83] "INDIANS AND MEXICANS,"[84] "INDIAN BUTCHERIES,"[85] "Approaching Hostilities on the Sioux Frontier,"[86] "A FIGHT WITH INDIANS…TWELVE HUNDRED LODGES ON THE MARCH,"[87] "INDIAN MATTERS, Very Like War,"[88] "MAS-SACRE IN COLORADO,"[89] "Cavalry Attacked by Redskins,"[90] "Indians Attack a Camp of Miners,"[91] "THE SIOUX WAR, RED CLOUD'S INDI-ANS ATTACKED WHITE MEN ON THE BLACK HILLS ROAD,"[92] "Rumors of Indian Troubles,"[93] "THE INDIANS, CATTLE RAIDS BY FIFTY SAV-AGES,"[94] "INDIANS, A RAIDING PARTY,"[95] "THE INDIAN TROUBLES,"[96] "FIFTEEN MEN KILLED BY INDIANS,"[97] "FROM THE INDIAN COUN-TRY,"[98] "Suspicious Movements of Indians in Dakotas,"[99] "Warlike Complexion of Indian Affairs,"[100] "THE INDIAN TROUBLES,"[101] "Gen. Crook's Command Fights 1,500 Sioux, a Battle Not Magnificent, but Very Like War,"[102] "A SPIRITED FIGHT WITH INDIANS, MARKED GALLANTRY OF THE TROOPS,"[103] "WHICH INDIANS ARE HOSTILE?,"[104] "THE INDIAN WAR,"[105] "PROTECTION FROM INDIANS,"[106] "THE HOSTILE INDIANS,"[107] "THE SIOUX WAR, Daring of the Redskins, Indian Loss Unknown, but Undoubtedly Very Heavy."[108]

Beyond compressing the tension leading up to the Little Bighorn battle with impressive concision, these headlines paint Indians as belligerents and butchers, characterizing them as untrustworthy, warlike, racially inferior, mercurial, unpredictable, and sneaky—and they cast the frontier as wild, untamed, and dangerous. Whites, in contrast, had been forced to heroically stage a defensive war. All in all, neither in headline nor in story does any of the papers acknowledge that it was in fact Indians who were forced to wage a defensive struggle to protect their ancestral homelands. Instead, in a run-of-the-mill passage, the New York Times commented acidly that "These original inhabitants of the Black Hills have a foolish notion that they ought to receive some sort of an equivalent for the country surrendered, besides whiskey and disease which our frontier civilization offers them."[109] The New York Tribune reported on archetypal wanton

Indian conduct: "The Indians rode up the edge of the bluff on the north of the river and fired 200 shots down among the tents, horses, and wagons."[110] It was widely understood, as a basic premise of ongoing coverage, that "the enemy had begun the attack."[111]

"BOYS"

Custer donned buckskins, wore his hair long, let his beard grow, was entirely at ease in the saddle, and became a crack shot. Before his death, no press organ doubted him, of course, as in the assessment of the *Rocky Mountain News*: "It cannot be denied that Custer is a brilliant and brave leader."[112] But he wasn't merely a one-dimensional, born-again frontiersman in the press. He was also a liminal figure, as frontiersmen often must be, operating sometimes unsteadily along the sutures distinguishing yet reconciling the binary structures of two cultural constellations. Yes, he cut a splendid figure, but his clothes were chosen with perhaps too much care, his flowing and manicured locks and facial hair cut to not accidentally fit an image that Buffalo Bill Cody would later embrace, and Custer wasn't from the frontier as such (few were). He hailed from Ohio (or Michigan, his adopted state). In other words, Custer was a bit too much like Alan Ladd's portrayal of Shane in the 1953 classic revisionist film of the same name.[113]

Like Hollywood's Shane, Custer was coiffed, considered, calculated, and equally reckless (i.e., Shane bet the future of a valley full of settlers on the outcome of his duel with a gunfighter, played with serpentine sexuality by Jack Palance, in a saloon). He was a kind of crossover performance artist who made playing cowboy acceptable to many because, in the end, he was just like the nation as it imagined itself to be, a mythical cowboy in mind if not in deed. Where audiences were literally forced to look up to John Wayne (he was 6'4"), audiences could more easily identify with average-sized Shane (5'8"). Custer was also not the rough and ready frontiersman of James Fenimore Cooper's Natty Bumppo, which served to engender and alienate his detractors. The fussy attention paid to his carefully considered wardrobe was contrary to accepted male behavior, and it mildly feminized him.

He "was far from the unstudied and careless dresser whom his wife portrayed in her memoirs. The colonel's overindulgent application of perfume, lengthy curls, and gaudy outfits reflect contemporary class and gender anxieties," writes Kevin Adams.[114] Further, Custer's few, if vocal, detractors surely were irritated by his non-Christian behavior. "A new kind of hero was invented in Christianity. Christian heroes suffer, as do heroes of the ancient world, but unlike the ancients, the Christians' suffering *is* their sacrifice," writes Stephen T. Asma. "Pagan heroes want to be publicly recognized for their acts of heroism; they want honor as payment for their monster-killing services."[115] Custer, in short, by this measure behaved like a pagan by strutting in his fancy dress; he dressed like a pagan too. Yet, upon his death, the predominant press framing cast him as Christlike, an American messiah. He gave his life that the nation might live without sin.

Turner's frontiersman operates as an essentialized American Adam. Custer carried the whiff of what Roland Barthes identified as a second-order semiotic system, a semiotic expression one generation removed from the original.[116] Custer was glib, loquacious, his frontier behavior was sometimes rash and impetuous, even his admirers admitted, bordering on the irrational, even hysterical—stereotyped nineteenth-century female attributes. In short, given the gender constructions of the day, Custer was not all man, revealed by an anal fixation with his appearance. He may therefore be seen as a kind of homosocializing performance artist.

Like Tarzan of the Apes, America's greatest pulp frontiersman of the early twentieth century, Custer too was comfortable dining with dignitaries and at ease at the theater. Yet he was no Tarzan either. Born of aristocratic parents, Tarzan was in and of the jungle and, crucially, was never defeated. Custer's epitaph, in contrast, reads that Custer failed, though it must be said that in so doing he made the ultimate sacrifice by giving his life for the nation. Seen in this way, any lingering obsession with Custer seems out of place. Rather, one might suspect that he continues to attract those who can identify with, or are otherwise fascinated by, his not-so-sublimated homosociality.

Custer's cohort, like the brevet major general himself, were widely and affectionately known as "boys."[117] Such frontiersmen exhibited "real grit," as evidenced by their derring-do and masculine forceful-ness.[118] Sacrifice became central to their existence, and life on the fron-tier was much tougher than it was "in civilization," the *New York Times* explained.[119]

"GOD COMFORT THE BREAKING HEARTS THIS NEWS HAS CAUSED"

In the weeks leading up to Custer's death, the press molded the Indian wars as an ongoing frontier conflict, endorsing the myth, closely antic-ipating Turner's essay (released seventeen years later), but also paral-leling the frontier structure into which the press cast the Mexican War. The frontier as a space separating savagery from civilization in 1876 was every bit as explicit with Indians as it had been between the United States and Mexico in 1846, perhaps even more so because the public didn't have to be sold on Indian war. The majority of Americans who moved to the ever-shifting edge of settlement did so both directly to seek opportunity and indirectly to spread the perceived goodness of what their culture had to offer. Indians, like Mexicans, therefore only stood to benefit from America's divinely sanctioned Protestant expan-sionism. These articles of faith the press expressed as self-evident. God has always loved and still loves America best.

Of course the justification differed from 1846 to 1876, as did the scenery and the cast of characters. Whereas in 1846 much of the nation endorsed Polk's assertion that Mexico had invaded the United States, in 1876 it was with far greater unanimity that the nation believed it had been forced by Indians to fight a defensive war: "It will be noticed that the Indians began the attack";[120] or "The cause of this war...may be summed up in the words, 'Sitting Bull and the outlaw Sioux.'"[121] Such flagrant denials of reality constituted the proximate cause of ongoing war, but 1876 added a substantive new wrinkle because of Custer's death. News of his demise electrified the country as it rallied around the idea that Indians must once and for all be thoroughly crushed. Mostly, the response was a simple matter of turning up the rhetorical volume, way up. It was a question of degree more than of substance. White anger ratcheted higher while the tenor of the thought itself remained remarkably consistent.

Consider the lengthy and representative collection of headlines that the *Chicago Tribune*, as was common practice, piled one upon the other on July 6, 1876:

HORRIBLE!

The American Indian Exalts His Reputation for Satanic Ferocity.
He [Custer] Attacks an Indian Camp with Five Companies, and All Perish.
The Bodies All Mutilated, and the Scene a Hideous Slaughter Pen.
Three-hundred and Fifteen Men Against Five Thousand Devils.
The Gloomy Butchery Takes Place on the Little Horn River.[122]

The accompanying story, also emblematic of coverage, was predictable in every way: Custer, as frontiersman, was heroic, active, a doer ("Gen. Custer found the Indian camp...and immediately attacked... and charged"); the Indians were savage, obscene ("The Indians poured in a murderous fire from all directions....[123] The whole Custer family died....The Indians actually pulled men off their horses"); the white soldiers exemplified active, manly civilization ("THE SEVENTH FOUGHT LIKE TIGERS, and were overcome by mere brute force,"[124] though this was all conjecture since none lived to tell the tale). The gory detail in the report leaves little to the imagination, yet, at the same time, the framing is a considerable work *of* imagination. After all, the two sides were locked into a war precipitated by white invasion, white slaughter, including common rape and the habitual killing of noncombatants, all heaped upon broken treaties. The passage even admits that Custer launched the attack without provocation—yet Indians were the savages when they fought back? It was "HORRIBLE!" that all the whites died, yet Custer specialized in sneak attacks and routinely killed innocents, including unarmed men, women, children, and elders.[125] Even in the rare cases where newspapers printed articles chastising the United States for undue aggression toward Natives, the writers did not challenge American expansionism as such but simply complained about the way it was carried out.[126] It wasn't really a case of myth meeting reality and winning every time; rather, that myth substituted for reality. Or, to put it another way, what is real? Answer: what people believe is real. Thus, Indians were tagged as the aggressors, savages, et cetera, et cetera. So went the reportage, day after day, as it had to that point, year after year, decade after decade.[127]

On the second day after the news broke, Chicago headline readers encountered

TOO TRUE!
The Appalling Tale of Indian Butchery Officially Confirmed.
A Feeling of the Most Bitter Resentment Awakened in the Country.
General Demand that the Demons Be Pieganized into Harmlessness.
Some History of the Principal Wild Beast Called Sitting Bull....
A Sketch of the Life and Military Career of the Gallant Custer.[128]

And the lengthy news story fleshed out this mythical presentation:

We know his [Custer's] gallantry, and most likely he was smarting under recent criticisms, and more than ever determined to make a glorious record....What is the cause of the war?...may be summed up in the words, "Sitting Bull and the Outlaw Sioux.".…[T]hey kept up an unceasing war....This war has been waged defensively on our part for many years before the hills were entered by anybody....All attempts to induce these Indians to go upon reservations have thus far failed...the alternative being that if they did not the United States would wage war upon them. This step was considered necessary not only on account of the numerous murders of white people committed by these Indians, but because they were making constant attacks on the friendly Indians...[which] made it very dangerous to allow these hostile bands to remain any longer beyond the control of the United States authorities....On more than one former occasion the Indians have deceived the troops into one of these ravines...and were all massacred....Custer was an officer of great bravery and daring....In 1867 [Sitting Bull] threatened....In 1868 he attacked....During 1869 and 1870 he devoted himself principally to the slaughter of the Crows, the Mandans, the Rees, the Shoshonee, and all other tribes friendly to the whites…and frontier settlers.… He defies the Government and hopes that he can get the Sioux nation to join him. If only they will do this he promises to DRIVE THE WHITES BACK INTO THE SEA.[129]

Again, the pattern of coverage reveals an ongoing effort to weave a romantic narrative, a stitch here, a stitch there, all serving to reinforce the dominating tropes of the frontier myth—civilization versus savagery, American innocence, American superiority, American forbearance, Custer's status as frontiersman, Indian aggression, merited American righteousness. The coverage also adds a sharper focus to the enemy by fingering Sitting Bull, "A PREDATORY MURDERING VAGABOND,"[130] as the catalyst for the offensive Indian attack that felled Custer.[131] "The young warriors love war…and go to the hunt or the war-path—their only idea of the object of life," the *New York Tribune* observed days later.[132]

The *San Francisco Daily Bulletin* presented part of its initial response to "the dreadful massacre" in deep historico-mythic terms: "We recount the perils of the Pilgrim Fathers on the New England coast from Indians."[133] Indeed, "A THRILL of horror must have curdled the blood in the veins of our readers on seeing, yesterday morning, the reported wholesale slaughter of Custer's command."[134] Denver was "thoroughly aroused."[135]

"EVERY MAN IN HIS BRIGADE WORSHIPPED HIM"

Yet a paradox presented itself. Despite the barbaric Indian character, and if all the mythical assertions were true, how could Custer have died? After all, he was a frontiersman of the first order, as no paper failed to mention again and again. For example, "He was fearless, reckless of the odds against him.…He was always at the front, and never still."[136] The press responded to this conundrum in subsequent days by reminding readers that Custer had been cut from impeccable cloth, a frontiersman worthy of comparison to old "rough and ready" Zach Taylor. Such presentations reminded readers of the centrality of such men to America's ongoing birth on the frontier, naturalizing Americana through the timelessness of repetitive narration. Two hundred and nine may have died, but this was Custer's story every bit as much as Hollywood westerns and action films like to boil down the primacy of American civilization to one heroic heterosexual white male. Thus, readers wouldn't have been surprised to read in the *New York Times*, even though there was and remains little evidence to support such a claim, that "Custer was among the last who fell. But when his cheering voice was no longer heard, the Indians made easy work of the remainder."[137]

The *Chicago Tribune* gnashed, "In appearance he was the very *beau ideal* of the soldier—tall, lithe and sinewy, with free, firm carriage... in costume...blending of the toggery of the state general and the wild Western scout's fantastic trappings, his sombrero and velvet jacket and buckskin leggings, top-boots and monstrous spurs, his long, yellow locks, and his sweeping moustache."[138] Or, in the recorded words of a Seventh Cavalry captain printed the same day,

> When I first saw him he was about 6 foot 1 in height, smooth-faced except for a long moustache, and with golden hair hanging on his shoulders. When he was riding it was always blowing in the wind....He was a very striking looking man. He was one of those men who, when you saw him pass at a gallop, you instinctively turned to look at again.... He was very active....A private could talk to him as freely as an officer....Custer was always ready to listen....Every man in his brigade worshipped him, and would follow him through anything....I don't suppose any man in the Eastern army had those PECULIAR QUALITIES OF MIND AND HEART AND DASH.[139]

Custer sounded like a creature born of royalty but simultaneously rough and ready, maybe like Tarzan after all.[140] Here is how Edgar Rice Burroughs describes the sensationally popular Tarzan of the Apes, born to greatness in the frontier jungles of Africa:

His straight and perfect figure, muscled as the best of the ancient Roman gladiators must have been muscled, and yet with the soft and sinuous curves of a Greek god....A personification, was Tarzan of the Apes, of the primitive man, the hunter, the warrior. With the noble poise of his handsome head upon those broad shoulders, and the fire of life and intelligence in those fine, clear eyes, he might readily have typified some demi-god of a wild and warlike bygone people of his ancient forest. But those things Tarzan did not think because he was worried that he had no clothing to indicate to the jungle folks that he was a man and not an ape.[141]

Or consider Louis L'Amour's ruggedly sensuous Hondo, a revolving-door sort of frontiersman who, by different names, appeared again and again in L'Amour's widely popular pulp westerns.[142] These are the first lines of the book:

He rolled the cigarette in his lips, liking the taste of the tobacco, squinting his eyes against the sun glare. His buckskin shirt, seasoned by sun, rain, and sweat, smelled stale and old. His jeans had long since faded to a neutral color that lost itself against the desert. He was a big man, wide-shouldered, with the lean, hard-boned face of the desert rider. There was no softness in him. His toughness was ingrained and deep, without cruelty, yet quick, hard, and dangerous. Whatever wells of gentleness might lie within him were guarded and deep.[143]

Finally, chew over this passage from the opening paragraphs of Owen Wister's 1902 bestseller, *The Virginian*, widely considered to be the best, or among the best, of the western genre, which in turn deeply influenced Burroughs.[144] The novel relates in fictional form the Johnson County War[145] but presents an undistilled frontier narrative.[146] The opening chapter is titled "Enter the Man."

[H]e climbed down with the undulations of a tiger, smooth and easy…more beautiful than pictures. His broad, soft hat was pushed back; loose-knotted, dull-scarlet handkerchief sagged from his throat, and one casual thumb was hooked in the cartridge-belt that slanted across his hips. He had plainly come from many miles from somewhere across the vast horizon.…[T]he weather-beaten bloom of his face shone through it duskily, as the ripe peaches look upon their trees in a dry season. But no dinginess of travel or shabbiness of attire could tarnish the splendor that radiated from his youth and strength.[147]

In his memoirs, Custer himself drew from this common cultural well when he described a scout, one Wild Bill. It is as if he is describing himself as others had described him in the press:

He was a Plainsman in every sense of the word.…In person he was about six feet one in height, straight as the straightest of the warriors whose implacable foe he was; broad shoulders, well formed chest and limbs, and a face strikingly handsome; a sharp, clear, blue eye, which stared you straight in the face when in conversation; a finely shaped nose, inclined to be aquiline; a well-turned mouth, with lips only partially concealed by a handsome moustache. His hair and complexion were those of the perfect blond. The former was worn in uncut ringlets falling carelessly over his powerfully formed shoulders.…[H]e was one of the most perfect types of physical manhood I ever saw.[148]

Still, Custer died. But not in vain, "because no one could believe that a force such as Custer commanded could have met with disaster," the *Rocky Mountain News* opined.[149] His inglorious demise reenergized the myth and redoubled commitment to the central cultural truth: American imperialism, virtue itself, blessed by God, must not be impeded and cannot be stopped. The nation returned the favor by deifying his sacrifice. Ultimately, the frontiersmen would prevail, the sort of Holy Spirit of America's secular creation religion, with or without Jesus Custer, the papers all agreed. Why? Because "gallant pioneer hunters and frontiersmen are already eager to attack the Indians, and know how to fight Indians in Indian fashion."[150] In short, the spirit he personified endured and was reinvigorated by his imaginary sacrifice.

And *if* Custer was taken to task for his behavior, and he was ("THE CAUSE [of his death was] HIS FEARLESS DARING," a *New York Tribune* headline put it,[151] and the *New York Times* said "Custer was rashly imprudent to attack such a large number of Indians"[152]), such arguments were ultimately half-hearted and lost in the flood tide of imperial discourse, that is, the compulsion to frame the story in mythic terms. These sorts of negative assessments, and after all the *New York Tribune*'s was actually a kind of backhanded compliment, appeared in every newspaper. They presented an infusion of empirical reality—after all, as with any film genre, while the audience willingly suspends disbelief, certain rules still apply. For example, the Harry Potter series allows for wands and wizards, rom-coms insist that silly love will win out, sci-fi that time travel is possible, and so on, yet each genre carries its own internal logic. Again, in the Potter series, magic, yes, but the dead don't come back to life, rom-coms don't allow for graphic decapitation, and in proper sci-fi purple dinosaurs cannot fly around in dugout canoes. So too there are rules in America's creation story, where the frontiersman prevails, yes, but recklessness borders on the unforgivable because it threatens to reveal a principal untruth upon which the myth relies. Failure, it would seem, was not an option (remember what Vietnam did to the American psyche?). If Custer sinned by undertaking too risky behavior, it was not the particular behavior that centered on pillage and conquest and left him dead that now lay in question; rather, it was pillaging and conquering in an inappropriate way that earned him criticism. Breaking the genre's playbook invited a kind of religious cognitive dissonance, say, as if you were to question whether the Christian God had nonconsensual sex with a married virgin.

That said, the solution came all too easily. If empirical reality intruded upon the myth, as in the case of Custer's espied mythically unbecoming conduct on June 25, 1876, empirical reality took the blame, not the myth. Nobody faulted Custer for attacking the village on the Bighorn River with the intention of destruction and annihilation because he had an open invitation to do so, according to the normative American worldview; instead, he was temporarily found lacking by some because he died while attempting to rampage and kill. But mostly because he died. Still, the papers mourned, "God comfort the breaking hearts this news has caused."[153] And were readers really to conclude that he was at fault in any way? Coverage suggests not. "Custer dropped squarely into the midst of no less than ten thousand red devils and was literally torn to pieces."[154] The *Rocky Mountain News* labeled it "promiscuous slaughter."[155]

CONCLUSION

Custer's work and the more general enterprise of assisting the opening, prospecting, felling, stealing, and settling of the west, problematize Turner's version of the myth. In particular, the cadence is wrong. We find no individual effete easterners going west to experience stripping down and rebirth. Instead, as the historical record shows, indeed as newspapers reported, people moved west in numbers, driven by unremarkable, quotidian impulses, to slake the thirst for various kinds of opportunity and the chance ultimately to better their lives. And that they were, especially in the postbellum period, afforded a modicum of government protection and, further, that the protectors were committed to the destruction of the Plains Indian way of life, which naturally meant taking Native lands, bear little resemblance to Turner's romantic tale wherein Indians simply disappear when inconvenient to the master narrative. Press coverage duly reported the empirical versions of events, which you might expect to have called the myth out; instead, the news framing crafted the enterprise, on the whole, as essentially wholesome, necessary, and divinely sanctioned, if entirely imaginative. In this way, the whole becomes more than the sum of its parts. Custer became an American Jesus Christ because he gave his life for the nation, much as Tarzan, or the Virginian, or Lieutenant John J. Dunbar in Kevin Costner's *Dances with Wolves* offered their lives for the greater good while wiping the slate clean of imperial hubris.

Custer's death also complicated the fiction that providence smiled on white conquest. The "boy" had behaved poorly, it seems, but wasn't the better story his immolation on behalf of the nation? By and by, the mythical discourse took it all in stride because it abides as it must. Casting Custer as an American Jesus, of course, was full of holes, which is not more than to say that the frontier myth itself didn't and doesn't measure up to empirical reality. So what? Jesus Custer made at least as much sense as the idea that God granted the land to America or that Indians were devils. In other words, it simultaneously made no sense yet made perfect cultural sense. "We have now an Indian war in full blast," erupted the *San Francisco Daily Bulletin*, speaking for the press. But, again, it was a question of degree, for the war had been ongoing since, as the paper noted, the days of the Pilgrims. Yet this more obstreperous tone carried the day. And so the creation story came to read more like the hard-edged canter of the Old Testament for a time (i.e., more unquestioned violence), but the myth itself endured as a kind of American children's Bible story. "The best use to make of an Indian who will not stay upon a reservation is to kill him," the *Chicago Tribune* reminded readers on July 7, 1876.[156] Or, two days later, "The only heroic Indian is a dead one....A single flap of the eagle's wings will avenge them."[157] Or "Their habits and instincts [are] the same as wild beasts, and as such they must be treated until extermination or absolute submission is the result."[158]

But wait just a minute, the American Jesus had died! But don't worry. He would rise again, because the frontiersman was always rising again. And military conquest would continue to pave the way for ongoing creation and re-creation:

> The attractions of the minerals and the opportunity for stock-raising in these Territories will increase the emigration there steadily and rapidly. It would be folly to resist it, and cruel to subject the emigrants to an unequal frontier struggle with roving hostile Indians. These Territories can only be made safely inhabitable by ridding them of the savages, and the interests of civilization demand that this shall be done....Fortunately, this policy may be carried out

without doing the Indians any injustice; on the contrary it will be the most humane to them.[159]

Presented in this light, Custer was humanized by his imperfections.

The "boy General" was a known and well-appreciated rule breaker and lousy student, yet he was blessed with natural smarts, the kind of "boy" Americana loves. He resembled a Hollywood action star. This obviously contributed to his charisma. In the real world, he defied authority for love (and was court-martialed for it before being drawn back into service),[160] at Westpoint he played pranks when he should have been studying, he defied convention by dressing in provocative and unusual ways, and he was oh so brave, daring to the point of recklessness, and successful enough that the term "Custer's luck" gained wide currency. In short, in news portrayals and, for that matter, in his self-portrayal for *Galaxy Magazine* and his memoir, *My Life on the Plains*, Custer was a frontiersman all the way, precisely as Beverly J. Stoeltje frames the archetypal hero: "If and when our hero returns, he regales the folks back home with stories of his exploits, which include the discovery and conquest of exotic lands and people....Brave pioneers will follow his route and settle the newly conquered land, bringing their ideas of civilization with them and imposing it in the name of some ideologically rationalized enterprise."[161]

The *New York Times* eloquently expressed the prevailing press sentiment in a passage on July 8, 1876, that speaks poetically of the innate superiority of organized, unified whites playing defense against aggressive savages, heroic loss/sacrifice for the glory of a greater cause, and the profound belief that white American conquest was entirely in accordance with the nature of things: "The companies had successfully thrown themselves across the path of the advancing enemy, and had been annihilated. Not a man escaped to tell the tale, but it was inscribed on the surface of these barren hills in a language more eloquent than words."[162] And those mythic hills were American through and through. Turner couldn't have phrased it better than the *San Francisco Daily Bulletin*: "The soil belongs no more to the Indian than to the wild animals which feed upon its herbage or upon one another, and...those who cultivate must take possession, and those who do not must give way."[163] In a short piece titled "Comment by the New York Journals," the same paper recorded that "On one proposition all seemed to agree, to wit: that the policy of the Government should be made one of deadly aggression, looking to the total extermination of the treacherous Indians."[164] Custer, through his sacrifice, enabled total mythical victory.

Finally, then, Custer was an American messiah. If he was flawed, and he was, his faults only served to magnify his humanity. Like Christ, he died in a gruesome fashion doing God's work. He sacrificed what was most precious of all things, his special life, for true believers. He died so that others might be delivered to the promised land (and they were) and forgiven their trespasses. And in life he served as a shining example of how an American might personify behavior favored by his (civil) religion. Custer was famed as an "Indian killer"[165] and consequently was no cheek turner, yet he provided for America a model of deportment and sangfroid that was Christlike in the ways he embodied and epitomized America's providential mission, adjusted as required to accommodate the times. And, like Christ, Custer bridged generations, he welded past with future, and he had really good hair. He rang true. He was a man for his times. As Sam Elliott's character the Stranger says of the Dude in *The Big Lebowski*, "He fit right in there."

CHAPTER 4

THE MEXICAN REVOLUTION: "A CHAOS OF THE LAND"

"Latin America doesn't matter."
—*Richard Nixon to Donald Rumsfeld*[1]

*That is how to deny our own history. We have transformed
our imperial way of life from a culture that we built and
benefitted from into an abstract self-evident Law of Nature.*
—*William Appleman Williams*[2]

News judgment, politics, history, and myth predisposed the U.S. press to take a significant interest in the Mexican Revolution, 1910–20, especially during the years of most intense fighting, 1913–16. From the murder of President Francisco I. Madero in February 1913, which renewed fighting, to Francisco "Pancho" Villa's cross-border raid on Columbus, New Mexico, in March 1916, which elicited the second U.S. military intervention in three years (and heralded an end to revolutionary fighting), American reportage of the civil war next door proved good for the news business. Seemingly endless tales of danger, loss, death, survival, mayhem, savagery, and bravery sold papers. The revolution was front-page news across America throughout 1914.

With respect to politics, the press evinced a clear and present sense that the civil war challenged and possibly threatened American political and economic interests in Mexico, further raising the news value.

After all, the two countries shared a 2,000-mile border, and unrest in northern Mexico threatened to spill into the American southwest, an area taken from Mexico in war within living memory (1846–48). Plus, Americans had invested heavily in Mexico after Porfirio Díaz established his long-running presidency/dictatorship, from 1876 to 1910.

The weight of history remained burdensome, too, given the short (to Mexico) years since the United States had seized half of Mexico's territory as booty of war in 1848. Further, Mexico's internecine conflict confronted the first premises upon which American foreign policy had always been constructed: manifest destiny and the Monroe Doctrine. The former championed jingoistic American expansionism, bathed in the syrup of alleged divine sanction and aggressive social Darwinism.[3] The latter openly challenged European interference in the hemisphere—but in favor of budding U.S. hegemony.[4] In this way, the Mexican Revolution issued a call to arms for a certain kind of American conception of the world and its sense of place for both countries in that order of things, a project to which the press contributed importantly and ineluctably.

Enter the frontier myth. With respect to Mexico, it married the Monroe Doctrine and manifest destiny in ways that may have been unhinged from empirical or historical reality—for example, that the United States had a divinely sanctioned need/right to expand at others' expense or that U.S. military intervention augured positive outcomes or that Mexicans were racially inferior to Americans—but were nonetheless palpable in press coverage and spoke eloquently and directly to the frontier myth.[5] Of course, since Turner's 1893 essay had been published, the world had changed. By 1915, the automobile had become popular, telephones were emergent, airplanes had been invented, and the United States had become a major regional and burgeoning world power. And of course the world was at war by 1914. New ideas abounded too—jazz, Freud, Einstein. In short, as ever, things changed. Yet in one important way they also remained, if not the same precisely, then as least contiguous.

This is important because, not infrequently since the end of the Vietnam War, one encounters the assertion that the frontier myth faded away with the closing of the frontier in 1890, as identified in the census noted by Turner. But the myth did no such thing, and Turner himself argued, after all, that the conditioning effects of the process of settling the west, as he understood it, would endure because they had become effectively hard-wired into the national character. And, while he confused empirical reality with a long-held cultural vision, he was right. Two American presidents of the early twentieth century, Theodore Roosevelt (1901–09) and Woodrow Wilson (1913–21), embraced Turner's ideas and acted upon them even as they interpreted them to fit their own particular worldviews.

The lower forty-eight states may indeed have achieved a patina of settlement by 1890, but they were hardly full. They aren't exactly full right now, as I recall from my drive across I-90 last year on my way to spend Christmas with family in Idaho. Part of the problem lies in the way that we were schooled. Like many, I learned at university in the 1980s that American "isolationism," beginning with George Washington's legendary farewell address, prevailed in the decades leading up to the Second World War. According to what I was taught, America was a lone wolf and eschewed getting tangled up in international affairs. But in fact the United States repeatedly intervened in the affairs of Latin American countries during this time. Such a casting of isolationism reflects a larger American worldview in which Latin America didn't count for much because, as suggested in the title of Lars Schoultz's excellent study, the region was "Beneath the United States." From just 1890 to 1932, the United States invaded, landed troops, and/or occupied Argentina (1890), Chile (1891), Haiti (1891, 1914–34), Hawaii (1893–today), Panama (1895, 1901–14, 1918–20), Nicaragua (1896, 1898, 1899, 1907, 1912–23), Cuba (1898–1902, 1906–09, 1912), Puerto Rico (1898–today), Guam, (1898–today), Honduras (1903, 1907, 1911, 1912, 1919, 1924–25), Dominican Republic (1901–04, 1914, 1916–24), Mexico (1914, 1916), Guatemala (1920), and El Salvador (1932).

Nevertheless, Latin Americans frequently looked to the United States, as did each of the three political candidates battling for victory in the Mexican Revolution as it entered its most decisive phase, 1913–15. Support from the United States, the three leaders calculated, could be secured with effective propaganda. This included, most importantly, diplomatic recognition, but it also included access to financial backing, arms, and possibly the passage of troops for strategic purposes through the southwestern United States. As a result, Victoriano Huerta, former commander of the Mexican armed forces, who had successfully plotted the murder of President Francisco Madero in February 1913,[6] "First Chief" Venustiano Carranza, former governor of the northern state of Coahuila, the haughty armchair general who claimed civilian leadership of the revolutionary movement,[7] and Francisco "Pancho" Villa, a social bandit-cum-revolutionary hero who had risen from abject poverty to lead the nation's greatest armed division, organized and staged complex propaganda operations in the United States.[8]

After Madero's murder, Huerta, Carranza, and Villa engaged actively and energetically in media self-promotion while attempting to denigrate one another in the American press.[9] Huerta's efforts stumbled and then simply collapsed months before he fled the country in July 1914. He was never able to overcome the label of murderer, tarred in the media by Villa and President Wilson (and by historians) with responsibility for the assassination of Madero. Carranza's public relations operations met with modest success, but this occurred only well after his troops had soundly defeated Villa in battle over the spring and summer of 1915. Villista propaganda, on the other hand, was highly successful, both in terms of reorienting American press opinion from condemnatory to congratulatory as well as ably achieving similar results with U.S. diplomatic personnel.

Villa effectively leveraged three propaganda elements to his advantage. First, he gained an earlier start than his rivals, who then struggled to overcome a media frame of his shaping (i.e., that they were "savages"). Second, the key thrust of Villista propaganda championed Villa in tropey mythical Americana. In this way, he came to epitomize, insofar as a half-breed Mexican could, an Americanized Mexican frontiersman. Third, Villista propaganda energetically and ruthlessly Othered Carranza and Huerta as so many stereotypical savage Mexicans, the antithesis of the frontiersman, which in turn, in comparison, further bolstered Villa's image. The combined results helped deliver a knockout blow to Huerta and then left Carranza reeling after the summer of 1914, with little hope of winning the propaganda wars. In short, judging by the tone and content of the U.S. press in late 1913, all of

1914, and as late as the spring of 1915, Villa won American hearts and minds—even as he would come to lose militarily on the battlefields of the revolution.[10]

The military struggle notwithstanding, Villa had more than competing propaganda messages with which to grapple. He also confronted a none-too-subtle predilection by U.S. press outlets to portray Mexico and Mexicans in stereotyped ways. In 1913, Mexicans in the press tended to appear much like Mexicans in pulp fiction westerns and in newly emerging movie westerns, in fact much like Mexico and Mexicans always had in the American mass media and public mind.[11] In other words, the news imagery of 1846–48 endured and even thrived, and it eventually caught Villa up.

"DOMINANT FACT"

The U.S. print media had long been nursed on the ethnocentric, colonialist dogmas of manifest destiny and the hegemonic implications of the Monroe Doctrine,[12] and expressed indignation, horror, and vicarious fascination as it bore witness to the violent turbulence to the immediate south. The American press—and, after all, to Americans this medium served as the primary source of information about Mexico—expended much energy and many resources to cover the news story of revolution.[13] Here again agenda-setting theory and recent research suggest that the media functioned not merely to frame the story for American readers, that is, to tell readers *how* and *what* to think: rather, the reporters and political leaders were also hewn from Americana, hence a consonance among reportage, policy, and public opinion, though the fit was (and is) never perfect, as witnessed by opposition in 1846 to President James Polk's warmongering or criticism of "boy General" George Armstrong Custer circa 1876. President Wilson himself endorsed the phenomenon of agenda-setting in a press release printed in the *New York Times* in March 1916.[14] In short, the press tended strongly, as it had in 1846–48 and 1876, to reflect the sociocultural milieu from which it had emerged—hence, to put it in contemporary terms, a racist nation begets a racist press, a sexist nation begets a sexist press, and a growing empire ineluctably begets an encouraging imperial press.[15] The corresponding imagery operates as a kind of palimpsest, conjuring up "news" that in fact narrated the revolution from a well-established and well-trod collection of American tropes (e.g., we hate imperialism because...) and denials (e.g., we do not support imperialism because...).

The result—given a climate in which an American vision championing its racial, cultural, and historical superiority to all people of mixed-blood ancestry in the Americas (i.e., half-breed, mestizo, colored) had flourished for two centuries—lent to a none-too-subtle predilection in the press to Other Mexico and Mexicans in the strongest of terms. The mainstream press exhibited this tendency both generally and specifically, as occasion warranted. In the former case, strongly pejorative stereotypical images remained predictable in the years leading up to Villa's raid on Columbus in 1916, though they seldom lacked creativity. In the latter case, the singular media rise and fall of Mexican revolutionary Villa provided an example that effectively established the pale of the stereotyping in three acts.

First, the press identified in Villa a model that demonstrated the clarity of its vision if viewed through a mythical lens.[16] In short, *qua* Mexican, he was presented as a garden variety savage in the mold of reports from 1846 or of how Sitting Bull was portrayed in 1876. Second, defying the conglomeration of heavily clichéd images the media employed to interpret Mexico, the press shortly came to distinguish Villa as an individual of substantive merit (though still stereotyped). Remarkably, he became for a time a kind of Mexican frontiersman. And third, after Villistas crossed the international border to raid Columbus in March 1916, the press reverted to the most negative of framings.[17] The savage came roaring back.

This engenders a second reason why a consideration of these images is crucial. To the extent that a free press and the shape of foreign policy in a democratic society reflect the will of the electorate, how the press interpreted Mexico during the revolution sheds light on the nature of American self-perceptions and the cultural premises upon which American foreign policy has been built, especially since, as noted, many scholars identify the closing of the frontier with Turner's essay. But, as discussed, Turner himself was less glib than prophetic in his assertion that the myth would endure: "He would be a rash prophet who should assert that the expansive character of American life has now entirely ceased. Movement has been its dominant fact, and, unless this training has no effect upon a people, the American energy will continually demand a wider field for its exercise."[18] Three principal sorts of interrelated depictions prevailed and bore striking resemblance to reportage on the Mexican War and Custer's demise. In the first case, the press personified Mexico and Mexicans as racially inferior, the basic idea being that a country of espied half-breeds must necessarily lack civilizing tendencies. A second press depiction imagined that Mexico and Mexicans were culturally retrograde, stuck discernibly in an earlier, backward stage of historical development. A third tendency depicted Mexico and Mexicans as morally infirm, savage in nearly every respect.

A BREED APART

According to the press, Mexico's perceived racial problem stemmed from its ethnic heritage—mestizo, a mixture of Spanish and Indian lineage, a "half-breed" in the parlance of the day. The celebrated American novelist Jack London reported from Mexico for *Collier's* magazine and clearly identified race as the fundamental problem underlying all of Mexico's presumed ills. He well expressed the prevailing American press sentiment about the effects of racial mixing, *mestizaje*:

> Mexico is an Indian country....Sixty-five per cent of the inhabitants are pure Indians; 15 per cent are pure Spanish, Americans, English, and other foreigners. The remaining 20 per cent are mixed Indian and Spanish....And it is precisely this 20 per cent half-breed class that foments all the trouble, plays childishly with the tools of giants, and makes a shambles and a chaos of the land....The "breeds" are the predatory class. They produce nothing. They create nothing.[19]

Forum magazine endorsed this assessment and went so far as to provide its readers with lists of attributes that allegedly characterized and differentiated the American from the Mexican. Charging that

Mexicans were natally "inclined toward crime,"[20] and claiming that Mexicans' "mixed" racial makeup predisposed the nation to civil strife, it complained that the Indian component of Mexico's "mixed" blood had long washed away any beneficial effects gained by Spanish lineage—itself weak and listless compared with the northern European bloodlines common in the United States. That said, the six features that characterized the Mexican were as much cultural as racial in origin:

1. Mainly of Indian type;
2. Illiterate;
3. Mainly of illegitimate birth;
4. Inefficient as workers;
5. Intemperate;
6. Quarrelsome.[21]

Americans could be summarized in four lines:

1. Loyal submission to the will of the majority;
2. Candid recognition of the inalienable rights of the minority;
3. A cool, sober judgment;
4. A very high standard of education and morals.[22]

In short, the press suggested that Mexicans functioned as the antithesis of American normality—and the border separating the two nations served as an unambiguous frontier, a point of demarcation that closely adhered to and promoted well-established American notions about how the mythical frontier imaginatively sorted out the civilized from the savage. An editorial cartoon from the February 20, 1913, issue of the *New York Tribune* (Figure 4.1) captures the sentiment. First, it expresses a common stereotype in which eternal and universal justice—that is, American justice—was presented as a female, dredging a common and long-standing stereotype of the feminine.[23] But Mexico resided so far from civilization that she had become a butcher, as evidenced by the bodies beneath the feet and blood-drenched knife she clasps triumphantly. The brief tagline "MEXICO—Viva What's His Name! Till the Day after Tomorrow!" scoffs at the very pretense of the existence of effective governance, let alone democracy, in Mexico. The country, the illustration implies, had simply lost its mind—and all sense of gender-based decorum to boot.

Francisco Madero ushered out thirty-five-year dictator Porfirio Díaz in the spring of 1911 and became president for fifteen months beginning in November. In February 1913, on the eve of Madero's assassination by reactionary Huerista forces, an event that would plunge the nation more deeply into civil war, the *San Francisco Examiner*, flagship of the William Randolph Hearst media empire, published an illustration (Figure 4.2) that

Figure 4.1. *New York Tribune*, February 20, 1913

expresses a variety of the press imaginings of Mexico. The cartoon reduces the country to an energetic but ultimately hapless single male figure, depicted as a scrawny and ungainly ersatz cowboy-esque character. Commenting sharply that Mexicans seem to lack self-control and good sense, it suggests that the light of progress, the irruption of civilization, will elude Mexico so long as the country continues to saddle itself with violence and havoc (as signified by the pistol, torch, and stereotyped garb). But is this condition a reflection of poor choices made or simply innate? The depiction suggests both possibilities. In the former, clearly all the character need do is drop the accoutrements of savagery and step off the treadmill of wasted energy. Choosing more sensible, less patchwork clothing might be a good first step and signify the ability to make better decisions. In the latter case—and either associating Mexicans with animals or representing them in animal form was common during this period—the rendering associates Mexico with a lower life form (the yapping mutt), implying that perhaps Mexico's problems stemmed from biological deficiencies. Either way, the civilized world, the world of "progress," seemed elusive.

Two years later an editorial sketch published in the *Los Angeles Times* (Figure 4.3) reinforced the *San Francisco Examiner* pictorial. In this case, Mexico is again presented as unable to control its predilection for bedlam and "anarchy." Yet while the signifiers here differ—torch and liquor bottle (*polque*, a misspelling of *pulque*, a spirit fashioned

Figure 4.2. *San Francisco Examiner*, February 18, 1913

Figure 4.3. *Los Angeles Times*, March 30, 1915

from fermented juice of the maguey plant) versus torch and pistol—the message remains similar: Mexico is destined to languor in its defunct culture until, at the very least, it abandons its poorly chosen behaviors. Again the illustration wants to have it both ways—insinuating that the behavior may also be more systemic in origin. In this case, the shaded color of the Mexican skin suggests that race played a role in engendering the alcoholism, implied by the *polque* and wanton visage. A *Chicago Tribune* editorial addressed the matter bluntly: "Brigandage," it explained, is "in the Mexican blood."[24]

Echoing the darker side of Turner's geographically deterministic thesis, the *Chicago Tribune* in early 1914 observed that "On one side [of the Rio Grande there exists] shiftlessness, poverty, slovenliness, laziness; on the other side enterprise, energy, prosperity, and thrift. It is as if we were stepping from one century to another."[25] This should come as no surprise, the *Los Angeles Times* reasoned, for "The Mexican seems to have gained little or nothing in civilization in 400 years."[26] The *North American Review* asserted that "Mexico is not, in fact, a nation, but a country peopled by many tribes of Indians of varying degrees of development, none reaching what we would call civilization."[27] In other words, Indians were not simply backward but in some cases actually incapable of civilization, as the term was used by the media. Paraphrasing the famous comment by President Wilson that he was "going to teach Latin America how to elect a few good men," *Everybody's* magazine confidently asserted that "We must teach them how to respect us....Then we must teach them how to behave."[28]

A letter to the editor of the *Nation* captured the prevalent media sentiment this way: "The average [Mexican] peon is mentally a child and morally a savage....[The revolutionary leaders] are simply savages of superior intelligence...[and] they take the field because it affords them an opportunity to murder, rob, and torture."[29] A *Los Angeles Times* editorial cartoon (Figure 4.4) agreed that Mexicans were childlike—diminutive, spoiled, excessively emotional, weak, lacking self-control, given to tantrums—whereas Americans were hearty adults (symbolized by a vigorous Uncle Sam) and more appropriately interested in grown-up behavior (war, ironically, but in Europe).

Figure 4.4. *Los Angeles Times*, August 14, 1914

It is again worth noting the stereotyped *charro* dress, visible in three of the cartoons presented thus far (and in countless others)[30]—oversized dude sombrero, bandanna, cowboy boots. Cacti, too, help the viewer identify the imagined landscape. In their own right, of course, such signifiers may mean nothing more than what they are—a certain type of clothing worn by Mexicans and a particular variety of plant that, in fact, grows widely in Mexico. Yet, in their ubiquity, they also comprise pieces of a larger code of signification, a subtext that provides visual clues to reinforce the more direct message of the cartoons.

Figure 4.5. *Washington Star*, June 2, 1915

In this way, clothes signify cultural backwardness, and cacti represent the barren waste of Mexico and its supposedly less evolved culture. Consider Figure 4.5. Again diminutive Mexicans are clad in rags and stand in opposition to and beneath Woodrow Wilson, playing the role of beat cop. It reinforces mythical tropes and economically expresses the Monroe Doctrine.

In sum, in both text and pictorials, Mexico and the United States occupied competing sides of a frontier depicted by the press in mythical terms. Mexicans, then, tended to be stereotyped in plainly pejorative fashion in 1913 and 1914. But, at the same time, a notable exception emerged—one Francisco "Pancho" Villa, the semiliterate and erstwhile social bandit from the northern state of Chihuahua, who nearly won the civil war in 1914 before suffering disastrous military losses in the spring and summer of 1915.

"RISE OF VILLA'S STAR"

Early in 1913, the American press tarred Villa as just another Mexican savage, but his image blossomed favorably in 1914 in lockstep with his increasing battlefield successes and, notably, because of an effective propaganda operation that promoted warm friendship with and welcoming hospitality toward the United States.[31] This more positive casting endured until his military collapse in the spring and summer of 1915, at which point the press lost interest in him, as evidenced by a lack of news coverage.[32]

In 1913, the *New York Times* made the extraordinary claim that "Francisco Villa, a man who has been an outlaw and murderer for many years, and who is now leading an arbitrary and despotic reign of terror over Northern Mexico[,] is more cruel and barbarous in his methods than any tyrant in the world's history."[33] In a way, this passage may have partially excused his "savagery." After all, Villa was fighting, as *Everybody's* magazine put it, a "ruthless Indian war."[34] What might one have expected? Two months later the *Chicago Tribune* exhorted that "the murderer...is no better than [outgoing dictator Victoriano] Huerta, the murderer of President Francisco Madero." Tearing a page from Turner, it continued, "The everlasting issue of civilization versus savagery is joined." Reiterating post-Custer reportage, it added, "The bandit leaders must all be reduced."[35] Here the paper marginalized Villa by lumping him into a well-established "savage" category, and like one of Jack London's "breeds" he stood directly anathema to the influences of civilization. He stood opposite to America, in short, according to the press.

Yet Villa initiated a savvy and aggressive propaganda campaign that would help to turn the tide. He employed press agents, charmed, bullied, bribed, lied to, cajoled, and otherwise behaved as a canny politician intent on self-promotion.[36] And it paid dividends by the spring of 1914.[37] As the *Nation* observed, his popularity derived from "superior press facilities."[38] His image was becoming Americanized insofar as Villa was suddenly seen as exemplifying traits favored by Americans—he was brave, organized, tough, modest, exciting, a winner, tireless, and took initiative. And he dressed like a cowboy in his real life. He was becoming, in other words, a kind of frontiersman. The results shaded a character not so different from Rambo, Indiana Jones, or Hollywood's version of Davy Crockett. Further, Villa availed himself of rhetorical opportunities to play up his preference for peace and nonviolence—though he was an exceptional combatant—and his bitter opposition to tyranny and injustice. For example, the *New York Times* on its front page (which Villa sometimes seemed to own) quoted the general:

> Mexico has enough troubles of her own, and is not seeking a war with any foreign country, certainly not the United States. I have come to the border for the purpose of conferring and seeking advice from my good American friends.... Say for me that we want no war, are seeking no war, and wish only the closest and most friendly relations with our neighbors of the North.[39]

The *San Francisco Examiner*, initially much opposed to Villa, came to view him in the most favorable terms, for a Mexican, depicting him as a capable man of action: "General Villa, grimy with dust and sweat, a red bandanna handkerchief about his neck, participated. He rode up and down the lines swearing and cheering, cursing and calling upon the saints."[40] Further, while allowing Villa to speak for himself, it played up his humble origins, his earnestness, and his integrity:

> I am nothing but a plain soldier and the words you will hear me utter now will be the words of an uncultured man.... Senors, for the first time in my life I am going to propose a toast, and for the first time in my life I am going to drink a toast, and it will be the first time that I ever willingly let liquor pass my lips....You gentlemen should be proud that you are Americans; that you represent the press of the greatest nation on earth, ruled by the greatest man alive, President Wilson.[41]

By the spring of 1914, Villa's image had experienced a remarkable makeover. The *Literary Digest* purported, if hyperbolically, to speak for the entire press of the United States. A headline proclaimed "THE RISE OF VILLA'S STAR." The article championed his "born genius as a strategist and commander" and stressed how "tremendous is the personal triumph of Villa."[42]

Throughout 1914 and into 1915, via well-orchestrated propaganda, Villa continued to serve as probably his own best image choreographer. For example, he cabled the *San Francisco Examiner* in May 1914:

> I have no aspirations. I will go back to work as soon as I drive out that drunkard, Huerta. I am only a poor man. I wish only to see my countryman freed from tyranny. I am a patriot. Yet I am the man whom they call the bandit Villa. If I wanted money I could be the richest man in the world, for I have walked among gold, silver, and jewels.[43]

Such presentations conjured up attributes Americans held dear—honesty, abstinence, humble origins, the virtue of work, and a healthy suspicion of ill-gotten gain—and fit well with the paper's sweetening assessments, which lauded Villa for his power, his "genius," his political acumen—and his ruthlessness.[44] He was like the hero of *The Virginian*, the enormously popular novel of the same name, released in 1912 and churned out in film at least five times. Villa was almost

American—or apparently as close as the press would allow a half-breed Mexican to become.

In September 1914, the *San Francisco Examiner* cited Villa as being the most potent, capable, and popular force in Mexico.[45] Publisher Hearst used the front page to wax Villa:

> The one man in this Mexican conflict and crisis who has appeared to tower over all others in personal power and capacity, in the magnetism to lead, the mastery to command and the ability to govern, is Francisco Villa. There are many men in Mexico more cultivated than Villa, many better educated, many more trained in diplomatic services and in the gentler arts of government. But these qualities are not what is required....A strong hand is needed, a determined purpose, a masterful mind, an experience gained from personal contact with the mass[es]....These qualities Francisco Villa possesses as no other man in Mexico.[46]

All this from a publisher who six months earlier had been calling for aggressive U.S. military intervention in Mexico to reinstate liberal rule.

Like the *San Francisco Examiner*, the *Chicago Tribune* sharply changed its portrayal of Villa. And, with no visible trace of irony, it went so far as to express mild astonishment at it:

> It is not to be wondered at that the personality of "Pancho" Villa, with its strange contradictions, is one that appeals to the imagination to a greater degree than any other man now in the public eye....Perhaps it was this appeal that drew newspaper writers around him and thus gave him a publicity which other big figures in Mexican affairs have missed....[I]t is about him that are woven the most romantic and fantastic stories, all interesting and some true....He is good "copy" anyway you look at him.[47]

As "good 'copy,'" Villa exhibited key mythical frontier traits. For example, he earned credit for disavowing any interest in becoming leader of Mexico because frontiersman are natural leaders. The press highlighted the story of his lack of political ambition yet portrayed him as nonetheless politically savvy and a natural, physically dynamic leader. Typically, such framing included references to his humble origins, his self-reliance, his commitment to formal education (even better, he was self-taught) and to uplifting the downtrodden, his love of the ideals of democracy, his bravery, his honesty, his decency, his admiration for American politics and things American, and his violent opposition to unnecessary authority and authoritarian rule (i.e., Huerta and Carranza). Photograph after photograph on the front pages presented Villa as a cowboy, typically astride or in the company of a horse. In short, collectively, this violent cowboy was depicted increasingly under conventions of the frontiersman. At the peak of his formidable press popularity, Villa stood tall in the saddle.

Like the *Chicago Tribune* and the *San Francisco Examiner*, the *New York Times* followed the general press reframing of Villa. On one of many occasions, in late September 1914, just days after Villa formally disavowed Carranza and the civil war erupted anew, the paper reported that "VILLA WON'T RUN FOR PRESIDENT."[48] And it lauded him as honest and reliable, displaying true grit. Distancing itself from an earlier tendency to stereotype Villa pejoratively, the paper added that he was "a Mexican of an unusual type."[49] The "savage" and "murderer" had come a long way in six months.

The *Nation* expressed mild astonishment about the public transformation from cretin to frontiersman:

> [Villa's] rapid and steady emergence from the reputation of being the worst of cutthroats and patriotic leader, as well as a military captain of remarkable ability, is one of the most extraordinary phenomena we can recall in the history of any public age. A year ago, if anybody had said that the people of this country...would be able to find in the doing of "Pancho" Villa a bit of real comfort and solace amid the general gloom, he would have been regarded as the silliest of jokers....It seems that his conduct ever since has been that of a loyal citizen and a friend of peace and orderly government.[50]

But then Villa's fortunes declined precipitously in the late spring and summer of 1915. Villa lost badly on the battlefield to Carrancista general Álvaro Obregón (who would go on to replace Carranza as president in 1920). Villa's public persona as Americanized Mexican frontiersman, and the revolution itself as yet another installment of the ineluctable and timeless frontier struggle of civilization quelling barbarism, collapsed simply by being withdrawn from circulation. In defeat, Villa suddenly ceased to be newsworthy and all but disappeared from print. And so it seems as if this frontier western was badly plotted because he didn't ultimately prevail as frontiersmen are wont to do. And the myth, meanwhile, offered no alternative ending, no Custer/Christ–like martyrdom, because Villa remained alive but was no longer a player, no longer news. Instead, his mythical nemesis, the effete and haughty Mexican Other, Carranza, prevailed militarily and went on to secure de facto U.S. diplomatic recognition in October 1915. The result was that the news framing of the Mexican Revolution lost its positive mythical resonance, at least insofar as Villa had reoriented it. Then everything changed abruptly and dramatically and angrily on March 10, 1916, when news broke that Villistas had staged a daring cross-border raid at Columbus, New Mexico.

"INSIST ON DISINFECTING THEM"

Villistas raided Columbus, a small border town, killing seventeen Americans and razing a number of buildings.[51] Speaking with one colonial voice, the American press at once expressed shock and outrage, and the Wilson administration promptly launched a limited and unsuccessful invasion of northern Mexico to capture and punish Villa.[52] Meanwhile, in the American press in 1916, opinions of Villa, who had begun 1913 as a Mexican scoundrel but by 1914 had been reinvented as a modified Mexican frontiersman, plummeted. The Columbus attack earned him vitriolic damnation while the story consumed the front pages for several weeks. In short, the Columbus story brought his image slightly more than full circle. Suddenly, not only was Villa back where he had started—presented as just another diabolical Mexican—but also, because of his unprovoked attack on the United

States, the reframing took on an added urgency and increased vitriol. In other words, over three years his image garnered both the best and the worst of stereotyped Mexican depictions in the press, effectively illuminating the extremes of the mythical American imaginary in the print media.

Despite Villa's generally favorable portrayal in the press in 1914, it is important to remember that his country and countrymen received no less stereotyped coverage than they had before Villa began to shine in press reports. For example, in early March 1916, on the eve of the Columbus raid, the *Chicago Tribune* noted that, when considering Mexicans, the United States "must insist on disinfecting them, vaccinating them, and treating them to gasoline shampoos," a common delousing treatment for so many lice-ridden vermin.[53] At the same time, the *Los Angeles Times* openly called on the United States to "Fight disease on the border."[54] Further, it warned, Americans in Mexico were "in danger"[55] as "anarchy and starvation"[56] continued to plague that land. Meanwhile, the *New York Times* endorsed the idea of military intervention in Mexico.[57] In short, Mexico remained savage even as Villa was rehabilitated as a frontiersman, and it remained savage after his disappearance as a news item.

But far more damning images emerged in the days and weeks immediately after the raid. For example, the *New York Times* reported that Villa, formerly portrayed as a fine role model who elicited great loyalty from his men, suddenly became a despot who ruled "by fear" and was "secretly hated" by his men.[58] The 1914 pal of America, the paper noted, had with relish (yet inexplicably) issued orders to kill "all the gringos."[59] Then he had fled like a coward in retreat almost as quickly when it became clear that the United States would react militarily to the raid. Smearing Villa by likening him to an American Apache warrior loathed by the press, the *New York Times* reasoned further that Villa was now "prepared to wage the kind of warfare old Geronimo loved."[60] Additionally, the paper reported how, with much enthusiasm and viciousness, Villa engaged in torturing Mexicans who had allegedly "collaborated" with American interests.[61]

Yet the New York daily's portrayal of Villa as savage blanched in comparison to depictions in the *Los Angeles Times*. Here, in this most chauvinistic of publications, Villa became a stain on what it meant to be stereotyped as a Mexican. He was an "outlaw," devoted to "murder, arson, theft," and "death to Americans."[62] On the next page, the paper reported that Mexicans "fought like devils" and that Villa was prone to "blind rages."[63] The following day the paper reported that, despite his dangerousness, Villa was none too clever; through "apathy" and "gross inefficiency," he had allowed a mere woman to escape from his "wanton" clutches.[64] Cynically chastising other (unnamed) publications as having been swayed by Villa's considerable charm and propaganda—to which, as shown, the *Los Angeles Times* itself had earlier fallen prey—the paper summarized Villa this way later that day: "Villa has had a long, bloody and turbulent record.... Villa is the vilest kind of ruffian, in addition to being grossly ignorant. He can neither read nor write." (In fact, he was literate, having learned to read while in jail.) It lumped him in with "all of the uneducated people of Mexico, and that means 85 percent of them[,]...[who] hate the United States and are in such a state of primitive ignorance" that they repeatedly and stupidly "defy the hulking giant to the north."[65]

A cartoon printed from the *Des Moines Register and Leader* (Figure 4.6) supported the view of the *Los Angeles Times*. In it, Villa, cast as a spoiled brat, requires strong corrective action by Uncle Sam. The illustration equates Mexican behavior—and thereby the culture of Mexico more generally—with filth and immaturity. You will note that Uncle Sam, representing the United States, is larger, stronger, and cleaner. It provides a common expression of imperial projection and displacement: *I must really be clean if I need to clean you.* Villa, diminutive and childlike, desperately needs a bath, and Sam is giving it to him, in the fashion befitting a cartoon canine. Meanwhile, other key Mexican political figures as well as the revolution itself (symbolizing that the nation as a whole stands in need of ablution), having been corralled, appear to be next in line for moral scouring. Notice, too, the worn-out clothing and lack of footwear, emphasizing the godawful depth to which Mexico had sunk as a result of years of internecine conflict.

The *Los Angeles Times* proffered an angrier, more direct solution than elemental laundering (Figure 4.7). In a cartoon of March 15, 1916, as a response to the raid on Columbus, it promoted intervention with extreme prejudice. Here Villa and, indeed, all of Mexico are represented as a snake.[66] In a sense, the cartoon also bastardizes the Mexican flag, which features an eagle grasping a serpent atop a cactus. But the eagle also symbolizes the United States, so it is ignored, lest it invite confusion, and replaced by a gigantic boot belonging to Uncle Sam. Although the serpent, carrying negative Christian baggage (here a rattlesnake),

Figure 4.6. *Des Moines Register and Leader*, March 17, 1916

Figure 4.7. *Los Angeles Times*, March 15, 1916

is dangerous, and in this depiction appears set to strike, so powerful in comparison is Uncle Sam that he requires nothing more than his mighty boot to crush Villa and Mexico. In reality, however, the subsequent American military intervention proved unable to capture the wily revolutionary.[67] Yet the pictorial provides a measure of cultural accuracy about perceptions of imagined American superiority and, in the overdramatized characterization, a measure of American outrage at Villa. The situation was well summed up by a headline to a story in which a reverend expressed a common view: "Pastors Urge Villa Bandits Be Wiped Out: To Kill a Few Mexicans Will Save the Lives of a Lot Better People."[68]

Whereas the *New York Times* stressed the backwardness of Mexican culture as the proper context in which to place and assess Villa's villainy, and the *Los Angeles Times* tended to impart a sense that Villa and, indeed, Mexicans more generally suffered from racial inferiority compared with Americans, the *Chicago Tribune* smeared Villa and Mexico in equal measure and condemned both for an allegedly arrested and decayed culture and biological turpitude. For example, typical of this sort of coverage, an editorial suggested that Mexicans were capable of learning but that the country remained essentially "wretched." Why? Mostly because of the problem it shared with Cuba,[69] Nicaragua, Haiti, the Philippines, and American Indians[70]—inherent lowliness. Thus, they needed the United States, they needed manifest destiny. And again, like the *New York Times*, the *Chicago Tribune* likened Villa and Mexico to allegedly savage Indians—including Geronimo—whom the United States had forcibly had to smash some forty years earlier.[71] In short, Mexico constituted nothing more than a "savage tribe…weak and sick."[72]

BACK TO BASICS

In this way, the American press reaction to the raid on Columbus effectively delivered Villa back among his kind—stereotyped savage half-breed Mexicans. While he had never been able to entirely shed his Mexican skin in the press, still he came to occupy a position of some favor—but it is important to note that he always existed as a mediated and stereotyped construction.

Two days after the news of the Columbus raid became front-page news in the United States, the *Chicago Tribune* published an illustration (Figure 4.8) that in many ways summarized the press's portrayals of imagined American supremacy over Mexico and cogently exemplified the central rationale of manifest destiny—and it fettered such visions, necessarily and indirectly, to U.S. foreign policy. Here Uncle Sam deliberates about whether he should simply whip Mexico, again portrayed as nearly mad, clutching tightly to a bottle of liquor and a pistol. Such action is inevitable, and Sam indicates as much ("Eventually—Why not now?" he queries), as it was with U.S. colonial actions that rebirthed the seated children in the cartoon, some of whom appear to have had their skins bleached (Cuba and Nicaragua). Needless to say, once the United States whipped those lands into shape, they became reborn as

Figure 4.8. *Chicago Tribune*, March 13, 1916

tractable, pliable, teachable lads, the cartoon makes clear. This myth-ical hubris constitutes the stuffing of manifest destiny, of course, the notion that the United States has been inspired and sanctioned by a Protestant deity to wage war on what it considers lesser peoples.

CONCLUSION

Villa emerged in the press in 1913 as a darkened shadow, the per-sonification of Mexican Otherness, an inverted projection of the frontiersman. Remarkably, within a year, this framing had begun to fundamentally reconfigure itself so much so that, within another year, by the winter of 1915, Villa had emerged as a thoroughly mythical Americanized Mexican frontiersman. In this latter guise, he wasn't so different from Daniel Boone[73] or Shane or Clint Eastwood's cop char-acter Dirty Harry, other seminal American mythical characters. And his espied qualities, in time, closely came to mirror those the myth identified as commensurate with the frontiersman. For not only did Villa personify in reportage all the requisite characteristics, but also his propaganda presented him as the opposite of his rivals. In other words, if Mexico's Other leaders were the opposite of the frontiersman—as illustrated by Villista propaganda—and Villa was the opposite of those leaders, then by default he must also be a frontiersman. And he became just that, though always qualified by a reduction in his status because he was just a "breed," after all.

As a case study, Villa's image during this period illustrates the cog-nitive disconnect that has typified analysis of U.S.–Latin American relations. Traditionally, political scientists and many historians have applied a kind of rational actor model to this study. But it invariably comes up short. Neither the demise of Custer nor the Mexican War, or reactions to them, for example, can be fully understood without reference to cultural influences and, indeed, the frontier myth. The frontier thesis, which builds monuments to mythical American mas-culinity, just as readily augurs aggressive colonial behavior—precisely as Turner called for and sanctioned.

Press reports emanating from Mexico during the fiercest hours of that country's revolution, 1913–16, illustrate this point with some clarity. The revolution unfolded in the American press in ways closely paralleling a frontier western. This is not to suggest that the revolutionaries themselves fought in ways commensurate with mythical properties or that the outcome of the civil war was necessarily influenced by the myth; rather, the American press collectively cast and interpreted the revolution during this period in ways that resonated mythically in frontier tropes for American newspaper audiences, especially with respect to the media treatment of Francisco "Pancho" Villa.

CHAPTER 5

AUGUSTO SANDINO: "FLY IN THE OINTMENT"

*Nationalism is the product of a collective imagination
constructed through rememoration.*
— *Gayatri Chakravorty Spivak*[1]

*Humanity emerged from the stone
age dreaming of monsters.*
— *W. Scott Poole*[2]

T he Indian wars ended on December 29, 1890, as any American history survey textbook will tell you, with the massacre at Wounded Knee, South Dakota. On that bitterly cold winter day, Lakota Sioux assembled on the Pine Ridge Reservation to stage a ceremonial Ghost Dance. In one sense, the ritual represented a fairly typical human exercise in and manifestation of community building. At such gatherings, people came together and ate, talked, slept, loved, joked—and danced. But not this time. The context on this occasion was somber and desperate, distinct in two ways. First, the Paiute prophet Wovoka had widely predicted that the ceremony would herald the demise of whites by the forces of nature, though he didn't call directly for hostilities against the invaders. The Ghost Dance constituted part of an expression of his vision. It would prefigure a return of the old ways. Second, the Ghost Dance served as a kind of unrealistically hopeful nonviolent resistance. The ground was fertile enough for such thinking after the country redoubled its efforts to crush the remaining free Aboriginals in the wake of Custer's 1876 death.

These Lakota Sioux were the last free American Indians. All others had been killed or "pacified," a widely used euphemism meaning violently conquered by force of arms. And so centuries of warfare came down to these final moments: the Lakota, last of the last, the vestige of America's unvanquished Natives who had been wounded and killed and pursued and herded like animals and would now be forced, at the end of the barrel of a gun, to live on reservations. In this context, the Ghost Dance took on an additional significance.

As the Indians assembled, the authorities were on edge. The authorities were always on edge whenever Indians congregated, suspect of any large Aboriginal gathering, memories of Custer's death still raw for many, and stereotypes of Indian savagery as common as ever. And so they sought to disarm the Sioux, who were largely not armed to begin with. They weren't warriors as such; they were mostly people who just happened to be Indian. Reports vary on precisely what happened next, but there exists no debate that, after an initial shot, the U.S. Seventh Cavalry (Custer's own beloved unit) fired indiscriminately into the assembled group, killing as many as 300 men, women, and children. Some escaped and were pursued and slaughtered. And some of the wounded simply froze to death. In this way the Indian wars ended much as they had begun in the early seventeenth century, ignobly, engendered and characterized by white aggression and intolerance, and fueled by white anger elicited by the temerity of Indians to have ever fought back to protect everything they held dear.

Given the tenor and direction of this book thus far, I decided to seek out the most popular history survey textbooks used in American colleges and universities to get a sense of what students (apart from my own) read and learn about Wounded Knee.[3] The results were consistent and blunt. According to Gary Nash et al., the second most popular such book,

> Although the Sioux had raised a flag of truce and started turning over weapons, a scuffle led to a bloody massacre.

Using the most up-to-date machine guns, the army killed more than 200 men, women, and children. With such measures, white Americans defeated the western tribes. Once proud, independent, and strong, Native Americans suffered dependency, poverty, and cultural disorganization on reservation, in Indian schools, or in urban slums.[4]

James West Davidson and colleagues, authors of the third most popular book, provide slightly greater detail, adjust the number killed, but reach the same basic conclusion:

> Against such a dismal future, some Indians sought protection in the past. In 1890 a religious revival spread word from the Nevada desert that a humble Paiute named Wovoka had received revelations from the Great Spirit. Wovoka preached that if his followers adopted his mystical rituals and lived together in love and harmony, the Indian dead would rise, whites would be driven from the land, and game would be thick again. As the rituals spread, alarmed settlers called the shuffling and chanting the "Ghost Dance." The army moved to stop the proceedings among the Sioux for fear of another uprising. At Wounded Knee in South Dakota the army fell upon one band and with devastating artillery fire killed at least 146 men, women, and children....Wounded Knee was a final act of violence against an independent Indian way of life.[5]

Again, same general storyline and conclusion as Nash and his co-authors.

Offering greater detail and richer context, John Mack Faragher and his colleagues, authors of the fourth book on the popularity list, put it this way:

> In 1889, the Northern Paiute named Wovoka had a vision during a total eclipse of the sun. In his vision, the Creator told him that if Indian peoples learned to love each other, they would be granted a special place in the afterlife. The

Creator also gave him the Ghost Dance....The Sioux, among others, elaborated Wovoka's prophecy into a religion of resistance....Many white settlers and federal officials feared the Ghost Dancers. After decades of Indian warfare, however, white Americans took the Ghost Dance as a warning of tribal retribution rather than as a religious ceremony. As thousands of Sioux danced to exhaustion, local whites intolerantly demanded the practice be stopped. The U.S. Seventh Cavalry, led in part by survivors of the Battle of the Little Bighorn, rushed to the Pine Ridge Reservation.... The Seventh Cavalry pursued the Sioux Ghost Dancers and 300 undernourished Sioux, freezing and without horses[,] to Wounded Knee Creek....[A]n accidental gunshot from one deaf brave...caused panic on both sides....Within minutes, 200 Sioux had been cut down....For two hours soldiers continued to shoot at anything that moved—mostly women and children straggling away.

Faragher's conclusion, though more emphatic, varies little from those offered by Nash or Davidson: "The massacre, which took place almost exactly 400 years after Columbus 'discovered' the New World for Christian civilization, seemed to mark the end of the final conquest of the continent's Indigenous peoples."[6]

The most popular U.S. history survey textbook used in colleges and universities, by James L. Roark et al., provides arguably the starkest and most empathetic presentation:

Faced with the extinction of their way of life...[o]n the plains, many tribes turned to a nonviolent form of resistance—a new religion called the Ghost Dance. The Paiute shaman Wovoka, drawing on a cult that had developed in the 1870s, combined elements of Christianity and traditional Indian religion to found the Ghost Dance in 1889. Wovoka claimed that he had received a vision in which the Great Spirit spoke through him...prophesying that... whites would be destroyed in an apocalypse. This religion, born of despair and carrying a message of hope, spread like wildfire over the plains....The Ghost Dance was nonviolent but it frightened whites...near Wounded Knee Creek....As the Indians lay down their arms, a shot rang out, and the soldiers opened fire. In the ensuing melee, more than 200 Sioux men, women, and children were killed....It had taken Euro-Americans 250 years to wrest control of the eastern half of the United States from the Indians. It took them less than 40 years to take the western half.[7]

Of course, all of these studies suffer from the same dilemma that confronts every survey textbook—so much to say, so little space in which to say it. That said, Roark and coauthors do two things that distinguish their book from its competitors. First, it inexplicably posits Indigenous religious traditions as monolithic and shallow, the latter exemplified in particular by the assertion that the introduction of new ritual effectively constituted a whole new religion. Second, the paragraph continues and concludes, "The subjugation of Native Americans marked the first chapter in a national mission of empire that would later lead to overseas imperialistic adventures in Asia, Latin America, the Caribbean, and the Pacific islands."[8]

In short, Roark and his coauthors stand alone in suggesting that the Indian wars, or at least the cultural context in which they occurred, endured after 1890 and even in a sense prospered long after the Indians had been crushed. Let me suggest that this is quite a remarkable thing for a survey textbook to say. But here is the real question: are they correct, or are the three other leading textbooks correct when they say that the Indian wars concluded with the massacre at Wounded Knee?

Consider one example. Forty-four years after Wounded Knee the U.S. military again found itself waging an Indian war, according to newspapers and magazines. By that date, it had been engaged for six years in fighting a "roving" "band" of "Indians," "raiders" in the "wilderness." The band was led by a "swarthy" and "little" man who dressed like Indiana Jones (but was all bad) and was variously referred to as a "chieftan," "rebel," "criminal," "savage," and "outlaw." His "Indian" band "robbed," "murdered," pillaged, and "killed" Americans, favored the "surprise" attack to direct confrontation, was comprised of nothing but "criminals," was extremely dangerous, was constantly on the verge of falling apart, posed no real threat, had wide support, or had no support except from illiterate Indians. American policy aimed to "exterminate" these Indians. It employed "Indian scouts" to do so. To contextualize the importance of the conflict, the *Los Angeles Times* compared the struggle to "the memorable one which Gen. Braddock attempted to conduct against the Indians near Pittsburgh [in 1755; Braddock died]....The principal handicap they [marines in Nicaragua] suffer from is that they are bound to observe the rules of civilized warfare and that [their leader Augusto] Sandino is not."[9]

All told, it sounds very much like the makings of mythical frontier Indian war. It is set in the wilderness and separates "civilization" from "savagery." It pits white America against Indians. The Indians are by turns stupid, vapid, sinister, intemperate, well organized, aggressive, lazy, sneaky, and so on. In short, they are guileful savages who force America to take defensive action. In other words, it is reminiscent of the long story of America's ongoing rebirth.

Clearly, Roark and his colleagues are on to something. In their concluding lines, they identify Latin America. Apropos, because this Indian war occurred in Nicaragua. Now you may wonder, why would the United States have been fighting Indians in Nicaragua? Here again Roark hits the mark, much in the way that Frederick Jackson Turner did. Both identify a pattern of behavior, conditioned real-world historical events, grafted like a never-ending palimpsest to and with long-standing cultural visions. The story features frontier war tropes and promises salvation and eternal youthfulness through conquest. Only the setting changes, though Washington, DC, is much closer to Managua than it is to much of the American west, and the American southeast borders the Caribbean Basin.

Nicaragua was perceived as part of America's "backyard."[10] It didn't hurt that it was full of espied half-breeds and Indians. One result is that manifest destiny bolstered—no, compelled—American meddling in Nicaragua, and in this way the frontier myth remained alive and well, forty-four years after termination of the Indian wars in the lower forty-eight states, according to the printed press.

"GOD'S GIFT"

According to the press, America maintained its chosen status. But it also got to choose—and in this case it picked Nicaragua. *Time* magazine, just then blossoming as the most important news magazine in the country, in a 1935 article titled "TERRITORIES: God's Gift of Thought," observed that "God and His manifest destiny gave the United States the better part of North America."[11] An article a year later, "TERRITORIES: Unwanted Freedom," noted that in 1898 at the conclusion of the war with Spain "the Era of Manifest Destiny dawned as the U.S. launched its first important colonial program with foreign races."[12] In other words, as noted, the frontier was not limited to contiguous continental growth, calling to mind editorial cartoons of Mexico and Mexicans. The *Los Angeles Times*, the most important and influential daily west of the Mississippi River, lamented in 1927, "In no other country of late has the white man's burden fallen so heavily upon America as in Nicaragua...and nowhere else has it been necessary to do so much policing."[13] Indeed, the paper quoted General John Lejeune: "We are only here to pacify the country."[14]

In 1931, *Harper's* magazine, in many ways the doyen of progressive periodicals since its founding in 1850, put the case for intervention in less dire terms, casting it as the work of kindly and beneficent Uncle Sam: "We have marines in Nicaragua this long time [since 1912], and millions of newspaper-reading people have been perplexed to determine just what they are doing there." The answer itself was manifest, the question merely rhetorical. "We really can help the world," *Harper's* asserted. "We can do a lot of good things in the world....[We can do] the job that underlies economic reorganization and starting civilization on a new course with something of a new plan."[15] Yet this publication, indeed all the publications herein cited, as well as America's political class, simply did not link intervention or manifest destiny with imperialism. Although the United States had been built as an iteration of empire, *Harper's* cheerfully argued that "Empire can lead only to death and destruction, no matter how it may be glorified by rhetoric, synthetic emotionalism, and meretricious patriotism."[16] This is precisely how the practice of imperialism was conceived and "recoded," writes Stephanson. Imperialism was anathema to America, so "attempts were made to call it something else: empire of peace, empire of love, empire of the intellect, empire of liberty."[17] Anything but what it was.

"AS MENTORS"

Most discussions of Nicaragua in its national period gather steam while relating events slightly after the mid-nineteenth century. Like most of Central America, Nicaragua languished in relative neglect during the colonial period and for the first decades of independence after 1821 because it had little to offer Spain, and then later England, and then still later the United States. All that changed after the Mexican War, when the United States discovered a compelling reason to desiderate a more efficient means to link its Atlantic and Pacific coasts. Passage by sea around Cape Horn was protracted and dangerous, and overland travel was expensive. No transcontinental railroad would be built till 1869, and even then railroads obviously didn't allow for the passage of oceangoing vessels. Because of geography (i.e., low-lying connectable lakes and rivers), Nicaragua presented the best site for the construction of an isthmian canal, which gained an additional sense of urgency after gold was discovered in California in 1848, leading to the '49er gold rush. In fact, American pining for just such a passage dates as far back as Thomas Jefferson in 1788.[18]

Meanwhile, after several decades of successful nineteenth-century industrialization, wealthy American capitalists had grown restless and sought new investment opportunities.[19] Nicaragua was attractive for political reasons too: first, because it offered the best place to construct a canal to link the oceans; second, that self-same industrialization, which benefited from a burgeoning population, created a thirst for Nicaragua's natural wealth—principally things such as bananas (hence the loaded term "banana republic") and especially coffee. Mines also developed. Finally, Nicaragua presented a strategic plum entirely in accordance with the Monroe Doctrine, all the more so if a canal were to be built.[20]

At the same time, the love affair with liberalism that argued persuasively for open markets and few or no limitations on foreign investment as well as the suitability of American-friendly authoritarian regimes swept the region. But not, notably, Nicaragua. One result was that American capital poured into the Caribbean Basin, which included Central America, under the aegis of manifest destiny and the Monroe Doctrine—and it was largely welcomed with open arms by the long-bickering political classes, now disproportionately dominated by comparatively secular and decidedly free-market liberals. In 1927, the *Los Angeles Times* bragged that U.S. marines, who had occupied Nicaragua since 1912, "are the idols of all classes in the country."[21] In turn, American military occupation promised to enrich the region's natural governing class if only its members could put an end to internecine conflict among themselves.

The mestizo and *Indio* masses, meanwhile, counted for little in this story, apart from the notable fact that they were systematically pushed off their lands after mid-century as part of the greatest land grab since the initial European invasion of the sixteenth century, termed "the second conquest" by scholars.[22] Brian Loveman characterizes the context this way: "American racism and its connection to missionaries around the world made it easier to ignore international law and sovereignty in the western hemisphere and elsewhere. McKinley, [Theodore] Roosevelt, Taft, and Woodrow Wilson shared but slightly different versions of piety and patriotism, more or less sincere in each case but grounded in a belief in America's righteous cause and racial superiority."[23]

This suited investors particularly well, as it did in neighboring Guatemala, El Salvador, and Mexico. After all, investors sought to maximize profits—bigger was better—and, given the historical era, workers' rights were an anachronism, which neatly complemented a disposition among white Americans to view nonwhites as irrevocably inferior. This in turn helps explain the knee-jerk tendency to portray Nicaraguan Natives as frontier-style Indians. It made perfect mythical sense, after all—to do the Indians a favor by crushing them in the names of decency, goodness, and tough love and then profit from the venture. So, to quell and resolve the political quarreling between Nicaraguan liberals and conservatives, the United States dispatched marines. Better, too, if American marines accompanied investment, because the region's republics might then achieve the low-risk stability coveted by investors.

And that is what ultimately occurred. American money and marines came quickly to subjugate the region, a state of affairs that prevailed, with increasing intensity and commitment, beginning in the 1870s. By the First World War, U.S. dominance was well established. So effective was U.S. behavior that by the 1930s marines were generally no longer required because American domination had efficaciously fashioned investor-friendly self-policing authoritarian governments throughout the Caribbean Basin. As a result, the still popular idea that these were the days of much ballyhooed "American isolationism" is simply nonsense.[24] The United States has interfered and intervened in the Caribbean Basin more or less at will since it developed the power to do so, including eleven times in Nicaragua alone.[25] It effectively inaugurated what Grandin simply terms a "flexible system of extraterritorial administration...free from the burden of formal colonialism."[26] Nicaragua joined this narrative slowly and reluctantly but by the mid-1930s had become a model of manifest destiny in action.

In 1850, the United States, then an ambitious growing regional power, and Great Britain signed the Clayton-Bulwer Treaty in which both sides agreed not to individually pursue the construction of a canal. Yet both countries also meddled in Nicaraguan politics, Americans siding in particular with liberals and Brits with conservatives.[27] In 1855, liberals invited thirty-three-year-old American filibuster William Walker to aid their cause. Walker instead used the opportunity to his own advantage and in 1856 installed himself as president. He quickly won American diplomatic recognition and moved to relegalize slavery and decree English as the official language. One of his goals included bringing Nicaragua to American statehood. Perhaps not surprisingly, within a year he was forced from office and banished. Undeterred, in 1860 he tried to stage a comeback, seeking to enter Nicaragua via Honduras. Instead, he was captured and executed by firing squad. Walker's adventure created a backlash against the liberals that lasted until the election of liberal nationalist José Santos Zelaya in 1893, who governed as president/dictator until 1909.[28]

At the same time, as in Mexico and Guatemala, from the latter nineteenth century and into the twentieth century, Nicaragua witnessed a growing concentration of land ownership, as mestizo peasant farmers were pushed off their lands in favor, in particular, of large-scale coffee growers. Again, as elsewhere, liberals finally came to dominate politically. It is easy to overdraw the distinctions between competing members of the elite while the vast majority were frozen out; still, the differences were telling. Traditionally, conservatives supported the Catholic Church, whereas liberals came to see it as an impediment to progress, that is, as an encumbrance to their own dreams of achieving greater wealth and power. Liberals also sought to open markets, whereas conservatives tended to be more content with the status quo. Finally, liberals tended to be more welcoming to opening and broadening the limited democracy that existed in Nicaragua, though the result was the inevitable turn to *caudillismo*, traditional charismatic strongman rule, and rampant corruption despite written constitutions that promised democracy along American ideals. Nonetheless, in reality, the Central American republics were democratic on paper only. And, again, this suited both investors and the United States more generally by providing sought-after political stability, predictability, as well as an environment that promised high rates of return on investment. For obvious reasons, the United States also gained strategically. America's destiny appeared manifest indeed.

GUNBOAT DIPLOMACY

By 1909, the United States had grown tired of Zelaya's economic nationalism and pounced. And just like that, President "Taft ordered the overthrow of Zelaya."[29] As a liberal, Zelaya promoted secularization of society. For example, he took aim at the church's control of education. He was a positivist inspired, like Mexico's famous *científicos*, by the ideas of Auguste Comte and Herbert Spencer. Progress and order were thus key to achieving liberal goals, measurable primarily by how elites fared financially. But Zelaya was driven from office when he rankled the United States by refusing to grant it the exclusive right to construct any future canal in Nicaragua. In a sense, the point was moot because such a canal was already well under construction in nearby Panama, itself forcibly torn from Colombia with U.S. blessing and assistance. To make matters even worse for Zelaya, while spurning the United States on the canal, he approached France, Germany, Great Britain, and Japan, all without success. But the damage was done. Michel Gobat identifies this as the first of three key errors Zelaya committed. The second was that turning to Europe also violated the Monroe Doctrine. Third, he sought to reignite a latent desire for the political unification of Central America as a distinct political entity, as it had been from 1823 to 1838, but it potentially threatened American hegemony.[30] The United States found the excuse it needed to take action against Zelaya when his government executed two American mercenaries. Then, with Zelaya safely out of the picture, American marines occupied Nicaragua from 1912 to 1933, with a brief reprieve in 1926.

This was the time of dollar diplomacy and gunboat diplomacy during which the United States, according to scholars, came to see the Caribbean Basin as an "American lake" and established "protectorates, allowing them to remain nominally independent while exerting extensive control over their internal and external affairs...to establish its so-called informal empire," writes Gobat.[31] Such conduct constituted America's contribution to second-wave imperialism. Unlike the first imperialistic wave that began with Columbus in 1492 and focused on sending settlers from mother countries, second-wave imperialism sought simply to extract raw materials as well as gain strategic advantage. Thus, men with investment capital and men with guns to protect that capital became the new normal—hence the terms "dollar diplomacy" and "gunboat diplomacy."[32]

After conservatives returned following Zelaya's ouster, by 1916 the United States had its canal guarantee from Nicaragua in the form of the Bryan-Chamorro Treaty, which granted the United States the rights in perpetuity to any waterway built across Nicaragua. And investment dollars poured in. Nevertheless, within months of the marines' withdrawal in 1926, liberals were at the throat of the U.S.-supported conservative regime. And so the marines came storming right back. A truce was effected, and new elections were held. Yet a lone liberal leader held out—Augusto Sandino, the aforementioned swarthy savage chieftain of the roving Indians. Perhaps unexpectedly, Sandino professed deep affection for the United States, as demonstrated in his comments reported in *Time*: "Let them come to Nicaragua—as workers, not as bosses. I salute the American people."[33] More than anything, he was an anti-imperial Nicaraguan nationalist. In fact, when the marines withdrew again in 1933, Sandino lay down his arms.

He was assassinated a year later by the American-built and trained National Guard—"as mentors," *Time* had explained[34]—under the direction of Anastasio Somoza García, who in turn would seize the reins of government in 1936. Somoza subsequently created a brutal dynastic dictatorship, followed in office by his two sons, Luis Somoza Debayle (1956–67) and Anastasio Somoza Debayle (1967–79). "The United States supported the Somoza dictatorship because it believed that Nicaraguans were too politically immature for self-rule and vulnerable to radical ideas," David F. Schmitz writes.[35] Anastasio Jr. left office only when the Sandinista revolution, named in honor of Sandino, unseated him in 1979. When he departed, it is estimated that his family was worth roughly a billion dollars in a country where the average annual income was less than a dollar a day.[36]

"NOT CIVILIZED"

In sum, then, manifest destiny beset Nicaragua for more than a century. The media eagerly supported it. Basic problems with the region, explained *Time*, were the "backwardness and poverty of Central America's seven sequestered little nations." Any measurable progress, for example building infrastructure, was "largely due to U.S. Paternalism and funds."[37] It began unofficially in 1855 when William Walker, lone-wolf American filibuster, prophet, and ragged embodiment of the frontier myth, avatar of manifest destiny, briefly established himself as president of the republic before being driven from office. And it spanned the twentieth century. In those years, when the United States wasn't actively occupying the country, it aided and abetted the murderous Somoza dynasty that enriched itself and its cronies at the expense of the masses.

The press cast Sandino's resistance to U.S. hegemony by employing mythical frontier tropes to expose his folly and champion manifest destiny. In this way, while captured in the language of the day, Sandino and his supporters served effectively as garden-variety imaginary frontier

Indians. "The Indians of Nicaragua are uneducated, irresponsible, and anxious to war and pillage," explained the *Los Angeles Times*, "and when an irresponsible person like Sandino goes out and says, 'Come on boys, let's loot and rob,' they join him with alacrity."[38] The substantive difference between fighting early Sandinistas and the postbellum Indian wars simply reflects a change in geography. Comparable imagery leaps from news coverage with no particular subtlety. Nonetheless, apart from Walker's unsuccessful attempt in the 1850s, there was never any real question of America settling Nicaragua. But this did not in any way mean that the U.S. interest was somehow lessened. In fact, the mythical frontier has seldom loomed larger in America's foreign affairs than it has in its relationship with Nicaragua.

At one level, one might expect Americans to have been sympathetic to Sandino. He was often reported saying things, echoing Thomas Paine, such as "I want a free country or death, and rely on the bravery and patriotism of my followers," as reported in the *New York Times*.[39] But it didn't wash, and such language became not just empty but even evidence of his duplicity and lack of honesty. Clearly, according to media reports, he was brave, but then so were many of the "savages" Custer had faced.

A basic perceived problem with Sandino was the problem of Latin America (a key component as well, you will recall, of America's "Indian problem"): cultural stasis. *Harper's* reported,

> Stationary societies, Sir Henry Maine has said, are distinguished from the progressive by the degree to which they are bound by traditional codes of behavior. The savage dare not break the cake of custom.... Western civilization, however, owes its main triumphs to its habit of experimenting with taboos. It owes its discoveries to men who, in some special realm, have been deliberately skeptical about its orthodoxies.

Therefore, "[a]n Englishman must not doubt the necessity of English naval supremacy. A Frenchman must assert that the occupation of the Rhineland is the clue to European well-being. An American has no right to skepticism about the Constitution or the Monroe Doctrine."[40]

Another problem with Sandino is that he fought the United States for no good reason. The United States only had marines in Nicaragua at the invitation of its democratically elected government, the press stressed. Constructed this way, he opposed democracy, whereas "President Coolidge believes the United States still can be helpful to Nicaragua by assisting the people of that country to choose its government."[41] Indeed, "No one knows better than Sandino that the American marines are stationed in the southern republic for the sole purpose of guaranteeing it a free election," the *Los Angeles Times* sermonized.[42] And because the marines proved unable to capture or eliminate Sandino, General Segundo Chamorro pleaded in the press that "the United States should take over the government of Nicaragua for an indefinite period....[T]ranquility, including the suppression of Sandino, must come from the United States."[43] Correspondingly, in early 1931, the *New York Times* reported that "NICARAGUANS FEAR LOSS OF MARINES." The framing was crucial because it absolved the United States of the charge leveled by Sandino that the occupation of Nicaragua constituted naked imperialism.[44]

Sandino, likewise, wasn't really a patriot, the press held. Worse, the *New York Times* reported that he may have been insane, citing possible "lunacy," as well as guilty of "treason."[45] The *Los Angeles Times* painted him "as a rebel fighting without principles, or flag, waging a campaign of deceit."[46] This was echoed three years later in the summer of 1932 when a report alleged that "Sandino seen close at hand is an unbalanced man, and his work is not only futile and criminal but unpatriotic, because it breaks up the peace, retards the progress of the people, destroys property, both national and foreign, and brings about discredit" to the nation internationally.[47] In turn, the United States was entitled to inaugurate or continue military action, as in the case of a reported theft of $2 million "personally carried out by General Sandino." It constituted, therefore, "a formal act of militancy against the people and government of the U.S."[48] In this way, Sandino provided a most useful and relatively inexpensive form of leverage by which the United States could cement its grip on Nicaragua. He was merely a fly in the ointment of imperialism, a figure employed to rationalize it, yet, at the same time, deny and invert it.

Sandino was a loser. Despite his ability to hold out against vastly superior U.S. forces, in terms of training, quality and quantity of equipment, and simple number of men in the field, the press painted him as an inevitable failure, even though the marines could not defeat him. When news reports noted his victories, they came in two varieties. First, Sandino held a massive advantage in numbers, so the marines could hardly be faulted. Typically, this depiction cast the Sandinistas as cowardly because they would never engage the marines in a square fight, as in "Sandino with far superior numbers is reported to have attacked,"[49] or "The marines have practically given up hope of getting General Augustino Sandino into a decisive battle."[50]

Second, therefore, he was deemed a coward, according to the *Los Angeles Times*.[51] The paper often focused on his treachery and cowardice, as evidenced by his inclinations to "ambush" and "hide" from a fair and direct fight.[52] Sandino preferred the sneaky "ambush," again where the blame lay on his underhanded approach to combat rather than on the marines' lack of preparedness.[53] But then how could any civilized army be prepared to fight in such tangled, overgrown "WILDS"[54] and "wilderness"?[55]

Sandino was routinely disparaged as an "undersized, half-educated Indian."[56] To begin with, he was small in stature, which fed into the American stereotype of the Latin American Other as childlike.[57] For example, *Time* reported that "Sandino is just a little fellow prowling among the caverns of the mountains."[58] The *Los Angeles Times* reported that "the swarthy little leader" and "little letter-writer" was "AFRAID OF CAMERAMEN."[59] About two weeks after his murder in 1934, *Time* offered this description of a laconic and spiteful diminutive character: "A vengeful-looking little man, scarcely five feet tall, part Indian, part Spanish, he talked well, was silent better....U.S. newspapers uniformly called him 'bandit.' Sandino, a great hater."[60] He was "recalcitrant" and needed to be "severely repulsed."[61] In a representative *New York Times* story from midsummer 1927, quoting State Department officials, Sandino and his "band" were "nothing more than common outlaws" (the term "outlaw" is used four more times in the story and is otherwise ubiquitous in press coverage[62]) and "armed bandits" fighting in a "wild and unsettled territory." Secretary of State Frank B. Kellogg also labeled Sandino an "outlaw."[63]

"A SUPERABUNDANCE OF GREASE"

Latin America, Central America in particular, was fated to weirdness and oddity, the media said. "When night falls on the mountains south of the Rio Grande, human gnomes emerge from their huts and crannies. They are knobby-headed, big-eared, scaly-skinned creatures. Some of them are splotched with red, like rusty iron. Others are mottled with green, like stained copper....Worms, with the help of gnats, make gnomes of these mountain peoples."[64]

Moreover, and not unrelated, the region was inherently inferior because of that component of its makeup that was Indian. For example, Mexico consisted of two classes —"the upper class of nearly pure Spanish blood and the lower class of Indian only recently somewhat civilized," said the *Los Angeles Times*. Central America was different because of miscegenation—but no better. The Native component allegedly accounted for "very marked clannishness."[65] A travelogue in *Harper's* tendentiously cast Central America as stuck in "feudal times" and "medieval repose," and otherwise it was a monolithic "alien civilization." "Four out of five countrywomen will spoil any dish they set out to cook. A superabundance of grease, a lack of real butter or cheese, and primitive cookstoves, combine with ignorance to achieve an almost incredible mess at mealtimes."[66] *Time* termed Central American cuisine, which included "nauseating" monkey meat, "disgusting," but it was all that was available "when their civilized provender gave out."[67]

In terms of architecture, "monotony and absence of all peculiar human character in their design evokes a painful analogy to the ants' nests hanging in the trees or the formidable cactus hedges which oppress the eyes mile after mile with undeviating cruelty." Natives of Mayan extraction "groped fearsomely in the darkness of their ignorance." What conclusions might be drawn from such characterizations? *Harper's* sought to provide some answers:

> There will always be a difference between our attitude towards these lost peoples and our interest in European vestiges. To say that the Roman, the Goth, the Gaul, the island-born Britons have vanished is true; but their blood flows in our veins. Their laws and customs have come down

to us through the centuries. Their myths and folklore echo in our minds. But here, no matter how we dig, is nothing that our hearts can cleave to. Here is no ancient prototype for us. Their civilization was not, according to earlier conjectures, destroyed by a stupid Spanish conquest. We now know that the Maya era was about to perish of its own internal weaknesses before a Spaniard ever landed in Yucatan.[68]

This lengthy passage well expresses the sense of innate superiority the United States felt toward its diminutive neighbors. Interestingly, it also rebukes a core frontier tenet, that is, from the experience of frontier Americans were molded anew.

Notably, Republican President Herbert Hoover termed Sandino an "outlaw." The Hoover administration's promotion of manifest destiny and the Monroe Doctrine, clothed in frontierisms, found a welcoming forum in the *New York Times* under the headline, "HOOVER DENOUNCES SANDINO AS OUTLAW":

[marines are] protecting the lives and property of Americans and foreigners at ports in coastal regions....In Washington it is held there is no ground for any fear that Great Britain or any other foreign nation has any present inclination to intervene in any way in Nicaraguan affairs...pertaining to the Monroe Doctrine...bandits...a bandit cutting the head from a prostrate dead marine...bandits...raiding... [o]utlaws...not civilized...banditry...not civilized.[69]

Elsewhere in the same issue Hoover cited Sandino's "cold-blooded murder," which placed Sandino "outside [the] civilized pale." The Sandinistas represented no bona fide movement or political thinking; instead, they were guilty of nothing more profound, and base, than "merely some sporadic disorders fomented by a murderous band." Said Hoover, "I am confident Sandino will be brought to justice."[70] Appropriately, the *Los Angeles Times* observed, "His social position is a little like that of a train robber in the old days of the Southwest—a naughty boy."[71]

"THE BOYS ARE WELL LIKED"

Time likewise conflated the Monroe Doctrine and manifest destiny into a self-evident truth. *Time* wasn't unique in this respect. It was given a name when William Howard Taft was president: "dollar diplomacy."[72] For example, in early 1927, a story reported that more marines were being dispatched to Nicaragua and that, thankfully, "The British Government...gave notice that it would not transgress the Monroe Doctrine." Then it explained the details of what it presented as a mutually beneficial treaty in the works between the two countries (Nicaragua didn't participate) in six easy steps:

1. The United States would "undertake" to "preserve peace in Nicaragua and the continuity of the Nicaraguan Government."
2. The "right of intervention" was acknowledged by "mutual consent" (not including that of Nicaragua).
3. U.S. Customs officials would take control of the "rehabilitating of the finances of Nicaragua with dictatorial powers."
4. The U.S. government would support a $20 million private loan from unnamed "American sources" to the Nicaraguan government.
5. The United States would create and train a National Guard.
6. "[A]ll the foregoing considerations show that the arrangement Nicaragua desires, so far from forming part of an imperialistic scheme of U.S. aggrandizement in Central America, is nothing less than a highly humanitarian project sought by Nicaragua and not by the U.S."[73]

Thus presented, the Monroe Doctrine appears to have crossed the line distinguishing what Hegel identified as the laws of men to the laws of nature. It was as natural as it was "humanitarian." Just common sense, in other words, in the way that colonialism becomes naturalized and invisible to purveyors of it.[74]

The report strikes one as simultaneously naive and farcical today. To begin with, it cloaks the gambit on the premise that Nicaragua had bullied the United States into action, which in turn had agreed somewhat reluctantly lest its behavior be misinterpreted/revealed as imperialistic. Couching the presentation in legalistic terms was at the very least too obvious to conceal the real motivation and a fairly blatant admission that the imperial project at work, at some level, gnawed at itself. And "dictatorial powers"? Why not? Diminutive people of color had long since proven themselves elsewhere and everywhere incapable of fiscal management. This was simply an exercise in tough love. No point in sparing the rod. And, yes, the National Guard was created. It would later provide the launching pad for establishment of the Somoza dynasty. Such creations worked brilliantly, for in this case the National Guard effectively did the dirty work—and, later, much dirtier—that the marines had attempted to do, while at the same time allowing the U.S. military to step away so as to provide a denial of the charge of intervention (to be fair, such an arrangement was also cheaper, less burdensome, and less open to partisan political attack from the other imperial political party in the United States). Then, finally, came the paternalistic icing on the upside-down cake, that the imperialism was not really imperialism and that it was, in the final analysis, for the good of the country directly affected by, but without voice in, the treaty.

Yet *Time* preferred its interpretation, as in the case of the story titled "NICARAGUA: Vexations." Alluding directly to the phenomenon of media agenda-setting as well as naturalizing its own coverage, it reported, "As everyone knows, the U.S. Marines now in Nicaragua are there notably under the pretext that Nicaraguans themselves desire the U.S. to police the country."[75] Or, as in the issue published one week later, citing Major General John Lejeune, "Every American who is proud of being an American should be proud of the American Marines in Nicaragua." The article credited this as a "mature opinion." Lejeune went on to reassure all patriotic readers that "The boys are well liked by the Nicaraguans."[76] Indeed, "The boys have the situation well in hand," snorted the *Los Angeles Times*.[77] In the aftermath of a 1931 earthquake, *Time* agreed: "Relief U.S. Marines have been in Nicaragua since 1912. Nicaragua may be an independent republic on the statute books, but officials and citizens instinctively realized last week that U.S. responsibility in a Nicaraguan disaster is precisely like that of Great Britain in an Egyptian disaster."[78] Schmitz considers the "relief" mission in a way commensurate with most scholars: "Since marines were first sent to Nicaragua in 1912, the United States had sought to impose stability in that nation" solely for American gain.[79]

On another occasion, *Time* broadened its interpretation of the justification for military occupation. In a story titled "NICARAGUA: Most Gratifying!" from late 1928 on the Nicaraguan election, readers were reminded that Sandinistas, like Indians of old, were barbaric. They had committed "atrocities" in those areas "where it had been impossible to make U.S. supervision fully effective." It cited a report from U.S. election authorities that drew attention to "revolting cruelty," citing "victims hacked to pieces with machetes," plus "fingers severed in order to remove rings," "noses and ears cut off," and "bodies mutilated after death." The conclusion that *Time* drew was unambiguous: "Such atrocities would more than justify U.S. intervention."[80] Were that true, the United States would have had to intervene against itself to prevent deplorable but not uncommon savage crimes committed in the United States. For several decades, behavior no less heinous was visited upon American black males in the South for daring to engage their constitutional right to suffrage.[81]

Published news reports drew attention to Sandino's relatively small contingent of followers, usually identified as no more than a few hundred, as a means to diminish Sandino and depict him as a kind of Indian blackguard, as if to equate lack of identified popularity with inherent criminality. Yet, as noted, his successes in battle were frequently held to result from his numerical superiority. No matter, he led an "insurrection," by definition illegal.[82]

"CLEAN UP SANDINO"

Sandino was a communist. His supporters, mostly in Segovia, "being Liberals, either are in support of General Sandino or are afraid of him....[They] are now anti-American and have been converted to 'radicalism and Bolshevism' by General Sandino," reported the *New York Times*.[83] A representative of New York's state assembly, identified as an "anti-Communist crusader," thus argued for the need to "clean up Sandino."[84] Yet oddly the paper also reported in 1933, after marines had withdrawn and negotiations had begun to reach terms by which the Sandinistas would lay down their arms, "SANDINO NOT COMMUNIST."[85]

The *Los Angeles Times* struck a more consistent line in its characterization of Sandino as a communist supplied with American communist funds to purchase weapons "used to kill American Marines."[86] "REDS IN EVIDENCE" shouted one headline.[87] Alone among the press outlets herein surveyed and auguring the principal justification for Ronald Reagan's interventionist policies in Nicaragua some fifty years later, the *Los Angeles Times* smeared Sandino by alleging a tie to "soviet Russia."[88]

Sandino was not always accorded the title of general either. The *New York Times*, for example, conjuring up a direct link to the Indian wars and images of the aimless and wandering Indian, also called him a "former Liberal General and now chieftain of a band of marauders."[89] For the *Los Angeles Times*, he was a "bandit chief" who spread "terror."[90] Consider this passage from early 1928:

> Augustino Sandino, the Nicaraguan, was described today by Major Gen. Lejeune of the Marine Corps., as a "small time Caesar, who would rather be a big frog in a little puddle...than respected."...Lejeune said Sandino was a "brave man, but has a shady record, having served at one time with Pancho Villa in Mexico."...After a wild life in Mexico, the General said, Sandino returned to Nicaragua.... Sandino is about 28 years old and has been convicted of a violent crime...and was a member of Villa's raiding party at Columbus, N.M....He has unusual power over the illiterate Nicaraguans and habitually makes long speeches to them.

The story also claimed that Sandino identified himself as a "bloodthirst[y] Indian."[91]

In short, readers would have learned that he was opportunistic more than ambitious, amphibian-like (slimy? cold-blooded? lower-ordered?), untamed, a violent criminal, had attacked the United States directly while in league with Villa as his "loyal Lieutenant...with a band of cut-throats," chirruped the *Los Angeles Times*[92] (he would have been ten years old at the time of the Columbus raid in 1916), took advantage of the uneducated poor of Nicaragua, was unnecessarily verbose, and even self-identified as an Indian savage.

It is hard to imagine a better direct mythical framing of Sandino as a frontier savage and Nicaragua itself as a frontier separating the civilized from the barbarous. That Natives were inferior to Americans was widely understood. For example, the *New York Times* reported that Nicaraguans were basically unintelligent yet conniving and crafty. "The Nicaraguans are unskilled in commerce and industry, and politics is the best paying profession....The opportunity for graft...is an added whip to political ambition....[W]e took them under our wing."[93] Meanwhile, the support that Sandino evoked in the northern province of Segovia reflected "the sympathy which the little fellow always draws, irrespective of his cause, when he is embroiled with a big fellow."[94]

The inaccurate charge that Sandino fought with the Villistas must have titillated readers scarcely more than a decade after the attack on Columbus had been front-page news all over America and had elicited an eight-month U.S. invasion of northern Mexico.[95] In a full-page story, "WHAT LIES BEHIND THE NICARAGUAN CRISIS," the *New York Times* again took up the Villa angle. It called the Sandinistas "lawless elements, the same kind of irregulars who followed Pancho Villa." Sandino was a "fly in the ointment," a "hot-headed young soldier of fortune." Small wonder, then, that *Time* noted the urgency with which marines fought "to exterminate his forces," a peculiar choice of phrasing, out of place in describing warfare but not when eradicating vermin.[96] Similarly, the *Los Angeles Times* said that Sandinistas "infested" Nicaragua.[97] Another day, employing an old west trope, *Time* termed Sandino a "desperado," again noted Hoover's intention to "exterminate" him, and likened him to the "arch-desperado Robin Hood, tough little General Augusto Cesar Sandino."[98]

Not surprisingly, the *New York Times* presented the "lawless"[99] Sandino as entirely without political merit. One story widely quoted a former Nicaraguan diplomat to the effect that "Sandino is a bandit and his principal business is now robbery, murder, and assassination.... Sandino does not represent the opinion of any group of people, but is only a small bandit whose business is robbery and murder."[100] *Time* took a step further, employing the parlance of the popular gangster genre of the 1930s, and termed him "the No. 1 bandit."[101]

Sandinistas were also debased by their racial makeup, according to the press. The *New York Times* identified these "raiders"[102] as "brown-skinned, mild appearing men and women for the most part, whose ancestry is Indian, with an admixture of negro blood from the Jamaicans who drifted westward....They are alert-looking fellows of average stature, straw-hatted, barefoot and most of them wearing only a cotton shirt and breeches. They look harmless enough, yet can fight like fiends with rifles and machetes." In turn, these Natives fought the "civilized troops," that is, the marines.[103] And they skulked: "There is almost a grim humor in the way Sandino's bands have appeared and disappeared and reappeared."[104] Or, as in *Time*, "He continues to skulk...to defy President Coolidge."[105] Or another day, "Tattered bandits sneaked down across the Pis-Pis river."[106] Occasionally, a press report almost perfectly captured the gist of the frontier sentiment, as in this poetically compressive account by the *New York Times*: "Small roving bands of outlaws, which make occasional raids, murdering natives, have no central organization, consist mostly of unimportant leaders. There are indications that Sandino's support is crumbling....A roving band of outlaws has killed four natives and wounded two others near San Juan de Talhaneca, presumably for the purpose of robbery."[107] Appropriately enough, and reminiscent of George W. Bush's comments about Osama bin Laden, *Time* reported that President Coolidge employed a traditional western shibboleth: "Get Sandino dead or alive!"[108]

Sandinistas, meanwhile, stooped as low as spreading rumors that "Americans eat children," the *New York Times* reported, calling such rumors "propaganda" spread "among the Indians there."[109] Equally gruesome was Sandino's "strong desire to 'drink Yankee blood,'" noted the *Los Angeles Times*.[110] And Sandino was stupid and confused, too, the daily said. "This wandering paisano probably hasn't a very clear idea what he is fighting about or why."[111]

In tautological fashion and reeking of manifest destiny and the Monroe Doctrine, the case for intervention built upon the allegations, then, that Sandino was a savage of mythic proportions. In one of many examples, *Time* reported on "U.S. citizens killed by bandit followers of Rebel Augusto Sandino" in a

> slaughter....[T]he bandits fell savagely upon Logtown. Under a breadfruit tree they killed John Phelps....They cut his body to bits. They threw Joseph Luther Pennington... into a river, peppered him to death with shots. Back in the logging camp they woke up Ripley Davis...to murder him in cold blood, cut off his head and stick it on a fence post. Then they sacked the commissary....Total fatalities: U.S. citizens 9; other foreigners, 8.[112]

The *New York Times* cited an American legislator who said Sandino "has ambushed and killed American soldiers, has exacted payments from American citizens, has destroyed American property and has attacked cities and villages apparently for the sole purpose of ravage and loot." If it wasn't obvious to readers just how vital the mythical stakes were, in the same story *Time* noted that President Hoover "likened them to the Iroquois."[113]

"LEADER OF LOST CAUSES"

Marines withdrew in 1933, and Sandino then agreed to negotiate an end to his resistance and to lay down arms. At this point, the tenor of press coverage changed. While he was not fully rehabilitated in the sense that the image cast of him over six years could ever simply be undone, the media did turn to referring to him in "former" terms. That is, his savagery became identified as if it were an affliction he had overcome. For example, one typical muted description in the *New York Times* termed him a "Nicaraguan outlaw for five years....A rebel since 1927."[114] Still, lest any reader get the impression that Sandinista resistance had been anything but utterly futile, the *New York Times* presented Sandino's agreement to come to terms in the wake of the U.S. military withdrawal as weakness, a sign of American policy's victory. "SANDINO SUBMITS," one headline read. Further, appealing to and championing the Monroe Doctrine and manifest destiny, the paper issued a vague and somewhat smug conclusion: "If Nicaragua is on the eve of enduring peace, it is largely due to the attitude of the American Government and its adherence to a plan that had the approval of Latin America."[115]

Another way to assess these accomplishments was to laud the creation and training of Nicaragua's National Guard by the United States, widely understood by scholars today as a U.S.-trained and -funded terrorist organization working on behalf of a brutal and corrupt government. Sandino had been a hapless "LEADER OF LOST CAUSES," the *New York Times* reported two days after he was assassinated on February 21, 1934.[116] Yet if his cause had principally been to have the marines withdraw, it is hard to square such a conclusion. Nonetheless, the *Los Angeles Times* averred two days after the killing that his death had "prevented the establishment of a dictatorship with the notorious rebel as leader."[117] A day later it upped the rhetorical ante and opined that Sandino, "the fiery little leader," had been "KILLED FOR 'RED' ACTS" and his plan to establish a "semi-Communist regime."[118]

Of course, as with the stories of Custer and the Mexican War, the press duly reported on the political opposition to dispatching marines to fight Sandino.[119] An article in the *Los Angeles Times*, for example, cited a Democratic senator from Montana who attacked the "Kellogg-Coolidge policy...in behalf of an American-made puppet president foisted upon the people against their will."[120] Another day the Los Angeles daily pilloried opposition to U.S. policy and claimed that "Every once in a while some Democratic statesman stands up on his hind legs in Washington and demands to know why this great nation has gone to war against Gen. Sandino." The reason was entirely simple: "Canal Vital to Future of United States Reason Marines Fight to Clean Up Nicaragua, NATIONAL DEFENSE HANGS ON BUILDING WATERWAY."[121]

On the whole, such expressions are best understood as politically motivated because in 1934, when Franklin Roosevelt, a Democrat, took presidential office from the Republican Herbert Hoover, little or nothing changed except that it was now primarily Republicans criticizing a Democratic regime. To be sure, Roosevelt unveiled his Good Neighbor Policy, which promised less unilateralism and more multilateralism and figures prominently in every history survey textbook, but it was mostly empty rhetoric with respect to the Caribbean Basin. It certainly changed nothing in U.S. behavior toward Nicaragua. Within two years of Roosevelt's inauguration, Somoza initiated a murderous family dictatorship that would endure for more than forty years. And F.D.R. did nothing. In fact, he is famously said to have commented that well, yes, Somoza was a son of a bitch but at least "he is our son of a bitch."[122]

CONCLUSION

In the struggle against Sandino, the United States found itself playing rhetorical cowboy versus Indian, frontier-style, all over again, as it would later in Vietnam and in Central America once again in the 1980s. Turner had predicted as much insofar as he had prophesied ongoing U.S. frontier imperialism. Theodore Roosevelt's frontier vision likewise also remains central; after all, it was Roosevelt as much as any president who set the wheels in motion for a more vigorous and active, racist, mythically inspired pax Americana for the Caribbean Basin.[123] The *Los Angeles Times*, for example, noted the continuity of U.S. policy over time, dating the long-running marine occupation as but a "continuation of a policy inaugurated by Roosevelt."[124] Celebrated novelist Owen Wister described Roosevelt in *Harper's* as "always the outdoor man and the preacher militant; never old in soul, young to the end.... [He] shine[s] more brightly in our sky."[125] To be fair, neither Turner nor Roosevelt identified Nicaragua as such, but each promoted and adhered to a myth holding that American expansion was limitless, central to the ongoing project of nation building, and news portrayals bore this out with respect to Nicaragua. Of course, while not unimportant, Nicaragua was still small potatoes compared to the Indian wars that secured the lower forty-eight states. The substantive difference between Nicaragua and American Indians or Mexico's Pancho Villa reflects a function of geography. Similar mythical impulses were at work, drawn from the same well, but there was never any real question of America settling Nicaragua. Think of the Indian war against Sandino as a kind of mythical frontier-lite—same great taste but less filling. This did not in any way mean that the U.S. interest was somehow lessened. In fact, under Ronald Reagan's self-styled presidency, the frontier had seldom loomed larger in America's foreign affairs: the subject of Chapter 6.

CHAPTER 6

RAMBO'S VIETNAM: "YOU JUST DON'T TURN IT OFF"

It was the dawn of creation in the Indochina bush.
—Philip Caputo[1]

The movies gave us planetary fame. Without them, the Comanches would be an obscure chapter in Texas history books. With them, we live forever.... We're trapped in history.
—Paul Chaat Smith[2]

In the summer of 1969, I spent two sunny weeks with my grandparents in Minnesota, about forty-five minutes north of the twin cities. One morning a lanky, unshaven young man showed up at the door, cigarette hanging loosely from his lip, gunny sack slung over his shoulder, looking to hitch a ride. He was coming home from Vietnam, I heard him tell my grandfather. He had run out of money just an hour or so from the family farm, and he wondered if we could help him.

He had knocked on the right door.

Grandpa was a Lutheran pastor and a veteran. He fervently supported the war in Vietnam. So, needless to say, he was—we were—delighted to do what we could to help Steve. So we drove grandma's blue Chevy Nova—no, Steve drove it—all the way home. Grandpa puffed serenely at his pipe, and Steve, who steered with one wrist dangled over the wheel, chewed on one of the stogies that grandpa had given him.

Of course, because I was nine years old, I had no real sense of Vietnam. Yet I was enthralled by John Wayne's *The Green Berets* (saw it at the drive-in theater), released one year earlier. On the whole, as a boy I adored the Duke. He and whatever he stood for spoke to the boy in me. I thought that war was glamorous, a grand romp, kill some bad guys and be back in time for dinner. And I was heavily influenced by my larger-than-life grandfather. He badly wanted America to win that war, so I did too. I believed that gramps had been a war hero in his own right, again not really thinking about what that meant.

Steve was not reluctant to share stories with us, perhaps taking some pride or even comfort that we all obviously looked upon him with a certain wonder and awe, almost reverence. Remember, unlike today, this was a time when America's war of the moment had come under vitriolic public criticism. And no doubt we felt special that we were somehow taking part in the epic return to Steve's childhood home. As he drove, Steve spun tales of firefights and communist skullduggery and too many close calls to count, of how he had to shoot and kill a girl about my age on a routine patrol one day as they rounded a corner on a jungle path. There she was, staring them down with a Soviet-made machine gun. Luckily, her gun jammed, he said. That was all that saved him. Grandpa noted that Soviet weapons were often inadequate, and that is why it malfunctioned (he really, really, really hated communists). It didn't occur to me till years later that Steve had shot and killed a little girl, let alone that she had been armed to begin with or that the story had excited me when it probably should have frightened me.

But what stuck with me more than anything on that trip was Steve's reply to my shy question, "What was Vietnam like?" In a way, his answer was vague but also impossible and thrilling. It made perfect sense to me. "It was like cowboys and Indians," he said. It really was just like *The Green Berets*. Ha! And, when I remembered this years later, I thought that I had gained some key insight into the conflict: cowboys and Indians. But I had not, I learned at university. Turns out that everybody who looked into it discovered or already seemed to know that the Vietnam War was a frontier conflict.

The struggle has generated a substantive bibliography. For example, my recent search of "Vietnam War" on Amazon.com turned up 64,338 results, roughly one for each American who died in the war. It has given rise to countless movies, documentaries, memoirs, novels, songs, and nonfiction studies, and it has generated untold pages of journalistic coverage. And, as noted, many already knew what Steve had told me, that the war, from the ground up, was imagined as some kind of frontier blowup. Countless American GIs in Vietnam (and later in Iraq) spontaneously imagined that the conflict offered little more than a restaging of the Indian wars where GIs stood in for cowboys and "gooks"—as methodically detailed in Stanley Kubrick's brilliant cinematic assault on the myth in Vietnam, *Full Metal Jacket*—"played the Indians."[3] It was erected upon Puritan notions and held "that America's God-given purpose from the beginning has been to construct a Christian nation where one did not exist," writes William W. Cobb, author of *The American Foundation Myth in Vietnam*.[4] As a result, "'Indian country' came to signify everything from Indian land to enemy-held territory in Vietnam."[5]

Structurally, the Vietnam War narrative bears close resemblance to a frontier war featuring imagined cowboys fighting imagined Indians. As ever, the cowboys, while invading and occupying and pillaging, allegedly fought defensively in the name of democracy and freedom, whereas the Indians/Vietcong fought an offensive war against goodness and decency and so on. In short, civilization grappled with barbarism all over again. And the stakes were dire because the United States also fought in Vietnam to contain the growth of the cancer of communism, which was hell-bent on world domination, we were taught at school. Thus, America was fighting for its very survival all over again. Fortunately, by defeating the yellow-tinged red communism in Vietnam, America might rebirth itself.

Like the Mexican War, the conflict was importantly built upon a flagrant and deliberate mendacity, in this case the charge that in an act of war an American patrol boat had been attacked in international waters at the Gulf of Tonkin on August 4, 1964, by the North Vietnamese navy. This led Congress to pass the Tonkin Resolution, which gave President Lyndon Johnson the authority to wage undeclared war, but war nonetheless, in Vietnam. Arguably, the provocation that led to the blatantly imperialist Mexican War was less compelling because the border dispute was, well, disputed. But a brazen attack in international waters? The United States had every right to defend itself, especially given the heightened stakes during the cold war.

Yet it raises questions. Were the deaths of nearly 60,000 American boys and as many as 3 million Vietnamese, Laotians, and Cambodians an appropriate response to a minor incident at sea 10,000 miles from America's shores? To make matters worse, the United States proceeded to lose the war, even though its criminal president, Richard Nixon, would later declare victory in retreat. Was that minor incident at sea worth the political cost, when the war overwhelmed and nearly consumed the American political system, of electing Nixon in 1968, in part because he claimed to have a secret strategy to win the war, when he did not? Such hypotheticals probably get us nowhere, but please indulge me one more time.

What if the confrontation in the Gulf of Tonkin never happened? How would that change things? Well, in fact, it never happened.

In the words of Robert McNamara, the secretary of defense at the time, "It never happened." It was instead a fabricated prevarication, revealed publicly only years later, so as to gain the Johnson administration sufficient political leverage to launch an undeclared war. (It worked brilliantly, and he waged the fight like a good old Texas boy.) Suddenly, it sounds a lot like the Mexican War, a point that has not been lost on scholars who have studied the war and its rhetoric.[6]

Probably the key unanticipated side effect of the war, unanticipated because the United States did not expect to lose, is what became known as the "Vietnam Syndrome." The loss shook the United States to its core. It had never lost a war before (battles, yes, as with Custer, but not a war) and certainly not to a ragtag bunch of surrogate Indians.[7] Thus, the country itself was seemingly adrift as the struggle for civil rights raged and the Watergate scandal forced Nixon to resign in disgrace. Conservatives, in particular, took an almost perverse delight in laying the blame on liberals, in particular the media and the Democratic Party. These liberals, the story went, were soft on communism and had forced the United States to effectively fight with one hand tied behind its back. As movie character John Rambo famously put it, "Somebody wouldn't let us win," and he didn't mean North Vietnam. This malaise, to borrow a Jimmy Carter–esque phrase, was homegrown. Basically, it was the liberals who had prevented the United States from being allowed to win.

The results are well known. The syndrome in due course contributed to the sharp rightward turn in American politics.[8] Especially on the right, politics became overtly religious all over again as Republican country experienced its own sort of new Great Awakening. Witness Ronald Reagan invoking God with righteous and relentlessly grim geniality, and later George W. Bush claiming without blush that God had chosen him to rule and to fight. Indeed, as Andrew J. Bacevich has observed, "The world that John Rambo inhabits bears close comparison with the world of Ronald Reagan."[9] But the fights after Vietnam that the nation picked, like a sore that will not heal so long as you continue to pick at it (Grenada, Iraq, bombing Libya, meddling in Central America to prop up feverishly violent military dictatorships, and such), were easy, despite the rhetoric, significantly very much about winning, returning to form so as to demonstrate that Vietnam was an aberration, not because it was a bad idea, but because big bad government and hippies and feminists and such had made America lose that war. Culture wars after the 1960s consequently took center stage, each coalition angling for dominance.

"NOTHING IS OVER!"

Hollywood embraced the Vietnam Syndrome avidly after the hostilities ceased in 1975. Notably, during the conflict, only a single major motion picture tackled the war, John Wayne's hawkishly inept 1968 *The Green Berets*. It was so awful that his longtime collaborator John Ford, the legendary director who made the Duke an A-list movie star, said when asked about the film that Wayne directed that the Duke really should just stick to acting. Later followed a handful of films that struggled, in varying degrees of nuance, with deeper ideas—*Deer Hunter* (1978), *Coming Home* (1978), *Apocalypse Now* (1979), *Platoon* (1986), and *Full Metal Jacket* (1987). But it was the widely popular *Rambo* series, in particular, that spoke most directly to the heartland, both mythically and at the box office.[10]

In their own ways, these star vehicles for Sylvester Stallone nuzzle deeply into the primal fog of the frontier myth. Each in its way tears a page from Frederick Jackson Turner, but each, significantly, also narrates a captivity narrative, which prefigures and informs Turner.[11] Captivity narratives feature the abduction of American innocence, typically in the form of a white female kidnapped by savages on the frontier, in what John Tirman calls the "deepest scar on the national psyche."[12] Cobb terms them a narrative "descent into hell" and stresses that "the purpose of the captivity was symbolic 'regeneration.'"[13] The frontiersman, standing in for a virile and masculine America, saves her and kills the savage abductor. The violence is wholesomely revivifying. Custer's popular memoir, *My Life on the Plains*, published two years before his death, abounds with such vignettes.[14]

Early on, these savages were of course Indians. And, in reality, on occasion American females were taken in war, but it cut both ways since Aboriginal females were often also taken. Perhaps the most famous historical case, loosely fictionalized in the based-on-a-true-story kind of way in Ford's film *The Searchers* (1956), is that of Cynthia Anne Parker, captured at the age of nine, mother of Quanah Parker, the last great Comanche chief. Parker's father was Comanche, his mother white. She had been captured in east Texas in 1836 and, in contradistinction to the grisly and popular captivity stories that so enflamed passions during the colonial period, she had assimilated, married, and bore children happily in her new life. When she was liberated, "redeemed," as an adult in 1860, she was overcome by grief and longed to return to her Indian family, though she never got the chance.[15]

More provocative were the wholly and unabashedly fictional captivity narratives that flourished throughout the colonial and early national decades. The genre has flourished across the centuries, from James Fenimore Cooper's *Last of the Mohicans* to the story of Republican politician John McCain, from the *Tarzan* novel series to newspaper heiress Patty Hearst, from the Iran hostage crisis (real world but also fictionalized in the recent movie *Argo*) to Nintendo's Super Mario, from the films *Taken* and *Taken 2* to ambushed and kidnapped American soldier Jessica Lynch, whom the *New York Times* called "a 19-year-old female Rambo."[16] And, of course, to *Rambo*.[17] Rambo fights in each of the seminal 1980s franchise films to have the innocence taken captive by the Vietnam War redeemed. Violence naturally, inexorably occurs, and mythical rebirth beckons.

"SMELLS LIKE AN ANIMAL"

Rambo, First Blood, released in 1982, performed extremely well at the box office, earning $125 million while costing only $14 million to create.[18] Yet the film is an oddity. Critics labeled it poorly written, poorly directed, and poorly acted. And maybe it is embarrassingly vapid, just plain lousy, barely watchable. And yet. It is at the same time a superb and timely evocation of the myths tangled up with (and proffering an emotional tonic for) the Vietnam Syndrome. It strives gamely and with success, I believe, to reconcile them in ways that distantly evoke Hitler's infamous stab-in-the-back theory that homosexuals, Jews, and other alleged deviants were responsible for Germany's loss in the First World War. Together they had conspired, the idea ran wild, to stab Germany in the back. Likewise, America had been stabbed in the back. Wielding his lethal phallus, John Rambo sets the record straight, rights the wrong. "Rambo redeems the MIAs and American manhood."[19]

Like Shane, like so many Hollywood cowboys, Rambo appears as if from mythical nowhere, wandering down from the mountain. He enters our suspended disbelief ambling along and rounding a curve on an old gravel road, not unlike Henry Fonda's character Gil Carter in *The Oxbow Incident* (1943). David Cowart has argued that the mythic hero frequently appears as if from nowhere: "As the generation of the self occurs spontaneously, so the hero appears miraculously—often by virgin birth or without the physical process of birth at all."[20] And Rambo comes at you with everything he has and is on his person, not unlike the character Jake Sully in *Avatar* (2007). And he comes at you with a relentless narcissistic bent.[21] We know right away that he is potentially explosive, clad in an army jacket and blue jeans, bedroll slung over his shoulder, shaggy locks reminiscent of Kevin Costner in *Dances with Wolves.* As an actor, Stallone also wore the baggage of the *Rocky* franchise. In short, we know him. And here he is a lone wolf peacefully minding his own business in the rugged rural west. Nothing wrong with that. He quite simply represents what all American men dream of—youth, freedom, muscles, and lots of hair.

As the first three minutes of the movie elapse, we get kids laughing and playing in an unfenced yard, we learn that Rambo isn't a racist (he is in search of a black war bud, and he had at least one Latino war friend), and we glimpse the majesty of snow-capped mountains behind him—in a mythical sense, they've got his back. But his buddy has died. So he wanders into "Hope," anytown USA. And this is where the complication occurs. The setup is wonderful because we get only what we see, and our expectations supply the rest. We discover a handsome and youthful laconic man drifting in from a mythical landscape toting an uneasy burden (and it shows in Stallone, not normally considered much of an actor) of enormous potential. His clothes mark him as dangerous, clad in the reminder of a valiant and violent recent past.

Rambo, as you may well recall, is then accosted in increasingly more belligerent tones by the local sheriff, played with a certain tenacious self-possession by Brian Dennehy. And here we meet the Turnerian nemesis of the bloated, corrupted, selfish, and morally indifferent government. It was the untainted fodder for Reagan's speeches (next chapter) and Tea Partyers of today.

The sheriff wants to know if Rambo, by virtue of his existence, is "asking for trouble." Like any frontiersman, John Rambo is taciturn, restless, not at ease in society, and he is clearly bottled up with mortal promise and unrequited anger. What follows is cartoonish, of course, but capably drawn. If you were raised in North America, it's hard not to like Rambo.

"Why are you pushing me?" Rambo asks the sheriff, in one of his longer lines.

"We don't want guys like you in this town," the sheriff goads him. "If you want some friendly advice, get a haircut and take a bath."

And then the sheriff drops Rambo off well north of town, on the other side of a bridge. But it is a bridge too far, after all, and Rambo turns about and heads straight back toward Hope. This is America. He will go anywhere he damn well pleases.

So the sheriff arrests him, now physically pushing Rambo. Then he discovers a huge "hunting" knife, "a concealed weapon," on Rambo, which tells us that our hero is even more deadly than we may have suspected. But it is an elemental, essential manliness revealed here, not the man of guns but the man as a more basic extension of his phallus. At the most basic Freudian level, he doesn't need to ejaculate to kill you (i.e., shooting a gun); he can symbolically fornicate you to death just by stabbing you with a really big knife. This is effectively how the narrative develops too. As with the early confrontations, dustups provide the foreplay, the knife work begins the violent sexual act of redemptive rape, and consummation occurs when Rambo later takes out the big guns and shoots until he's laid out on his back.

Meanwhile, he is cuffed and taken to jail. Here he is roughed up a little, mocked a little. He is told he "smells like an animal." But this isn't really an insult; rather, it provides foreshadowing because the narrative strips Rambo to near-mythical animal savagery, necessary so the viewer can bear witness to the rebirth to come. To remind us of the mythical country we have entered, in the id of any building, the basement, one of the deputies says to him, "Right this way, partner."

The "pushing" continues apace. Rambo is forced to strip (get it?), he's beaten, and then he is roughly hosed down. Then, for reasons that make little sense, they attempt to shave him with a straight razor. Rambo, by the way, also suffers from post-traumatic stress disorder (PTSD). He has flashbacks. And the razor sets one off. Nobody understands him. Nobody tries to understand him. Nobody knows about or appreciates the sacrifice he made for America. Like the old marshal (Lon Chaney) says to Will Kane (Gary Cooper) in *High Noon* (1952), "They don't care. They just don't care." In this way, the Vietnam Syndrome is repackaged as a corrupted effete establishment sellout, and Rambo throws it down at the feet of ungrateful America, just like Ronald Reagan did.[22]

And then Rambo takes action against the immoral and crooked authorities who have pushed him too far. Now the film launches into a decidedly ungainly turn. Rambo beats up the cops and steals a motorcycle, a modern-day horse. What follows is clumsy. Put it this way, the fight scenes are amateurish, no *Bourne Identity* (2002). And not just because of when the movie was made. It doesn't even come close to the artfully manicured fisticuffs in *Shane* or the famous barn fight (with Gary Cooper suffering from a bad back) in *High Noon*.

Nonetheless, Rambo speeds away on the motorcycle and is pursued by the sheriff in his cop car. The chase culminates in the police car being wrecked and Rambo ditching the bike on a steep rock hillside. He then takes to the mountain and fashions a primeval sack shirt from an old tarp, looking much the primitive man now, a man at first principles we are meant to understand, Indian-like. He even goes preliterate in the sense that he ceases to speak. Stallone mostly grunts—"monosyllabic simplicity," offers Barry Langford[23]—and simply huffs and puffs through long sections of the film. He is now operating off the grid. He has gone off the reservation, running low to the ground. Meanwhile, the sheriff gets organized, and shortly a posse and dogs are closing in on our mountain man, despite his healthy early lead on them.

As the tension builds and the characters prepare themselves for the confrontation to come, we have time to consider the obstacles Rambo now faces. And they are formidable. The sheriff, and all that he personifies in mythical terms, stands in the way of decency, honor, and truth. The real America that Rambo signifies, we realize, has been snatched away while he was off fighting for the dear virtues America represents. And appropriately, suddenly, our mountain man has, well, not exactly miscalculated but nevertheless arrived at a metaphorical yet very real precipice—not of his own making, of course, because nothing is his fault any more than a two-year-old accepts responsibility, any more than the myth ever squares responsibility for its embellishments and urgings-on, that is, squares itself fully with reality. The dream is more comfortable, after all, as the Republican right has shown all too abundantly since Vietnam.

Even his three-day beard won't save Rambo now. To make matters worse, a chopper appears above, its passenger a crazed deputy determined to shoot Rambo off the face of the cliff. He tries. He shoots and misses, shoots and misses, Stallone whipping his head sideways to avoid rifle slugs, like Charlie Chaplin dodging bullets in the jail scene in *Modern Times*, except this time it would be unintentionally and absurdly funny if not for Stallone's uncannily humorless portrayal.

Finally, Rambo tosses a rock at the chopper, forcing it to sway, the shooter stumbles and falls to his demise, and Rambo leaps for safety. The forest gods save him from certain death as a cedar tree buffers his fall. He injures his arm. He grunts. He bleeds. He runs like a Cro-Magnon. He gets the deputy's rifle. He wants to make peace, but they insist on shooting at him from the top of the cliff.

By this point, the film as cartoon has fully taken over. We know Rambo has been forced to do what has to be done: make war to redeem himself but also to redeem America from the defilement it has suffered. If America's innocence was taken captive while he was away at war defending it, and if those who sent him to fight were corrupted government folks who stabbed the nation in the back, he's going to get some payback. It's inevitable. New rules.

As the one deputy who recognizes something special about him from the start, the one who thinks the sheriff takes the matter too far, says, "I knew there was something about that guy." Or, moments later, delivering to the audience a classic feel-good line, another deputy says that now "he's hunting us." And so it goes. Yet Rambo chooses to wound but not kill. Somewhat inelegantly, he explains to the sheriff, laying down a higher-road frontier gambit, "I coulda killed them all. I coulda killed you. In town, you're the law. Out here, it's me. Don't push it, or I'll give you a war you won't believe." Spitting diction that Ben Stiller would later ape to great comedic effect in *Tropic Thunder* (2008), he adds thickly, "Let it go. Let it go." But they do not believe him, and they keep pushing him. So he gives them the war he promised.

Along the way, Rambo's Green Berets commander, a certain Colonel Trautman, shows up. But he gets no respect. He warns the sheriff: "I didn't come to rescue Rambo from you. I came to rescue you from Rambo....A man who's the best with guns, with knives, with his bare hands. A man who's been trained to ignore pain, ignore weather. To live off the land." But to no avail. The pursuit continues.

"They drew first blood, not me," Rambo grunts out to Trautman later, after the fighting is done and he has blown up about half of the town and at length shot but not, importantly, killed the sheriff. But come on, Trautman reasons, "It's over. It's over, Johnny," not clearly indicating whether he means Vietnam is over or the conflict in the town is over or, perhaps, both.

Rambo erupts as he breaks down shortly into great sobs, spluttering out a kind of soliloquy. "Nothing is over," he roars.

RAMBO'S VIETNAM: "YOU JUST DON'T TURN IT OFF" 159

Nothing. You just don't turn it off. It wasn't my war. You asked me. I didn't ask you. And I did what I had to do to win. But somebody wouldn't let us win. And then I come back to the world, and I see all those maggots at the airport protesting me, spitting, calling me baby killer and all kinds of vile crap. Who are they to protest me?

He collapses and cries some more. And suddenly at this moment you realize you have witnessed an epochal turn, a point of cultural demarcation that nobody could have predicted. But there it is. Rambo breaks down, and he sobs like a baby. And in so doing it isn't that he vents some pent-up mythical rage so much as in his tears he regresses again to the level of a child, weeping principally because he didn't get his way and things didn't turn out the way he wanted them to. He did not get his way, and now he has the right to blame them, the liberals et alia. You have just witnessed how his frontier credentials, if allowed free rein, ultimately prevail. He is a winner. And he could have won Vietnam if only the U.S. government had let him, so the guilt is thrown back at the un-reborn. Manly tears, standing in for baptismal water, wash him clean.

And can you blame Rambo for any of it? Of course not. They kept pushing and pushing and pushing him. He had to fight back. And to fight back he had to strip down. Keep in mind, always the frontier Christ, he sacrifices for you, for all of us. And so if he wells up and breaks down, these tears are shed on our behalf as well. And this is entirely appropriate, and we are thankful for it. It is sometimes said that it was Bill Clinton's ability to feel your pain that made it possible for Bob Dole to cry publicly and without shame at Richard Nixon's funeral. This important cultural turn resonates in a variety of ways. For example, recall that, at the height of the Vietnam War in 1968, tears shed by Democratic nominee Ed Muskie effectively ended his run for the Oval Office (ironically, because the moment occurred as a result of Nixonian "dirty tricks"). Back in the day, real men did not cry openly—ever. But how times change. Watch *First Blood* again and you realize that it wasn't Clinton who granted the gift of tears to Dole, it was every bit as much Rambo. If Rambo could cry, darn it, any man could cry in public. And it begs the serious mythical question: can Rambo get it back for us, or is he all cock, no action?

"DO WE GET TO WIN THIS TIME?"

Some things are inevitable—death and sequels. In 1985, Stallone returned in *Rambo, First Blood Part Two*. He is still Rambo, of course, but somewhat more so. More jacked. This time his veins veritably pop from his muscles. And this time he is more homosexy, though he gets the girl (and she is promptly killed within seconds of their first and only dry kiss). He is more deadly. This time the body count rockets from one to fifty-eight or sixty-seven or sixty-nine, depending on who is counting.[24] And more captivity. This time it is not just imagined American innocence taken hostage but also includes actual MIAs and, egad, Rambo for a time. In short, it is a more frontier and more manly Rambo. And far more regenerative violence. More revisioned Vietnam.

The story picks up where it left off. Rambo wound up in jail pounding rocks, we are meant to understand from *First Blood*. Then Trautman appears and offers him a chance to have his sentence expunged if he agrees to a mission that would drop him beyond the frontier and deep into Nam, in-country, where he would recon to determine whether or not persistent rumors of MIAs being held against their will are true. If so, Rambo is to take pictures to verify their existence and then report to Trautman, who will in turn lead a rescue and extraction mission. Of course, we are meant to scoff at this—Rambo taking pictures? That is unnatural, and we all know it. But he agrees. It is the better option. Besides, you just know he is going to go rogue.

The MIA plot was both clever and timely for this film. Chatter about MIAs garnered a lot of media attention in the 1980s and early 1990s as the country spontaneously endorsed and even seemed to take comfort in the protomythical allegation that Vietnamese savages were doing what once Indians were believed to have done by nature: kidnapping innocent Americans and holding them against their will in deplorable conditions. Despite the Gulf of Tonkin lie upon which the war had been predicated, the captivity narrative coughed up a culturally appropriate justification for the war, after the fact, of course, but none-theless paradigmatically heartfelt. Reagan talked openly about MIAS in the 1980s,[25] and Texas billionaire Ross Perot, who had pursued the matter since the 1970s, made political hay with the idea during his two runs for the presidency in 1992 (he earned 19 percent of the popular vote, impressive for a third-party candidate) and 1996 (8 percent).

To say that Perot was passionate about the topic understates his expressed concern. For example, he took issue with Senator John McCain, who himself had spent five-plus years in a Hanoi jail and sat on the congressional committee that, from 1991 to 1993, investigated the MIA issue. According to the *Daily Beast*, Perot was convinced that "the senator hushed up evidence that live POWs were left behind in Vietnam and even transferred to the Soviet Union for human experi-mentation."[26] He's not the only one. Among a wide variety of authors, Bill Hendon and Elizabeth A. Stewart have identified and sought to document a massive ongoing cover-up of the MIA issue in a book that made it to the *New York Times* bestseller list in 2008.[27] Then there is the matter of those MIAs/captives who were ultimately released but, like McCain, spent long years in captivity, detailed in books such as Frank Anton and Tommy Denton's *Why Didn't You Get Me Out? A POW's Nightmare in Vietnam.*[28] Perot was sometimes dismissed as kooky and even a little bit bizarre. Perhaps the weirdest moment came when Admiral James Stockdale, his vice-presidential running mate and sur-vivor of seven years of captivity in Vietnam, turned off his hearing aid during the vice-presidential debate.

At any rate, *Rambo II*, the top-grossing film of 1985, conjures up a trifecta of captivity narratives. Rambo gets straight to it, pointedly and famously asking Trautman, "Sir, this time do we get to win?" Well, yes, kind of, Trautman says. "This time it's up to you." In short, according to one scholar, this is how "Rambo redeems the MIAS and American manhood."[29] Moreover, "it derives from…skillful retelling of an arche-typal narrative that has always exerted a powerful grip on our collective imagination."[30] Indeed, according to Ronald H. Carpenter, Americans saw many of their twentieth-century conflicts as frontier wars.[31]

But, first, the film gives us a gift in the form of Rambo's backstory, in a script written by Stallone and James Cameron (of *Titanic* [1997] and

Avatar fame), which further cements his frontier credentials. We learn that Rambo is a half-breed of Indian-German descent from Arizona, a "hell of a combination," which plots him from the mythically elemental dew of Americana, blessing him with the deep savage nature (with a dollop of Hun cunning)—the goods necessary to reorient and win the Vietnam War once and for all. Yes, and in Nam he recorded, we learn (not that Rambo would deign to count such things), fifty-nine bona fide kills (says Trautman), earned two silver stars, four bronze stars, two purple hearts, a Distinguished Service Cross, and the Congressional Medal of Honor. Kapow! And we hear in an aside that he is the "chosen one." Are you convinced now? If not, just watch him kill up to sixty-nine baddies. Quite rightly, Trautman dispels the doubters: "Rambo is…a pure fighting machine with only a desire to win a war that somebody else lost." Moreover, "What you choose to call hell, he calls home," Trautman zaps the softies sitting behind computer screens who obviously know nothing of real manliness.

Next up, in a tender moment we catch our narcissist aridly masturbating. In this intimate scene, the camera pans against the darkness of night, beginning with and highlighting his throbbing muscly shoulder as it tracks teasingly down his veiny, glistening, ropey arm to where he strokes his knife methodically back and forth, back and forth, on the sharpening stone. To turn an old phrase slightly, a good man is hard to find, but Rambo is a hard man good to find. He is hot yet somehow brittle, all man yet also metallic. "Rambo is nothing more nor less than a trendy incarnation of the traditional frontier hero—Leatherstocking on steroids…with Reds substituting for redskins," write Schechter and Semeiks.[32]

And Rambo has got only thirty-six hours. Nobody really expects him to find any MIAs. Except the audience.

As he is dropped from the aircraft, his parachute gets hung up, and he is forced to cut himself free of most of his equipment in order to survive. So he is forced into battle with only his Bowie-like knife, a bow, and some explosive-tipped arrows. This must have surprised audiences about as much as the fact that, guess what, he finds MIAs! They have been worked like slaves, scrawny and half-starved, penned up in a bamboo-shuttered cave teeming with spiders and rats. Rambo gets to them quickly enough, dashing along a stream, scrambling over rocks, running through jungle ferns, bandanna fluttering. He knows where they are because, senses keen, from afar he hears them moaning quietly.

The location is a classic frontier setting. Mostly untamed, dangerous nature, well beyond the pale of civilization. For example, Rambo bursts into a small clearing to pause beneath a tree. A dangling fat snake menaces him from behind, ready to strike. Unperturbed, he snatches it by the throat, scoffs, and carries on. It is cool because he kills only when it is called for. The Vietnamese, meanwhile, typify pure savage idiocy, so much fodder for his revenge. Violating every cherished nineteenth-century Protestant precept, they are by turns filthy (even their teeth), treacherous, dishonest, and heavy drinkers, delight in the company of whores, and lack vitality and discipline. Their Russian overlords are naturally more sophisticated and white but also more menacing, conniving, and, crucially, Godless.

Apart from throaty utterings, Stallone's principal approach to acting is to move his eyes sideways to express emotion. And to flex, at which Stallone excels. The plot and acting are, in sum, to say the least, hackneyed and predictable. But then, given the expectation established for us by *Rambo 1*, something unusual happens. And who would have expected that boy meets girl? His contact is named Co, also a half-breed. She is pretty, good at killing, and also longs for America. They are a perfect match. They can communicate. She speaks Hollywood Indian too.

Rambo spills his guts to her. He tells her that, after he returned from Nam to America, he discovered "there's another war going on." Not one to waste words, she queries, "What war?" He tells her it is a war against goodness and everything the returning soldiers stood for while fighting for America. But what about her? What's she going to do? "Maybe go America," she explains with prosaic economy. "Live the quiet life." (She obviously didn't see *Rambo 1*, i.e., *First Blood*.) She asks him, "What bring you good luck?" He brandishes, boing, his big knife. "I guess this." Later what really sets the mood for love is when she expresses her feelings for him: "Rambo, you're not expendable." It is a magical moment, to which he appropriately nods his head in a way that might easily be mistaken for a burp.

Next, once Rambo relays his news about the MIAS back to head-quarters, euphoria erupts. But the callow and deceitful civilian commander, Murdock, orders the mission terminated because Congress cannot handle the pressure of reality. The mission was nothing more than a cynical political exercise. Nothing more. Rambo was set up as a patsy. "It was a lie," Trautman decries to Murdock. "Just like the whole damn war." Well, yes, the war was a lie, but Trautman is not appealing to empirical reality; he is channeling Rambo's do-we-get-to-win-this-time frontier revisionist delusion. And, appropriately, Murdock is just a "stinking bureaucrat trying to cover his ass," Trautman says, launching a homophobic taunt. Murdock responds forcefully and with ironic truth, "No, not just mine, a nation's." In this way, the actual cover-up for the lie of Tonkin is neatly replaced by the covering of the ass. This recasting of the narrative—and, I mean, even Stockdale knew of the Tonkin deception when he was an admiral but says he was ordered to keep it secret—is what allows Rambo to "win this time."

This is a dark time in the film, then, because Rambo has been sold out and suddenly taken prisoner when the chopper that was supposed to rescue him with his lone redeemed MIA abandons him. Curse that rotten bureaucrat and those spineless tax collectors in Congress! Next thing, Rambo is strapped Jesus-like, arms tethered across a yoke, covered in leeches, dangling torso-deep in a pit filled with the effluent from a pig sty. Then he is taken for questioning by the "Russians" and, predictably, treated to a little torture to smarten him up. The devious Russians are merciless with electric shocks administered by a mean bastard turning a big dial. Rambo shouts out yet doesn't really flinch.

They cannot believe he can endure so much torture. Then, conjuring up a bit of trickery worthy of Mel Brooks's television series *Get Smart* (1965–70), Rambo agrees, if they unshackle him, to send a message via radio telling the folks back at HQ that there are no MIAS after all. You can guess the rest. He fights his way free, again saving the same emaciated MIA whom he drags around like a rag doll. Unexpectedly voluble, he denounces them, "Fuck you." To Murdock, he issues a warning: "I'm coming to get you."

Meanwhile, Rambo's Pocahontas has returned to help her man, disguised as a whore, and they escape, kiss, and agree to move to America.

And she is abruptly killed seconds later. "You not forget me," she implores with her dying words, prostrate in his arms. Rambo sniffles a moment and then goes full Rambo on the village and its savage occupants. One by one he picks off the Russians, dispensing lethal justice from the mud, the water, the air, the tall grass, by fire, arrow, exploding arrow, hand-to-hand combat, and, most improbably (no, excuse me, nothing is improbable with Rambo), chopper to chopper. He returns to HQ and receives a hero's welcome, but he eschews all praise and deflects it to the MIAS. Then he confronts Murdock, menaces him with the great knife, does not kill him, but warns him: "You know there's more men out there. You know where they are. Find them, or I'll find you." And that is about it.

To argue that the film is dopey and more than slightly ridiculous—and here I plead guilty—is ultimately unfair because such an argument misses the point. *Rambo II* works for the same reason that *Rambo I* worked, and *Rambo I* worked because it channels America's creation story in its most elemental form, the captivity narrative. *Rambo II* is slightly more charged because it is also more ambitious—three captivity narratives for the price of one, plus the love interest. Both films fittingly go over the top, in part because the production values are awkward and poorly effected. On the other hand, over-the-topness is called for because the frontiersman draws from a well of fantasy, denial, and illusion. *Rambo* is no more over the top, in this sense, than Moses was when he parted the waters, or Jesus was when he healed a leper, or Saint Rose of Lima was when she achieved sainthood while she really suffered from mental illness.[33] If you want to bash *Rambo* for stretching credulity, then all religion becomes fair game, at least insofar as the narratives are logically absurd and empirically nonsensical.

"COME TO TERMS WITH WHAT YOU ARE"

At the same time the United States was arming and training the Taliban (yes, *that* Taliban, of Osama bin Laden infamy) to resist invading Soviet forces in Afghanistan beginning in 1979, many Americans took pleasure in saying that Afghanistan was the Soviets' Vietnam. In *Rambo III*, Colonel Trautman lambastes the Ruskies for having ignored the lessons of history (not that "history" has ever stopped the United States from repeating the same imperial behavior—in fact, just the opposite, as expressed cogently in the idea that "trauma demands repetition," taken up in Chapter 1). "We already had our Vietnam. Now you're gonna have yours," he says.

Rambo III is somehow more Rambo than ever. It is tempting to say that it is too much Rambo, in fact, and in so becoming it transgresses the thin lines separating farce from cartoon and cartoon from propaganda. But, to be fair, all the *Rambo* flicks are cartoonish and amount to frontier propaganda insofar as they reek of the culture that made Stallone a very rich man. A case in point is the movie's dedication: "THIS FILM IS DEDICATED TO THE GALLANT PEOPLE OF AFGHANISTAN."[34] (You just know how much this gesture meant to them.) The word choice—*gallant*—offers an interesting throwback to the same phrase when it was used to describe American forces that invaded Mexico in 1846 or Custer's Seventh Cavalry as it warred and raped and pillaged in the 1870s. Gallant? The people of Afghanistan we meet in this film are mujahideen: that is, the future Taliban, not exactly Mayberry living.

Rambo, First Blood excused America from the debacle of Vietnam because it had been sold out, kidnapped, and cheated by "somebody" who "wouldn't let us win." Hence a captivity narrative. *Rambo, First Blood Part Two* offered no additional excuses but symbolically reenacted America's birth thrice—by redeeming American innocence that had been stolen by savagery, by freeing MIAs and thereby reinstating American manhood as well as erasing American culpability for the war, and finally by setting Rambo free and thereby laying out the welcome mat for future preemptive aggression, like having earned a kind of imperial rain check, redeemable whenever, wherever.

Rambo III, again cowritten by Stallone, begins with an image of the flag. Then we encounter Rambo earning money in an Asian martial arts contest by "stick fighting." This offers rough homosocialism as spectacle as the two near-naked brutes slash at each other with their rods, until Rambo beats his mate into submission and they become fast friends. Rambo donates the purse he earns to the monks at the monastery where he works as a kind of tin smith. He is content.

But America needs him because its foreign policy cannot succeed without the frontiersman, we learn. Well, we already know that, but we are reminded of it again. It is important that we be reminded that the myth operates precisely as religion, based on faith. So a doubting Thomas—in this case a skeptical and unmanly embassy employee—serves the purpose well of reminding us to keep faith too. Rambo's success depends entirely upon it. It is the suspension of disbelief twice—in the role of movies as fiction and in the power of the myth as religion.

Anyway, Afghanistan has been terrorized by Soviets who have killed "over 2 million civilians." These innocents were "systematically slaughtered by Russian armies" that employed every means at their disposal, including chemical weapons, the embassy guy says. But now, after nine years, with a little help, the Afghans have begun to take back their country except for one region ruled by a notorious Soviet cretin. Trautman wants to take him down, and he wants Rambo to help do it. Rambo declines. He says, no thanks, his war is over.

Trautman appeals to him by comparing Rambo to a great work of art. "We didn't make you this fighting machine, we just chipped away the rough edges." Nonetheless, thanks, but no, says Rambo. "You're always going to be tearing away at yourself until you come to terms with what you are," Trautman counsels. No, go away, says Rambo politely.

Suddenly, and I guess there is no escaping captivity in the *Rambo* series (and, like success, trauma also seems to demand repetition at the box office), Trautman crosses the frontier with his team, and all except him are killed in a few seconds; he is then taken prisoner at that notorious Soviet commander's fort. And in this way Rambo is drawn back into the game. He prefers peace but will fight if something noble and true and decent and white and male is at risk of becoming diminished. And he will do it all by himself. Reasonably, America's mujahideen allies are unwilling to risk it all to save one American who will only up and leave when his mission has been completed. But this is a mere plot device. Rambo is a lone wolf whose agency will enable full Afghan redemption.

In another way, too, Rambo is more Rambo. He is now even more jacked. Where *Rambo II* found him bulked up, muscles upon muscles, veins popping from his arms, Stallone somehow found another level for *Rambo III*. The muscles are bigger than ever, and the veins bulge not only across his arms but also across his chest and pecs. He struts (he gave up merely walking in *Rambo II*) in a way reminiscent of George W. Bush, arms flared slightly at the sides as the chest puffs outward. It is reminiscent of how you can hear in John Wayne's voice an attempt to lower the register so as to ramp up his masculinity, as in, say, the early scenes from *Red River* (1948) or when he is barking orders in the first filmic adaptation of *True Grit* (1969).

Feeling the heat from Arnold Schwarzenegger's growing popularity in the late 1980s, *Rambo III* also attempts to inject levity into the script. It doesn't work. For example, early on, when asked to explain his presence, Rambo tries a joke, "I'm no tourist." Or, when his guide says it is pure folly for Rambo to go in alone against the Russian fort and that he will "accept no responsibility," in an inside joke Rambo ruefully guffaws, "Sounds familiar." Another attempt occurs later when Trautman introduces this gambit: "How's the wound?" Rambo reminds him, setting up the joke, "You taught us to ignore pain." Trautman delivers the straight line: "Is it working?" Rambo flubs it: "Not really." Or, finally, in case you haven't caught on to the newly jokey Rambo, when they are at last surrounded by Soviets, with no chance of escape, and certain death awaits them, Trautman presents a jocular silver platter: "You got any ideas?" Rambo: "Surrounding them's out." Trautman: "Hell of a time for humor, John." He is almost on the mark here because the attempt at humor is hellishly unfunny.

In *Rambo III*, the frontier is redrawn slightly, more reminiscent of the American west with desert-like scapes and Indians/Afghans and their weird customs, riding on horseback and living in tents. The Soviet commander is a pure bully. "Out here I have no superiors," he crows, not unlike the scene in the gorgeous and vastly superior film *The Man Who Shot Liberty Valance*, where Valance (Lee Marvin) announces venomously, as he prepares to beat Ransom Stoddard (Jimmy Stewart) nearly to death for trying to protect an old lady from hooligans, "You want law? I'll teach you western law." And a beating commences.

Trautman challenges the commander and seeks to reveal his, and thereby then-contemporary Soviet, hypocrisy with words: "You talk peace and disarmament to the world, and here you are wiping out a race of people." Never mind that this is precisely what the United States did to grow from thirteen to fifty states over 150 years—"ethnic cleansing against Native American peoples," as one scholar describes it.[35] Picking up and mimicking President Reagan, Trautman claims that the "freedom fighters" have turned the corner in Afghanistan and that they just need a little Rambo help to get rid of this last Soviet creep. "They'd rather die than be slaves to an invading army," Trautman zings the commander, again apparently unaware of the eighteenth and nineteenth centuries in the U.S. west. "You can't defeat a people like that."

The rough stereotypical homoerotic onanism of *Rambo II* surfaces again here but primarily as the projection of homophobia. Apart from the camera's utter fixation with Rambo's torso, probably the best evocation is offered by Trautman's challenge to anal rape. In a deep, dark dungeon where Trautman is strung up, in itself a thinly disguised symbolic anal cavity, the Soviet commander menaces the American colonel and demands to know, apropos of nothing, where the Stinger missiles are. Trautman says they are "close," teasing him. This gives the commander pause. He moves in. While you aren't exactly on the edge of your seat at this point, it begs the question: is Trautman really going to give them away? "How close?" rasps the commander. "In your ass!" Trautman smacks him down. Right, my exploding missiles are in your ass, now hit me again! In turn, not so subtly the commander shoves his pistol against Trautman's mouth. This scene is really a kind of dance. The disagreement between the two men, as with the superpowers they represent, lies not in regard to the substance of the tune they follow but in regard to who gets to lead and who has to play the role of bitch. But not to worry. The commander is a polymorphous whore, whereas Trautman, we know, has eyes only for "Johnny."

Making no effort to shy away from enhanced mythical obviousness, *Rambo III* also ramps up the religious tones that undergird the *Rambo* series. This cuts two ways. By heaping ever greater invective upon the Russian *qua* Other, we come better to know and deplore evil. This helps prepare us—as if we need it—for the second coming. What I mean is that Rambo in a muddy way is compared both to God ("Who do you think this man is? God?"), which he is not, of course, but also as the "chosen one," all of which speaks to long-ago Puritan notions, albeit in a sloppy manner. Yet it serves the point well enough: on behalf of America, Rambo fights the old frontier battle. One Afghan leader explains it this way: "Holy warriors. To us, this is a holy war. And there is no death for the mujahideen because we have taken our last rites and consider ourselves dead already." Last rites? That is a Catholic custom, and these are Muslims.

The captivity narrative in which innocence is redeemed is also more complicated here. Sure, we know that Soviet forces exterminate, rape, pillage, and sucker children to early deaths with booby-trapped bombs disguised as kids' toys. All that is innocent and good the Soviets contaminate and defile, yes, we get that. But Rambo is also dogged by a brave Afghan boy who has lost his parents and brother to the war. It is the oldest trick in the book, of course, but it works well enough. The boy will not go away, and we know deep down that, because Rambo's face is incapable of showing emotion and/or Stallone's face is incapable of acting, Rambo loves the irascible kid, as Shane in the 1952 classic loves his young protégé Joey or Dunson loves Matt in *Red River* or Rick loves Carl in *The Walking Dead*. The paternal line must continue, after all.

The kid complicates things because we know full well that the horrors of war are no place for a boy who should be able to spend his time playing with GI Joe dolls or playing cowboys and Indians or playing with his plastic light saber. Anyway, predictably, the kid, we see, is brave. But he is just a kid after all, and this is a theater of men, so in turn the boy is injured, and Rambo has to drop everything and ensure the lad's escape to a safe place. Then he returns to uncapture Trautman. But now suddenly Rambo and Trautman are surrounded, and it appears as if all is lost. As if! In a classic coming-of-age moment, the boy figures prominently as the mujahideen come riding in to save the day.

Yes, you read that right. The cavalry ride in at the last moment to save our hero and his sidekick. Rambo takes to a horse, too, as he effectively saves them all from Soviet destruction. As Studlar and Desser put it, "Attempting to deliver its audience from the anxiety of the present, Rambo would seek to restore an unreflective lost Eden of primitive masculine power."[36] This holds true for the series. The nod to Eden is particularly insightful because Rambo is in fact a religious figure inasmuch as the frontiersman invariably acts like Adam, Christ, and/or Moses, creating, sacrificing, delivering. In fact, he is much like Kevin Costner's John J. Dunbar in *Dances with Wolves*. Both characters are stripped down, reborn (in Rambo's case, again and again), the Natives are redeemed (at least in *Rambo III*), Rambo gets the girl (in *Rambo II*, though not for long), he saves innocence (always), he redeems captives (always), and he becomes a better Indian/Vietnamese/Afghan fighter than the Natives (always). This is because he is the essential man for his times, "he fits right in there," to borrow again that line from *The Big Lebowski*.

CONCLUSION

The *Rambo* films work so well because they are caught up in and reinforce a self-referential loop. Any creation myth has an internal logic, and it is because the series so articulately and closely adheres to the frontier myth that the wildly implausible becomes believable, the idiotic conceivable, and the imperial invisible. We cheer for Rambo even as some of us dismiss the film as lightweight, even puerile. The point is that Rambo gets us, he really gets us. And we get how he gets us, and we are grateful to him for it at a deep level. He is nature's man in just the way that Henry Nash Smith noted: "The idea of nature suggested to Turner a poetic account of the influence of free land as a rebirth, a regeneration, a rejuvenation of man and society constantly recurring where civilization came into contact with the wilderness along the frontier."[37]

Moreover, the *Rambo* series provides a means for America to take a war that it lost, refashion the conflict as a captivity narrative, and win it. In so doing, the loss becomes pinned on the effete, the feminine, the corrupted, the overcivilized city/eastern types. It is, in short, unadulterated frontier. In this way, the myth endures and prospers even as technology changes (though phallic weaponry remains a constant), the geographic setting changes (though the line separating civilization from savagery endures), the faceless face changes (Mexican, Nicaraguan, Vietnamese, Soviet—they are all still just stereotyped mythical Indian stand-ins), and so on. In other words, the myth abides in spite of significant historical change and in the face of empirical reality for precisely the same reasons that Christianity and Islam and Cree belief have survived. They endure because people continue to believe. And people believe because, once adopted, signs and wonders abound everywhere for true believers. In this way, Rambo completes the circle and brings us home. He tells us a story that we already know to be true. He is America's avatar of creation.

CHAPTER 7

RONALD REAGAN'S NICARAGUA: "THIS SHINING CITY"

Frontier rhetoric of constant vigilance against
fearless and savage Indians made the need for
armament seem crucial. Even when pioneers did
not encounter hostile Indians on their travels west,
settlers tended to "reimagine" such Indians.
— Abigail A. Kohn[1]

I was with the Enemy eleven weeks and five days; and not
one Week passed without the fury of the Enemy, and some
desolation by fire and sword upon one place or other.
— Mary Rowlandson[2]

In 1986, the Iran-Contra affair unearthed the unsavory revelation that the Reagan administration had funneled profits made by secretly and illegally selling arms to terrorist hostage takers in Iran to the Contras in Nicaragua, who sought to overthrow a democratically elected government commonly known as the Sandinistas.[3] President Ronald Reagan was a cold warrior through and through and believed that if Nicaraguan leftists, inspired by Augusto Sandino's refusal to capitulate to imperial aggression fifty years earlier, as well as Catholic liberation theology that preached social justice were not stopped, then communism would shortly be banging on America's back door via Texas. He identified the Contras, mostly mercenaries and castoffs from the disestablished and brutal Nicaraguan National Guard, as the "moral equivalent" of America's founding fathers. (Reagan uttered similar words of praise for the mujahideen, in effect the Taliban, when he welcomed them to the Oval Office for a public relations event in 1982.) He contended that the "evil empire" (i.e., Soviet Union), to which he linked the Sandinistas, would stop at nothing in its quest for world control. And so one result was that the Reagan administration sought to destroy the Sandinistas. For Nicaragua, however, it was manifest destiny and the Monroe Doctrine all over again.[4] As David Dent writes, "of all the countries in Central America, Nicaragua has suffered the most in the hands of Washington policymakers."[5]

Funding the Contras via secret sales of arms to a known belligerent of the United States violated the law. And, for a moment, it appeared as if the scandal might bring down Reagan. But despite heated congressional hearings and an enormous amount of publicity, it simply (and perhaps predictably, in hindsight) blew over. Even though at the same time the CIA engaged drug dealers "as middlemen,"[6] it blew over. In part, this outcome derived from Reagan's growing popularity, which increased sharply over his two terms in office and continued to soar after Reagan left office, according to Gallup.[7]

Democratic legislators who controlled Congress also proved unwilling to plunge the nation back into another Watergate-like trauma, which had forced Richard Nixon out of office in 1974 just two years into his second term. The sentiment held that the country simply could not endure another such body blow. As with Watergate, protecting the sanctity of the political system trumped the sense that criminals, irrespective of their station or office, should be punished. While lawmakers held that they were acting in the best interests of their constituents and of the country as a whole, the contempt in which Congress is held today suggests another outcome. Moreover, as late as 1989, more than 40 percent of Americans had no idea which side the United States supported in Nicaragua, let alone what the competing sides represented.[8] To be fair, at least some of the confusion resulted from a highly orchestrated propaganda campaign—successful agenda-setting—by the

Reagan White House,[9] while Reagan in turn claimed that those who opposed his policies themselves employed "concerted propaganda."[10]

The Sandinistas, meanwhile, played rough. With noteworthy success, they had taken up arms against and defeated the Somoza family dynasty that the United States had backed more or less unflinchingly since 1936. But they also governed of necessity, at least during the Contra war, in a heavy-handed way. Their many international supporters argued that Sandinista rule simply reflected the intense pressure felt as a consequence of American attempts to destroy the Sandinistas by wrecking the country's infrastructure. This was achieved, in large part, not only by indirect war via the Contras but also by the CIA's wreaking havoc on the economy and infrastructure and pressuring other countries to shun and punish Nicaragua, "in accordance with the premise that support for freedom was self-defense."[11]

The Contra war, funded covertly by the Reagan administration and by private U.S. donors in an effort orchestrated by the Reagan regime, was mostly staged from neighboring Honduras. Perhaps a better way to assess the Sandinistas is to consider their behavior after Reagan left office and after the Soviet Union collapsed. From this vantage point, it turns out that the Sandinistas were in fact democrats after all and not flaming totalitarian communists. For example, in 1990, as the Soviet Union fell apart, the Iron Curtain came down, and nearly two years after Reagan left office, the Sandinistas endorsed, staged, and lost a free election.

"THE MOST PEACEFUL, LEAST WARLIKE NATION IN MODERN HISTORY"

Reagan's first career was as a Hollywood actor. Reagan played in dozens of films, including the role of George Armstrong Custer in the 1940 film *Santa Fe Trail*. He served as president of the Screen Actors Guild during the 1950s, a time in which it actively sought to root out communists and communist influences in Hollywood. He secretly provided information to the FBI, a list of names of people he thought might be communists or communist sympathizers. He never became a big star, and by the early 1960s, after having joined the Republican

Party, he became a spokesman for General Electric and then a vocal supporter of Republican presidential candidate Barry Goldwater in 1964. He was tapped to run for the governorship of California. He ran and won in 1966 and 1970. He won the presidency in 1980 and served two terms.

Central mythical themes and frontier phrases recur in Reagan's speeches with such regularity that it becomes possible to discern a clear and consistent frontier narrative at the heart of his popularity, demonstrating that the frontier myth has endured and even thrived not merely in the printed press and Hollywood but even in the White House and, in this case, the espoused words of America's most popular modern president. His speeches, delivered with consummate skill (Reagan was not called the "great communicator" for nothing), leave virtually no mythical stone unturned. By channeling deep Americana, he was able to disarm and deflect many of his opponents; his supporters, meanwhile, lapped it all up.

The addresses sketch a romantic frontier zone, bend a knee to the founding fathers, tear a page from muscular seventeenth-century Massachusetts Bay Protestantism, and rhetorically endorse rebellion, manifest destiny, and frontier universalism—"the oldest hopes of our Republic…for all of humanity,"[12] as Reagan framed it in the 1982 State of the Union Address—wrapped tidily, simplistically, and consistently in a series of neat rhetorical binaries. Turner had likewise channeled long-standing visions of America's creation, its sense of special mission.

Reagan consistently cast Central America as a shadowy and savage landscape where Soviet and Cuban communists prowled, pitting totalitarian darkness against the light of America's blessed civilizing impulses. But, of course, communists were relative newcomers. The origins of such a vision lie much deeper in the fabric of Americana. America needs an enemy as much as strong needs weak, right needs wrong, white needs colored, God needs Satan, and civilization à la Turner needs the savage.

The source of his take on American exceptionalism will come as no surprise to those old enough to remember Reagan. He said it was vetted and reborn on the "frontier of freedom"[13] and lay in its blessed compact with God. Channeling seventeenth-century Puritan notions, as presidential candidate he addressed the Republican National Convention in 1980:

> More than anything else I want my candidacy to unify our country....They [Democrats] say that the United States has had its day in the sun....My fellow citizens I utterly reject that view....We need rebirth....The United States is unique in world history...[and has] a special kind of compact.... Three hundred and sixty years ago, in 1620, a group of families dared cross a mighty ocean to build a future for themselves in a new world....[T]hey formed what they called a "compact."...That set the pattern...[on] sacred honor to found this nation.[14]

In short, even before taking office Reagan evinced a rhetorical addiction to spouting Puritan shibboleths wrapped up in well-established mythical frontier garb. Grounding himself in this way was of key significance in his attempts to appeal to Americans, as his speechwriters knew all too well. But it also served the political purpose of presenting himself, like the Puritans, as a Washington outsider, which holds a natural appeal to voters. The genius of his approach is that it simultaneously ensconced him as an outsider, rhetorically, and a consummate insider, for no American rhetorical current runs deeper than the myth of creation. It was, in a way, a clever expression of Protestantism—Reagan made an end run around the established order to fashion a more direct relationship with the public. Like Reagan, the Puritans had come as outsiders but remained undaunted, of course, as they built nothing short of a mythical new world, "beloved and blessed."

"We are not a warlike people," Reagan told the convention, despite centuries of evidence to the contrary. "Quite the opposite," he insisted. "We always seek to live in peace. We resort to force infrequently and with great reluctance." As evidence, he noted that "four times in my lifetime America has gone to war"—the First and Second World Wars, the Korean War, and the Vietnam War (he was born in 1911).[15] "We were never the aggressors," he averred in 1983.[16] "We do not start fights. We will never be an aggressor," he offered in 1982.[17] However, most reputable accounts identify dozens of military engagements during his lifetime, almost all of which were initiated by the United States. For example, by the time Reagan was ten years old, the United States had dispatched troops to, invaded, and/or occupied, in alphabetical order, China, Cuba, Dalmatia, Dominican Republic, First World War, Haiti, Guatemala, Honduras, Mexico, Nicaragua, Panama, Soviet Russia, and Turkey.[18] But this was normal. Frontier conflicts, such as that waged against Nicaragua, simply did not count. It was not a matter of denying them, which would have required some acknowledgement that something, anything, had happened; instead, it was as if they were simply unseen, much like the Indian wars of the late nineteenth century, barely noticed except when things occasionally went wrong (e.g., Custer). Indeed, "America is the most peaceful, least warlike nation in modern history," Reagan gloated in an address to the Republican National Convention in 1984.[19]

It followed that he saw the Indian wars as Puritans might have, certainly as Turner had. "Here was virgin soil [and] an abundance of land," Reagan quoted Thomas Jefferson.[20] In a 1988 address, as was his usual custom, he returned to his opening frontier themes:

> It is impossible to capture in words the splendor of this vast continent which God has granted as our portion of this creation. There are no words to express the extraordinary strength and character of this breed of people we call Americans....They are the kind of men and women Tom Paine had in mind when he wrote—during the darkest days of the American Revolution—"We have it in our power to begin the world over again."...I believe that this generation of Americans today has a rendezvous with destiny. Tonight let us dedicate ourselves to renewing the American compact... the spirit that blazed with zeal....The spirit is still there, ready to blaze into life if you and I are willing to do what needs to be done....The time is now to recapture our destiny....Can we doubt that only a Divine Providence placed this land, this island of freedom...[to aid] freedom fighters of Afghanistan [mujahideen] and our countrymen held in savage captivity?[21]

Turner was eloquent, as you will recall, but no more stirring than Reagan's speechwriters. The "Teflon president" (so tagged because nothing objectionable that he said appeared to stick to him) could read a speech like no other president in living memory. And the speech here included many of the myth's central tenets, for example that Americans were God's chosen people and inhabited a providential land. This allegation is so profoundly American that it reaches further back than Turner all the way to the Puritan founders whom Turner himself repackaged and regifted.[22] It mines pure gold of an imagined "rendezvous with destiny," a common theme and a phrase that Reagan also employed in his address to the Republican National Convention eight years earlier.[23] Further, (white) Americans were racially unique, "a breed" apart (which nods unpleasantly to the racial divide that saw people of color vote overwhelmingly for Reagan's two presidential opponents) because of their favored status with God. Moreover, Americans had a divinely sanctioned ("Can we doubt that only a Divine Providence...") purpose to fulfill: "The time is now to recapture our destiny."

Reagan, like some latter-day Moses, would lead Americans to the promised land of the future that expressed a throwback to, or simply reinhabited, an imagined past. His efforts consistently nodded to the early literary foundations of the frontier myth when he tapped into a most curious minor national fixation on the immediate post–Vietnam War years, an updated captivity narrative, the idea that untold numbers of innocent American POWs, à la *Rambo II*, remained against their will in Vietnam.[24] Reagan carried these themes forward reliably for eight years and appealed to Paine's ideas like clockwork.[25] He doted on and defended "America, this shining city on a hill," invoking John Winthrop's famous words.[26]

"WE'VE PUSHED CIVILIZATION FORWARD"

Reagan's frontier setting wasn't the actual old west, but then it never had been because the mythical old west never really existed anywhere except in the imagination. Yet it remained as fecund as ever. And his speeches embraced and endorsed this tack and situated the frontier as a place where "civilization" was pitted, as ever, against "savagery." The "frontier" is a place where "we've pushed civilization forward," Reagan explained in the 1984 State of the Union Address. "Our goal is to build on our pioneer spirit."[27] It is a place of "raw, untamed wilderness" such as that which had confronted George Washington when he "placed his hand upon the Bible."[28]

And, that said, Americans should have been mindful of the perils threatened by the frontier because, as Reagan spoke to Congress in the spring of 1983, "El Salvador is nearer to Texas than Texas is to Massachusetts. Nicaragua is just as close to Miami, San Antonio, San Diego, and Tucson, as those cities are to Washington."[29] The stakes were high, he earlier and famously warned Britain's Parliament, always pitching a simplistic binary in favor of a more nuanced worldview, because "totalitarian" governments, the natural "enemies" of democracy "have refined their instruments of repression." Also, ever ready to burnish a mythical platitude, Reagan found America's Godless enemies, like so many Indians or Mexicans of yore, waging a "barbarous assault on the human spirit." Consequently, the risks were dire as well as religious, as they always had been. It was God versus Satan all over again.

Meanwhile, Reagan identified those Central American revolutionaries who fought to decolonize their countries from American hegemony "for what they really are—Cuban-backed guerrillas who want power for themselves." Indeed, he returned to his essential and teleological mythical point that humankind has an "instinctive desire for freedom and self-determination." But not to worry, he counseled British legislators, the story would end much like a sappy Hollywood production: "[T]he forces of good ultimately rally and triumph over evil." The "great civilized ideas" would prevail— "individual liberty, representative government, and the rule of law under God."[30] Ever stalwart, Reagan bragged that "we have not been afraid to characterize our adversaries for what they are." "They" were "evil."[31]

Such were the stakes in his articulated views, and dozens of his speeches retill the same mythical soil. "There is sin and evil in the world, and we're enjoined by Scripture and the Lord Jesus to oppose it with all our might," Reagan told a meeting of evangelicals. As a result, the frontier of Nicaragua had the makings of a site for a holy war. "Yes, let us pray for the salvation of all those living in that totalitarian darkness—pray they will discover the joy of knowing God. But until they do...they [the Soviets] are the focus of evil in the modern world."[32] Given such views, did the Sandinistas ever stand a chance? Reagan answered this question again and again, as when he addressed the Contras directly, echoing his 1985 State of the Union Address: "We say to you tonight: you are not alone, freedom fighters. America will support with moral and material assistance not just your right to fight and die for freedom but to fight and win freedom...in Nicaragua...for the security of our frontiers." Lest America not shame itself, he continued, "let no one say that this nation cannot reach the destiny of our dreams."[33] For obvious reasons, he chose not to describe or explain how the Contras specialized in castration and torture, for example how "some earned a reputation for using spoons to gouge their victims' eyes out."[34]

Instead, immorality haunted the Caribbean Basin, Reagan preached. Soviets had infested Cuba, and then Cubans, in turn, had spread communism like a cancer to the tiny island of Grenada.[35] "You just give me the word and I'll turn that fucking island [Grenada] into a parking lot," Secretary of State Alexander Haig told Reagan.[36] A single paragraph in the 1985 State of the Union Address got right to the point:

> The Sandinista dictatorship of Nicaragua, with full Cuban-Soviet bloc support, not only persecutes its people, the church, and denies a free press, but arms and provides bases for Communist terrorists attacking neighboring states. Support for freedom fighters is self-defense and totally consistent....I want to work with you [Congress] to support the democratic forces whose struggle is tied to our own security....They're dreams we can make come true.[37]

In this way, the Sandinistas were Othered, enemies of freedom and democracy, corrupted by the darkness of communist totalitarianism, and preternaturally aggressive. America's "freedom fighters" rather obviously stood in for the opposite. Where did this universal love for freedom originate? God. It was "the love of freedom that God places in each of us and whose defense He has entrusted in a special way to this nation," according to Reagan.[38]

But it wasn't all God and love versus the Sandinista Other. The situation was messier because the Soviets were much like Hitler and, more generally, Nazis, Reagan stressed.[39] It cut two ways. First, because of the efforts of the United States, he explained, "I can tell you tonight, democracy is beginning to take root in El Salvador, which, until a short time ago, knew only dictatorship."[40] But he neglected to note that it was an authoritarian government of American making, one that not so secretly employed death squads against its civilian population, killing tens of thousands. Reagan termed the government a "blessing."[41] Second, and this was his real point, rebels in El Salvador, "trained by Nicaragua and Cuba,"[42] presented a Nazi-like threat to America.

Meanwhile, in the face of "the generosity and the good faith of the American people," the ungrateful Sandinista government, guided by Godless Marxism-Leninism,

> has imposed a new dictatorship. It has refused to hold the elections it promised. It has seized control of most media and subjects all media to heavy prior censorship. It denied the bishops and priests of the Roman Catholic Church the right to say Mass on radio during Holy Week. It insulted and mocked the Pope. It has driven the Miskito Indians from their homeland, burning their villages, destroying their crops....It has moved against the private sector and free labor unions.[43]

So continued Reagan's frontier cant. Remarkably, perhaps shockingly, this litany of charges bore close resemblance to U.S. history and Reagan's own behavior as president. For example, the seizure of Aboriginal lands and the wanton massacre of Indians comprise the basic story of the creation of the United States, Alaska and Hawaii included. Or consider Reagan's own assault on organized labor[44] or his ongoing sophisticated propaganda operations that actively sought to punish those who disagreed with his views. Further, while the Roman Catholic Church itself was riven with political divisions disguised as doctrinal disputes on the question of Central America, several priests actually served in Sandinista governments.

"AMERICA'S NEXT FRONTIER"

Reagan's assertions consistently appealed to the Monroe Doctrine and manifest destiny:

> Closer to home, there remains a struggle for survival for free Latin American states, allies of ours. They valiantly struggle to prevent Communist takeovers fueled massively by the Soviet Union and Cuba. Our policy is simple: We are not going to betray our friends, reward the enemies of freedom, or permit fear and retreat to become American policies—especially in this hemisphere....In this springtime of hope, some lights are eternal; America's is.[45]

Toward these ends, Reagan additionally summoned one of the central insights achieved by America's foreign policy brain trust during the cold war, when the future of the planet hung uneasily in the balance: that is, he referenced the domino principle, the idea that if one country fell to communism then its neighbors, like dominoes placed on end, would necessarily topple as well.[46] Plus Reagan lied to the country and claimed that "We do not seek its [Sandinista government's] overthrow. Our interest is to ensure that it does not infect its neighbors....The goal of the professional guerrilla movements in Central America is as simple as it is sinister: to destabilize the entire region from the Panama Canal to Mexico."[47] But "stability" and "freedom" and "democracy" had long been coded language for American domination, its manifest destiny. Latin American republics were peopled, after all, by mere children.[48] But this was his story, and he stuck to it with sunny optimism, a soothing avuncular sound, and a guffawing, parson-like visage.

And then Reagan ratcheted the volume ever upward: "Must we sit by while independent nations of this hemisphere are integrated into the most aggressive [Soviet] empire the modern world has seen?"[49] But, in point of fact, the region had already fallen prey to such an empire—the American empire.[50] Yet, as ever, Reagan implored America to deny empirical reality in favor of frontier ideology, keeping the faith with its own ongoing (and past) behavior. Anticipating the Bush Doctrine of two decades later, he earnestly pressed his audience: "The national security of all the Americas is at stake in Central America. If we cannot defend ourselves there, we cannot hope to prevail elsewhere. Our credibility would collapse, our alliances would crumble, and the safety of your homeland would be put in jeopardy."[51]

In his 1985 State of the Union Address, Reagan reiterated his frontier vision and presented it, with respect to Nicaragua, in syllogistic form. It worked like this. (A) The United States, because God's light and favor shone on it, is a peaceful, Christian democracy; (B) Sandinista Nicaragua personifies the opposite of all things American; (C) ergo, the Sandinistas live in atheistic darkness and are warlike and totalitarian.[52] This constituted his mantra, and he stuck to it through thick and thin, when his popularity was low, as it was early in his presidency, through the Iran-Contra affair and beyond. In fact, in early 1987, when Reagan acknowledged that he "took a risk with regard to Iran" that "did not work," he nonetheless remained devoted to his cold warrior vision for Central America. "Nicaraguan freedom fighters never asked us to wage their battle," he cried. "There must be no Soviet beachhead in Central America."[53] Reagan's views were widely shared in Washington, yet for Nicaraguans the cold war *qua* justification rang hollow because American interventionism had been the rule in Central America for half a century before the Soviet Union even came into existence.[54]

Mirroring a natural enough cultural progression dubbed by Beverly Stoeltje as "from westward expansion to expansion into space,"[55] Reagan painted his desire to militarize space with a mythical palette, his so-dubbed Star Wars initiative:

> We can develop America's next frontier. We can strengthen our traditional values. And we can build a meaningful peace to protect our loved ones and this shining star of faith that has guided millions from tyranny to the safe harbor of freedom, progress, and hope....Just as the oceans opened up a new world for clipper ships and Yankee traders, space holds enormous potential for commerce today.

Later in the speech Reagan restructured this appeal: "America was founded by people who believed that God was their rock of safety. He is ours. I recognize we must be cautious in claiming that God is on our side, but I think it's alright to keep asking if we are on His side."[56] One might wonder if the priests and nuns murdered by death squads engendered by Reagan's policies thought the same thing.[57]

"A SPECIAL KIND OF COMPACT"

Turner presented geography as a determining factor in giving rise to the exceptional American character, whereas Reagan, appealing to Puritan theology, characterized the land as a gift from God to his chosen people, a refuge, if you like, from sin and immorality. Therefore, more in keeping with the Puritans, Reagan averred that Americans were already blessed. And as such they weren't compelled so much mechanistically, as Turner had it, to expand and simultaneously improve the world as they were, in Reagan's view, duty-bound to spread the word, in a kind of Wilsonian vein, an expression of millennialism that loops directly back to manifest destiny,[58] in effect to deliver the world in magnanimous rebirth. Thus, these two themes, blessedness and rebirth, became tangled up in Reagan's Puritanical messaging.[59]

His acceptance speech at the Republican National Convention in 1980 laid the groundwork for his sermons/speeches, as noted. Reagan pitched reaching across the aisle, as presidents often do, but not in the way that, say, Barack Obama has, as a practical means to compromise and negotiate or as an appeal to reason. Instead, Reagan sought to blur political lines as an effect of "those values that transcend person and parties...a special kind of compact...for the sake of this, our beloved and blessed land...which God has granted as our portion of this creation." Then he added his rhetorical appeal via Paine. But now I am repeating myself. And why not? That's what Reagan did with ruthless, effective, and unclouded determination.

His ongoing call for sacrifice should be seen in Christian terms. At the heart of it, Reagan asked of America that it behave like a frontier Jesus:

> The time is now, my fellow Americans, to recapture our destiny, to take it into our own hands. But, to do this will take many of us....I ask you tonight to volunteer your help in this

cause....Can we doubt that only a Divine Providence placed this land, this island of freedom, here as refuge for all those in the world who yearn to breathe freely....[W]e begin our crusade joined together in a moment of silent prayer.[60]

Or "You all know that some things are worth dying for. One's country is worth dying for, and democracy is worth dying for....Something else helped the men of D-day: their rockhard belief that Providence would have a great hand in the events that would unfold here; that God was an ally in this great cause."[61]

And so Reagan faithfully preached on for eight years. But, really, was the United States actually blessed by God? According to him, you bet it was. For example, in his first inaugural address, he spoke of American democracy as "nothing less than a miracle." American exceptionalism, tautologically, "makes us special among the nations of the Earth." Reagan again called for Christian sacrifice from "You, the citizens of this blessed land."[62] It followed that "All of us together must bear the burden." And he again championed his presidency as offering the country mythical rebirth, a "new beginning," as he often put it, or "national renewal,"[63] to put a (Theodore) Rooseveltian stamp on it.[64] "We are a nation under God," Reagan said, "and I believe God intended for us to be free. It would be fitting and good, I think, if on each Inaugural Day in future years it should be declared a day of prayer."[65] Soldiers who fell in battle, "our fallen heroes," in particular, he noted in comments made in January 1983, "gave more than can ever be repaid. They're now part of the soul of this great country and will live as long as our liberty shines as a beacon of hope for all those who long for freedom and a better world."[66] In his 1987 State of the Union Address, Reagan insisted, "Let's stop suppressing the spiritual core of our national being. Our nation could not have been conceived without divine help."[67] It followed, then, that in his view "America is in the midst of a spiritual awakening and a moral renewal."[68] The results would invigorate the nation as they always had: "Our economy is not getting older and weaker; it's getting younger and stronger."[69] Here Reagan echoed one of the signature lines from John Ford's seminal 1962 film, *The Man Who Shot Liberty Valance*, "Go west and grow young with the country."

In his first inaugural speech, Reagan also returned to the theme of rebirth, employing one of his most common rhetorical strategies, an appeal to authority in the form of a key historical personage. In particular, his speeches extolled the virtues of "fathers" George Washington and Thomas Jefferson, who actively awakened the "infant nationhood," and by employing them as avatars of peace and all things American and Reaganian he was able to link ordinary American soldiers/heroes with the founding fathers and American martial behavior in the Second World War and the Vietnam War: "Each one of those markers is a monument to the kind of hero I spoke of earlier." In this way, "we love our country" and "our countrymen," we "reach out a hand when they fall," but, like a stern cleric, he warned "potential adversaries" that "our forbearance should not be misunderstood."[70] The latter phrase parrots one of the central charges of President James Polk's successful war appeal to Congress.

"THAT'S OUR SONG"

Reagan positively crowed in the State of the Union Address in 1984 that he had helped steer America back on track toward its destiny "under God." He mocked and teased: "Some questioned whether we had the will to defend peace and freedom. But America is too great for small dreams. There was hunger in the land for a spiritual revival; if you will, a crusade for renewal....Americans were ready to make a new beginning."[71] While such effusions were brilliantly mythical, they were of course of dubious empirical accuracy. With respect to Nicaragua, by 1984 the secret and illegal funding of the Contras had commenced in violation of the Boland amendment[72] and in violation of international law. Nicaragua's harbors had been mined, and the Reagan White House was well on its way to decimating the country's infrastructure.[73] In reality, that "new beginning" was mostly the repackaging of manifest destiny. But while such repackagings strike one as being of the highest order, once, twice, thrice they eventually become facile because they deliver platitudes and avoid substance more or less altogether. For example, Reagan waxed banally in his second inaugural address:

My fellow citizens, our nation is poised for greatness. We must do what we know is right, and do it with all our might. Let history say of us: "These were golden years—when the American Revolution was reborn, when freedom gained new life, and America reached for her best....[W]ith heart and hand let us stand as one today—one people under God, determined that our future shall be worthy of our past.... There's no story more heartening in our history than the progress we've made toward the brotherhood of man that God intended for us....It is the American sound. It is hopeful, big-hearted, idealistic, daring, decent, and fair. That's our heritage, that's our song. We sing it still....We raise our voices to the God who is the Author of this most tender music. And may He continue to hold us close as we fill the world with our sound...to a waiting and hopeful world.[74]

Reagan told the British Parliament that "we live now at a turning point" in the fight against America's communist foes, even embracing as allies on his mission "the so-called new philosophers in France" (he does not identify them, and it makes you wonder whether he meant to imply that he had been reading, who, Foucault, Barthes, Derrida?). And Reagan invoked Thomas Jefferson to champion the idea of revolution with the aim of achieving democracy, as in, first, quoting Margaret Thatcher, "a little rebellion now and then goes a long way," which drew hearty laughter, and, second, advancing his view that "the democratic revolution is gathering new strength" around the planet. It was a bravo political performance.[75] "Ronald Reagan approached politics as if it were theatre," William LeoGrande has observed.[76] Ever one to blend his sense of American exceptionalism with what he understood as universal, modernist, teleological certainty, it figured, after all, that it was "man's instinctive desire for freedom and self-determination" that compelled the struggle (okay, maybe he hadn't been reading those "so-called" French philosophers). One might sum up his statements in London on that day in this way: "The march of freedom and democracy...will leave Marxism-Leninism on the ash-heap of history as it has left other tyrannies which stifle freedom."[77] The "turning point" idea was absolutely central to his messaging and key to his popularity.

Casting himself as some kind of Moses who might lead good Christians to the promised land, Reagan petitioned the Old Testament as if it offered insightful and timeless historical lessons: "Since the exodus from Egypt, historians have written of those who sacrificed and struggled for freedom—the stand at Thermopylae, the revolt of Spartacus, the storming of the Bastille, the Warsaw uprising in World War II. More recently we've seen evidence of this same human impulse in one of the developing countries in Central America."[78] Of course, Reagan was referring not to the actual democratic, decolonizing revolution that had occurred under the Sandinistas in Nicaragua, whom he sought to overturn, but to El Salvador, which would indeed fall into revolution after Reagan left office only to throw out the authoritarian and murderous government he had funded, armed, propped up, and grossly termed "freedom fighters" and "revolutionar[ies]." Nevertheless, he espied "man's instinctive desire for freedom" as rewarded implicitly by his policies. Thus, he found at work in God's manifest plan a "crusade for freedom." Spiritual rebirth beckoned: "Let us tell the world that a new age is not only possible but probable."[79] And again, "The Bible tells us there will be a time for peace," but first sacrifice, meaning, for all intents and purposes, that war was necessary: "With God's help we can secure life and freedom for generations to come."[80] Grounded in the assertion that Americans were God's chosen people, he concluded, in the face of incontrovertible evidence to the contrary, including plain common sense, that "We have never been aggressors. We have always struggled for freedom and democracy....We have no territorial ambitions. We occupy no countries."[81] Was Reagan lying or just ignorant?[82]

For him, the pull of nationalism remained strong. "How can we not believe in the greatness of America?" Reagan queried. "How can we not do what is right and needed to preserve this last best hope of man on Earth?"[83] In one address, he quoted William Penn: "If we will not be governed by God, we must be governed by tyrants." Then he again quoted Thomas Jefferson, the slave-holding president who fathered a child out of wedlock with a sixteen-year-old slave: "The God who gave us life, gave us liberty at the same time."[84]

Clearly, for Reagan, the nation had been chosen by God, who also threw in the unoccupied real estate. Thus, Americans were special and blessed. Their enemies—for example, Sandinistas—were correspondingly, as usual, dark and dirty and in need of punishment and reform and rebirth. And why not, like oldtime Protestants, banish playing cards and outlaw dancing at the same time? Nonplussed, Reagan wrapped it neatly, if awkwardly, in parlance that would have done Rudyard Kipling proud:

> The task that has fallen to us as Americans is to move the conscience of the world, to keep alive the hope and dream of freedom. For if we fail or falter, there'll be no place for the world's oppressed to flee to. This is not a role we sought. We preach no manifest destiny. But like Americans who brought a new nation into the world 200 years ago, history has asked much of us in our time. Much we've already given; much more we must be prepared to give. This is not a task we shirk from; it's a task we welcome…a destiny and a duty.[85]

Reagan here raised the universal hubris of the frontier myth that a shining America stands in for humanity as a whole and for all time, "our mission," as he labeled it in 1985.[86] The passage effectively denied the history of American policy in the Caribbean Basin, conjuring it up simultaneously as a kind of white man's burden as well as a gift from above, rather than as the expression of self-interest. So the claim that "we preach no manifest destiny" was not so much patently untrue, and more a rhetorical appeal to utterly deny (or at least project) reality and, at least as important, to remain true to the mythical vision that had dispatched America to Nicaragua in the first place—conquest in the name of peace, dictatorship in the name of freedom, gaping social inequality in the name of stability, racism in the name of capitalism. David Schmitz characterizes the behavior as "paternalistic racism that categorized non-western European peoples as inferior, vulnerable to radical ideas, and therefore in need of a firm government to maintain order and block communism."[87] But perhaps this was not surprising given Reagan's view that Americans are God's chosen people.

Further, Reagan identified history, as always, like a Puritan, as if it existed principally to mark America's compact with God, which remained unrequited and therefore required yet greater sacrifice, not to be "shirked." So, though it wasn't manifest destiny by name, it was instead "destiny and a duty." Was there any difference?[88] No, not really. Reagan's constructions again and again posited American behavior as the will of God, the requirement of duty, and placed America face to face with an implacable, offensive, and aggressive enemy. "Freedom prospers only where the blessings of God are avidly sought and humbly accepted," Reagan explained. "The American experiment in democracy rests on this insight....Freedom prospers when religion is vibrant and the rule of law under God is acknowledged."[89] Was this an "insight" or the projection of a wish? Does it apply equally to Islamist states? Did it apply to American Indians who actively embraced Christianity yet still endured frequently lethal colonial treatment? Did it apply to American slaves?

That said, contradictions on no occasion troubled Reagan in his public utterances. For example, though it might seem apparent now, by the 1980s and after the debacle of Vietnam, an idealist might have had cause to consider the Monroe Doctrine an empty old relic of days gone by. But it was never this way for Reagan. According to the words he spoke, the Monroe Doctrine lived and breathed and inspired and guided and rewarded.[90] "Our commitment to a Western Hemisphere safe from aggression did not occur by spontaneous generation on the day after we took office. It began with the Monroe Doctrine in 1823 and continues our historic bipartisan American policy."[91] The appeal to historical authority as a kind of established, unquestionable monolith was thereby entirely fitting, though for reasons different from those Reagan supplied. American policy had indeed long reflected bipartisan consensus about the Caribbean Basin that America should and would dominate, that tiny Central American republics should and would get in line and identify American interests as their own. Or else. That poverty and the absence of political freedoms should prevail in the basin was a given, the scholarship shows. It gives one pause to wonder, again, was Reagan basically misinformed about his country's past behavior? Did he really believe the words others wrote on his behalf? Or was he simply a not-so-closeted imperialist who employed frontierisms to pursue political goals deemed otherwise not obtainable? Or was he just mostly asleep at the wheel?

It is instructive to consider his rhetorical and financial support of the mujahideen, whom he distinguished as "genuine," democratic believers in "freedom." Reagan recognized them as "freedom fighters" who constituted the "moral equivalent of the founding fathers." But, wait, it gets crazier. As is well known today, the mujahideen engendered the Taliban and in some cases were one and the same as the Taliban. Yet his words hardly reflected a slip of the tongue, after all, because the United States worked actively over several years to thwart Soviet activity in Afghanistan. Reagan even dedicated the 1982 flight of the space shuttle Columbia to the mujahideen. He couldn't see the future, of course, any better than he could assess the past, though he talked about it ceaselessly. In short, it leads to a rather stunning question: did Reagan have any idea what he was talking about? Given his willingness to lie or hide from reality, his charm, his calculated friendlessness, his need to dominate, his desire to win, Reagan may well have been a highly functioning psychopath. Indeed, recent research, which received wide circulation in the press, suggests as much.[92]

Upon his death in 2004, both *Time* and *Newsweek*, before the Internet knocked the stuffing out of such publications, ran identical front cover close-up photos of a tanned, fit-looking, grinning Reagan decked in white cowboy hat. The point was not to be missed. He had draped himself in frontierisms, and now he was being remembered as such by the fourth estate. In his 1988 farewell address to the Republican National Convention, Reagan strutted his imaginary cowboy pedigree:

> We lit a prairie fire a few years back…all across America.…
> But we can never let the fire go out or quit the fight because
> the battle is never over.…There is still a lot of brush to clear
> at the ranch, fences that need repair, and horses to ride. But
> I want you to know that if the fires ever dim, I'll leave my
> phone number and address behind just in case you need a
> foot soldier. Just let me know, and I'll be there…as long as

this sweet country strives to be special during its shining moment on Earth.[93]

Amen.

"I'VE THOUGHT A BIT"

One of Reagan's special complaints about his arch-foes was what he termed "one-party authoritarianism that institutionalizes the concentration of power."[94] That said, when you consider the remarkable consistency of American behavior over 150 years toward Nicaragua, it is hard to distinguish how an American one-party authoritarian state could have managed it better. Manifest destiny and the Monroe Doctrine put Nicaragua squarely in the crosshairs, and America acted in a culturally appropriate way by subordinating the tiny country while trumpeting phrases about freedom and democracy and capitalism; and so it remained under Reagan. And the phrases weren't empty, either, though in practice they generally played out in ways opposite to how many Americans actually understood them. When Nicaraguans foolishly took America at its word—for example, as noted, Reagan liked to extol the virtues of a "little revolution" in the face of repression—in the names of freedom and democracy and capitalism, it was smacked down. That Reagan chose not to accept empirical reality did not mean, of course, that he was rudderless either. Far from it. He simply followed an alternative mythical frontier reality. It supplied all the answers. Like any religion, it always does so as long as there are preachers to preach and believers to believe.

His 1988 farewell address to the nation probably got as close as any to the truth of the essential mythical Reagan:

> The past few days when I've been at that window upstairs, I've thought a bit of the "shining city on a hill." The phrase comes down from John Winthrop, he wrote it to describe an America he imagined. What he imagined was important because he was an early Pilgrim, an early freedom man.... I've spoken of the shining city all my political life, but I

don't know if I ever quite communicated what I saw when I said it. But in my mind it was a tall, proud city built on rocks stronger than the oceans, windswept, God-blessed, and teeming with all kinds of people living in harmony and peace.... That's how I saw it, and see it still.[95]

Reagan's words struck deep chords in the United States. The most popular history survey textbooks used at American colleges and universities express it well but slightly overstress his popularity as president. Gary Nash et al. note Reagan's "enormous popularity" and attribute it to factors such as his ability to portray "an old-fashioned cowboy image" and "a pleasing manner and a special skill as a media communicator."[96] John Mack Faragher et al. agree and identify Reagan as a transformative president. "No other twentieth-century president except Franklin D. Roosevelt left as deep a personal imprint on American politics as Ronald Reagan."[97] James Roark et al. concur and observe that Reagan was even able to appeal "to Americans who opposed his policies."[98] James West Davidson et al. mostly agree with these assertions and cite Reagan's important role in helping bring "about a major political realignment, only the third since the Civil War."[99] In short, and again, Reagan was extremely popular. He won two impressive electoral victories to boot.

Yet the sections in these survey textbooks devoted to describing his presidency paint a slightly baffling picture because his popularity seems highly improbable. To begin with, as noted (and if you are a certain age you will remember), his policies were actually unpopular, his administration was wracked by sleaze, Reagan fell asleep at meetings, his attention drifted such that he had trouble coherently answering questions at press conferences, he coddled evangelicals but didn't attend church or expend political capital pursuing evangelical goals such as school prayer, his administration flouted the law when it defied Congress and secretly funded the Contras in Nicaragua, he vowed never to negotiate with terrorists—"nor will we yield to terrorist blackmail"[100]—yet his administration did precisely that when it secretly swapped arms for hostages with notable public enemy Iran. How could Reagan possibly have been popular?

CONCLUSION

Yet he was popular and became more so in the years after he left office. Nash et al. are correct in suggesting that his folksy yet classy style, mixed luminously with mythical frontier—Nash et al. call them "cowboy"—tropes, best explains American jubilation with the "Gipper," Reagan's nickname derived from the 1940 movie *Knute Rockne, All American*. Perhaps nowhere was this clearer than in his words aimed at Central America, in particular Nicaragua. A close reading of his foreign policy speeches reveals clearly that they were, for lack of a better phrase, mythical frontier speeches that endorsed and promoted manifest destiny and the Monroe Doctrine and even bore close resemblance to John O'Sullivan's 1845 remarks. It was thus the appeal to America's own creation story that Americans swooned over. In this way, Reagan's lyrics were not so much speeches as they were simultaneously tender and stern sermons as well as nostalgic lullabies to a past that never existed but that mythical Americana remembers ever so fondly.

Greg Grandin shows that "Reagan's Central American wars can best be understood as a dress rehearsal for what is going on now [2006] in the Middle East."[101] But then, arguably, America's mythical frontier wars are always dress rehearsals for the next conflict and can be traced back to founding Indian wars. As Reagan put it, "The calendar can't measure America....America isn't finished. Her best days are yet to come."[102]

And so again one is reminded that myth and religion overlap closely. They explain where we came from, what we ought to be doing now, and where we are going. The frontier myth plays most heavily on origins but also provides a script for behavior through characters such as the frontiersman archetype as well as a constant reminder that, because the frontier mechanism is universal, expansion of the frontier constitutes and inaugurates the future. In short, America and American ideas and ideals will expand indefinitely. So, when Reagan artfully embraced and so ably promoted them, the effect was to depict his presidency in quasi-divine terms. His critics like to mock him as a B-level actor who starred in the role of a lifetime as a C-level chief executive. Yet his speeches suggest that Reagan wasn't acting, that is, playing make-believe, any more than devout Christians are faking it. Of course, speeches are always calculated and arguably cynical in a narrow political sense, but the evidence shows that his words, his inner political self, and his public behavior cast him as a kind of rhetorical president-frontiersman, in effect a hybrid American Jesus-Moses. Yes, of course, people knew he was just a man, but by so capably channeling the American divine he became mythological before our very eyes and ears.

With genial and sometimes jaw-dropping simplicity, Reagan saw American democracy as goodness itself, and one-party rule, which he tended to conflate with communism, as sinister. His insistence that one-party rule was a central tenet of communism and totalitarianism, which he equated, strikes me as perhaps the ultimate expression of frontier delusion and hypocrisy. None of the American-supported regimes in Central America was in fact democratic. Most were run by thugs and butchers dressed up as generals who called themselves presidents. Further, U.S. policy toward Nicaragua for more than 100 years reeked of the one-party variety. From Democrat to Republican and back again, from Roosevelt (Republican) to Roosevelt (Democrat) to Reagan (Republican), America waged frontier war on tiny Nicaragua.

For Reagan, the world then faced a stark binary choice between "good" and "evil" or, as he put it, "morning again in America" and "darkness." He explained in his famous "Evil Empire" speech in 1983 that "There is sin and evil in the world, and we're enjoined by Scripture and the Lord Jesus to oppose it with all our might." In the same speech, he issued an urgent warning to avoid "the temptation of pride" so as to be ready and able to choose "between right and wrong and good and evil."[103] Remember, America remained a "shining city on a hill." In this way, as Pfitzer notes, and in Reagan's hands, "The frontier myth has maintained its validity as an allegorical device for explaining the spiritual mission of the culture."[104] As Williams argued decades ago, manifest destiny and the premise upon which the frontier thesis is based—that is, imagined American exceptionalism and virtuosity—are one and the same.[105]

CHAPTER 8
CONCLUSION: "WAKE-UP CALL FROM GOD"

*I'm driven with a mission from God. God would tell
me, George, go and fight those terrorists in Afghanistan.
And I did, and then God would tell me, George,
go and end the tyranny in Iraq....And I did.*
—George W. Bush[1]

*What's wrong with sentiment? What's wrong with
mythology? Both are palatable substitutes for reality.*
—Linden MacIntyre[2]

Prior to September 11, 2001, planes had never crashed into the
World Trade Center. That was new. Likewise, Sioux, Cheyenne,
and Arapaho warriors had never wiped out George Armstrong
Custer prior to 1876. No Mexican army had invaded the United States
before 1846. Mexican revolutionary Pancho Villa had never ravaged
the United States before 1916. No "half-breed" communists had ever
severely molested American interests in Nicaragua prior to Augusto
Sandino in the 1920s. No Vietcong had ever attacked the United States
in international waters prior to 1964. No communists had ever infil-
trated and threatened American vital security from tiny Nicaragua
prior to Ronald Reagan's presidency.

I mean, yes, they had.

They had because in popular culture these frontier conflagrations reprised structurally, emotionally, and psychologically the same birthing conflict that gave rise to the American nation, born in war against Indians and heavily flavored with then-prevailing Puritan religious views. Each of these frontier wars rests upon a grand and frequently eloquent mendacity that proffers a kind of cultural amnesia. Such rituals of renewal contain within themselves an invitation, a promise, even a compulsion to forget everything that went on before. To begin anew means to wipe the slate clean, to willfully and purposefully forget. So sometimes the mendacity occurs as a gross distortion of the truth (as in the allegation that Mexico had invaded the United States), sometimes a specious assertion (as in the idea that invading Americans were fighting a defensive war against Indians), sometimes imperial hubris (as in Mexico and Sandino's Nicaragua), sometimes a blatant fabrication (as in the charge that North Vietnam had engaged in an act of war against the United States in international waters), sometimes a cynical sly wink (9/11 and WMD). Although it is easy to be lured under the umbrella of myopic nationalism, and even fascinating to get lost in the endless study of charges and countercharges of quotidian politics, such tacks blind one to the startling structural commonalities among America's regenerative wars. As Eric Hobsbawm observes, "Nationalism requires too much belief in what is patently not so."[3]

There also exists the long-established chronicle in American popular culture of positing the United States as the victim of vicious surprise attacks, when the sucker punches arrive seemingly out of nowhere and have neither reason nor context to guide them. For some, it has a name: "blowback." But American nationalism prefers to remember the past selectively and in such a way that befits its creation story, the frontier myth. On closer examination, all of the frontier conflicts began with an imagined or manufactured prevarication that, once swallowed, took a back seat to the frontier autopilot, which in turn supplied an emotionally primal tale to remind Americans of their duty to remain true to the cause, neatly bottled in that old saw "remember the Alamo."[4]

You may well recall George W. Bush's symbolic cowboy invocations after 9/11 in reference to the hunt for Osama bin Laden, the comments about "let's smoke him out" and "wanted: dead or alive." Those cowboy barbs quickly morphed into a barbed deception, precipitating the second hot war directed at Iraq since the end of the cold war. Poorly conceived because the untruth was tastelessly conspicuous, the two-fold falsehood claimed that bin Laden was in cahoots with Iraqi leader Saddam Hussein and that Hussein had been stockpiling weapons of mass destruction. Nonetheless, in the wake of the 9/11 attacks, Bush acted with enthusiastic public support. Hence the war against Iraq. And so it seems again that reality too must abide the myth, for despite outing of the lies the wars dragged on well beyond Bush's presidency and into Obama's second term.

Still, the frontier wars do not correspond exactly in every detail to one another, let alone the Turner thesis, any more than any Christian sect maintains perfect harmony with the Bible. How could they? Turner's essay isn't a prescription so much as an imperfect, affectionate declaration of faith. Myths are neither static nor immutable. And this malleability grants them substantive additional weight. As Teofilo Ruiz notes, "the most common individual and communal form of resistance to…or rejection of the suffocating grip of history is through some form of religious experience, either mystic rapture or communal feeling translated into millennial dreams or utopian fantasies."[5] In certain respects, the history of Christianity illustrates this with some precision.[6] The trouble, to quote John C. Lyden, is that "there is no absolute distinction between religion and other aspects of culture, and that we have a tendency to label certain sorts of activities as 'religious' chiefly because they fall into patterns that we recognize from religions with which we are familiar."[7]

The religious myths bound up in and deriving from the Bible have been remarkably flexible over nearly two millennia and have been adapted to suit a wide range of cultures and behaviors, often pitting pious Christian against pious Christian in bloody fights to the death. Yet, at least in their own eyes, those fighting could remain true to their religion, to their Bible, to their God. In this light, you might think of this study as a creationist reading of the frontier myth across some of America's wars.

Richard Hughes offers a terrific example that illustrates how Christianity and the frontier myth are still tangled up to this day. He quotes evangelist Pat Robertson's reaction to 9/11. Robertson termed 9/11 a "wake-up call from God." He read it as a sign that "God almighty is lifting his protection from us." Reverend Jerry Falwell, with whom Robertson was speaking, agreed and added that "The abortionists have got to bear some burden for this because God will not be mocked....I really believe that the pagans and the abortionists and the feminists and the gays and the lesbians...I point in their face and say, 'You 'helped this [9/11] happen.'"[8]

Again, like Christianity, frontier wars draw from an assortment of not unlimited historical markers, and in this way real-world events—the Alamo, Custer, Indians, captivity stories, Pearl Harbor, the twin towers, and so on—have been framed in such a way as to channel the mythical drama. In other words, American culture has processed these vastly different conflagrations in surprisingly similar fashion. Importantly, they also share another constant in that they gird or expand America's imperial base, as William Appleman Williams presciently argued decades ago when he said that imperial growth was America's "lowest common denominator."[9] Viewed from a rational perspective, America's behavior in the frontier wars might be better understood as a form of what Noam Chomsky terms "state terrorism," and he singles out the United States as its chief purveyor.[10]

"BURROW AND HIDE"

My argument has stemmed from three observations. First, there exists the never-ending pattern of war since 1776, suggesting a deep psychological need to fight. Second, the patterning—portraying battles as defensive maneuvers against the savage Other, as noted—repeats itself without reference to temporal concerns, and the gambit is always some variety of how the savage Other attacked without provocation. Myth is eternal: it seduces and elides linear time. One result is that the Alamo or Pearl Harbor or 9/11 maintains cultural currency and emotional resonance, just so long as we choose to remember. Third, I have borrowed and applied two ideas from psychohistory: nation-states have explicable psychological makeups, and trauma demands repetition. We tend to know this anecdotally, that abused children are more likely to abuse others. Or that a nation born in violence becomes imprinted with a need to relive the trauma, which, for America, has been life-affirming.

One might fairly expect that the frontier myth remains an active, even vital, component of the nation's well-being. And it does. The creation story compels the United States to launch defensive wars. In this way, it remains forever (and ever) innocent, guiltless, and pure. The result remains crucial to ongoing nation building, for nation building itself may sound boring; instead, the American nation experiences the excitement of ongoing religious rebirth, bathed in violence. As Richard Slotkin has observed, "A violent history begets the expectation of future violence."[11]

Reagan sought to marry the political right with evangelicalism. It won him two terms in office and fashioned him as a legendary president. Much of his success may be attributed to his relentless evocations of frontier tropes. Immediately following 9/11, Bush the younger sought to pick up where Reagan had left off and to arrange a political marriage of neocons and their notions of preemptive foreign policy with evangelicalism. It worked, too, because Bush, like Reagan, also articulated a deep belief in frontier religion. That religion, dating back to the Puritans, was built upon several basic presuppositions. First, the nation was chosen by God. Ergo, despite fussy posturing about doing the right thing, whatever Americans opted for was already the right thing because they were, by definition, already blessed. As Greg Grandin writes, "In a universe of free will where good work is rewarded and bad works are punished, the fact of American prosperity was a self-evident confirmation of God's blessing of U.S. power in the world."[12] In Reagan's day, it was precisely the shared sense that they (Americans) were being persecuted—that is, his core, conservatives and born-agains—that made them natural allies, plus they had common enemies: liberals and/or secular humanists, commies, and people of color.

Second, God's work would then play out on and in the chosen land. It consisted, for the Puritans, of battling things Satanic. Thus, the land itself came to personify a kind of Manichaean spirit, bifurcated by us (God's chosen) and them (Satan's minions). The "them" were Indians or Indian stand-ins, for centuries in fact. Enter Turner and his frontier thesis, which artfully blended matter and spirit in a way that made absolute cultural sense in the nineteenth century. And when the war to conquer "them" Indians took more than two centuries, the results had a profound effect on contributing to the emergence of a culture bent on expansion because it could be understood as following God's plan to defeat Satan as well as a culture that loathed "Indians." This became the basic operating system for American growth and imperialism. Symbols and characters from the world as it is—cowboys, Indians, western landscapes, disdain for things European, and so on—blended easily and readily with religious sentiment. Hence the frontier myth. Hence Davy Crockett,[13] the boy General, Buffalo Bill, Tarzan, Roy Rogers, *Shane*, John Wayne, Ronald Reagan, *Dances with Wolves, Avatar, The Walking Dead*, and W. Bush.

Who doesn't remember the words of Bush as he let loose his so-called war on terror by invading Iraq? And a close reading of the speeches of Bush and Dick Cheney confirms the trend. Mark West and Chris Carey observe that the "Bush administration placed itself as heir to the Reagan presidential frontier."[14] In particular, the Bush regime chose after 9/11 to employ a frontier discourse because of its deep cultural resonance. The evidence speaks volumes. Bush:

> It's an enemy that likes to burrow and hide....We're hunting him down, he can run but he can't hide....[T]he noose is narrowing....Any outlaw regime will be confronted....You know you're in pretty good country when you see a lot of cowboy hats out in the crowd....I love coming to this state. It's a state where cowboy hats outnumber ties.

And so on. West and Carey find that Bush styled himself in the mold of a "frontier sheriff" and sought to hitch himself to Reagan's rhetorical wagon. Cheney did, too, and actively sought to meld the two presidents. For example, said Cheney of Bush, "I saw [in Bush] the conviction and moral courage of Ronald Reagan." Yet, the authors point out, Bush's cowboy genes were bogus.[15] Bush bought his Texas ranch only at the last minute, and his upbringing was as a spoiled private school/

Yale/Harvard brat. As Erik Baard argued in 2004 in the *Village Voice*, "George W. Bush Ain't No Cowboy."

The neocons lusted for a catastrophic event that might provide them with a chance to realize their goals. For them, 9/11 served as just such a fortuitous calamity. While Bush and Cheney employed frontier rhetoric with as much commitment as, if less consistency than, Reagan, they also benefited mightily from a docile corporate media that not merely chose to accept the Bush Doctrine uncritically but also spontaneously framed 9/11 and the response to it as a frontier event—as the media had in 1846, 1876, 1914–16, and so on. Thus, the president widely considered by historians to be among the lousiest of American chief executives enjoyed great popularity immediately after 9/11. Just think about it. The man bought a ranch in Texas and started wearing cowboy boots and cowboy hats at the very moment he launched his presidential campaign. He began using mythical language at exactly the moment he needed to defend and shore up support for his frontier payback wars. In this way, Bush capably, for a time, channeled America's deepest myth. But he was not alone. Newspapers did it. Hollywood too.

"THE MOST BEAUTIFUL FILM"

But wait. Didn't 9/11 change everything? Wasn't the world born anew?

Arguably, yes. Everything changed in the way that mythical rebirth always reboots things. That *is* rebirth. In itself it is neither original nor unique to the United States. But what makes it distinctly American here is the backstory that accompanies it and the ways in which American culture reacts more or less as it always has reacted—the frontier genre conventions, best exemplified in the western that tied the myth loosely to American material history, and the regenerative violence, which spins imperial gambits into defensive, who me? struggles for survival itself. The cultural response to 9/11, according to John Mead, has been "a sort of boldly definitive American experience for the dawning of a frightening new world. What we actually get is a series of well-drawn and entertaining clichés culled from the lexicon of American tough-guy iconography and adventure yarns: frontier and war stories, thrillers and westerns."[16]

Consider the gussied-up *Avatar*, released in 2009, the highest grossing film of all time.[17] It offers a veritable frontier playbook writ with nearly pitch-perfect timbre for traumatized post-9/11 audiences, "a film littered with references to 9/11 and its iconography, to the War on Terror and to the subsequent wars in Afghanistan and Iraq."[18] Director James Cameron prepared for the script, which he wrote, by studying the ten most popular Hollywood films of decades past and then sought to layer in features from them into *Avatar*. It worked brilliantly. Audiences loved it because the film is one of those "stories we tell ourselves and the ones we like to hear, especially when it comes to imagining the future, [which] remain inherently settler colonial stories."[19] It broke box office records.[20] Mainstream film reviewers writing for newspapers and popular magazines tended to gush over it. David Denby in the *New Yorker* put it simply: "James Cameron's *Avatar* is the most beautiful film I have seen in years."[21] Roger Ebert cooed, "He has silenced the doubters by simply delivering an extraordinary film...sensational entertainment."[22] In a less popular venue, Craig Detweiler in the *Journal of Religion and Film* exclaimed that "Cameron's glorious creation makes us value God's creation anew."[23] "*Avatar* is a familiar story," wrote Carol Linnit. "The success of *Avatar* as a story relies on the audience's ability to identify with the Na'vi...[who are] crafted in response to a general social nostalgia for the sacred....It is meant to be enjoyed as a visual feast."[24] Everybody agreed that the film is visually stunning.

Many noted how *Avatar* resembles so many other films: *Dances with Wolves*, which won the 1990 Oscar for Best Picture, *Last Samurai*, *Man in the Wilderness*, *Little Big Man*, Disney's animated *Pocahontas*, and others.[25] Cameron said he drew consciously on "pulp classics like Edgar Rice Burroughs...[and] Rudyard Kipling."[26]

There was never any need for Cameron to beg, borrow, or steal from more than one film because *Avatar* merely conjures up a futuristic *Dances with Wolves* in space. The latter, directed by and starring Kevin Costner, relates the story of a Civil War hero who, because of his sheer and appalling bravery and willingness to sacrifice his life, is granted the right to a new posting anywhere in the "realm." He chooses to go west, "[t]o see the frontier before it's gone," he explains with anachronistic clairvoyance. And so he goes forth and settles at an abandoned fort nestled deep in Indian country.

He is a nice guy, this Lieutenant John Dunbar, contemplative, open-minded—in fact, he is a liberal, offering just about the right feel for Bill Clinton's coming rhetorically liberal yet actively centrist presidency. In a series of minor escapades, Dunbar meets, greets, and befriends the Lakota Sioux who live not far away. To Costner's credit, the film endeavors to portray the Lakota for what they were—what most people are most of the time—human beings who live in groups where love, nurture, honesty, community, and such carry the day. Nothing wrong with that.

Where the film drew intense criticism, including my own,[27] derived from a couple of things. First, the Sioux aren't the only Indians in *Dances with Wolves*. Their enemies, the Pawnee, who also presumably loved, nurtured, and so on, are cast as classic stereotypical savages on several occasions in the work. Well, okay, so the Sioux had enemies. But it gets much worse than that because the story exemplifies a term critics applied to *Avatar*, a "white messiah fable," in the words of David Brooks.[28] And, in fact, Dunbar behaves as a white messiah.[29] He is Jesus-like in a contemporary way, teaching, gently leading, self-sacrificing, delivering, you name it. The catch is that he offers a kind of salvation, not to Indians but to white audiences, whom he delivers from guilt. The suspension of disbelief, on which film relies, has seldom felt so uncomfortable.

As he gets to know the Lakota, Dunbar comes to admire and even love them. He becomes one of them, shown cleverly enough in the film as he slowly yet deliberately discards his military regalia and dons Sioux apparel, language, and values. In short, he is stripped and reborn as something better, deeper, more honestly American, Turnerian, the film teaches us, than the bad old army and corrupted easterners. Fair enough too. This is a well-worn story, after all, and Costner tells it with tender affection from a revisioned kinder, gentler imperial point of view.

But then comes the messiah. In rebirth Costner emerges as the essential Lakota. He becomes a better Indian than any of them. He is magnanimous about it in a paternalistic and demeaning way. He grants them agency in a world that lies beyond their ken, simple folk that they are. He engineers, for example, a crushing defeat of the Pawnee via superior technology (repeating rifles) and strategy. Ta-da! He is the liberal frontiersman who washes away—and this is exactly what Ebert argued[30]—all the bad blood, all the racist colonial crap that Hollywood had spewed since day one. In one move. Dunbar took America back to the starting line, to a kind of ground zero, in such a way that it could now reimagine its history with Natives.

Costner's film was a big hit. Its resonance with audiences reemulated its cultural origins; that is, it drew thirstily from precisely the same mythical well from which Cameron drew for the New Agey garb in *Avatar*, right down to the conclusion where, though the Indians have won a temporary reprieve, you know that the bad guys will come back. But not to worry, the point of each film is to open your heart and let the regenerative properties of righteous violence wash you clean. To look to the future, because that is always what America does best, even if it forfeits the past in the form of erasure or revision. America looks to the future with hopey-changey, bridge-to-the-future idealism.

"AS ONE LIFE ENDS, ANOTHER BEGINS"

Avatar is simpler. In the year 2154, Jake Sully, an incorrigible paraplegic marine vet, winds up on the frontier of Pandora. Like in *Dances with Wolves*, dastardly Americans are pouring in because they covet the land and its resources. Not unlike Custer's pushing violently into the Dakotas on behalf of white gold prospectors.[31] Beneath its surface, Pandora holds energy riches in the form of awkwardly termed "unobtanium," desired by an aggressive and intolerant corporation supported by an aggressive and intolerant American military contingent. Trouble is, again as in *Dances with Wolves*, Pandora has a population of Indigenous "humanoids," tall, lanky, blue-skinned folks called the Na'vi. They do not want to give up their land. But the corporation wants it. Conflict ensues.

In his elemental role, Jake is reborn as a frontiersman and then leads his wards to sweet vindication, wrested violently. He gets "his legs back" this way, literally and figuratively, in perhaps the only attempted artful turn in the film. Through the wonders of future technology, his DNA has been spliced with Na'vi DNA to create his own avatar. This leads

Jake to love (a princess, what else?) and the opportunity to achieve something Dunbar cannot, the semblance of victory. Smacking of tragedy and evoking tears, the emotional payoff of *Dances with Wolves* collides with empirical history: Indians were militarily conquered. *Avatar*, plotted in the boundless future, sets no such imaginary constraints and thereby grants Cameron, among other things, the option of a sequel (now in preproduction). Although it runs more than two and a half hours, the movie is taut.

Avatar dives straight into the mythical frontier. Rugged Jake, played by Sam Worthington, gets lucky. "I never thought I'd be going there," he drawls. Worthington plays the character straight up in unperturbable cowboy fashion. He is told that going to Pandora offers him a "fresh start. On a new world," no less. Planting mythical seeds, Jake thinks out loud in his running voice-over and ruminates, "One life ends, another begins." He is tough, and he is cool. "There's no such thing as an ex-marine."

Colonel Miles Quaritch, a strikingly portrayed muscular baddie with a terrible scar across his face, acted by Stephen Lang, furthers the mythical setup. We find Jake on Pandora at his first meeting with his fellow soldiers. The colonel angrily erupts as he frames the mythical civilization-versus-savagery narrative into which the cast (and audience) have been thrust: "Out there beyond that fence every living thing that crawls, flies, squats in the mud, wants to kill you and eat your eyeballs....We have an Indigenous population of humanoids called the Na'vi. They're fond of arrows dipped in neurotoxin....[T]hey are very hard to kill." In short, we discover early on that Pandora is a lot like imaginary Indian country and that the Na'vi are a lot like Hollywood Indians. "Not so much any Indigenous people, but rather any number thereof," notes Joshua Clover.[32] And, yes, they even wield bows and arrows, we learn in the first three minutes of the film. But they are not, at least not yet, of Dunbar's variety because we have been warned by the colonel that they shoot poison arrows and need "killing."

Quaritch's corporate counterpart, Parker, of diminutive stature, augments the colonel's sentiments by cynically aping American rhetoric à la Vietnam War or post-9/11 conflicts: "Look, we're supposed to be winning the hearts and minds of the Natives....[T]hey'll start

trusting us....[R]elations with the Indigenous are only getting worse....
Those savages are threatening our whole operation. We're on the brink
of war." In this way, *Avatar* is framed by "post-9/11 rhetoric....The
destruction of Home Tree is replete with imagery from footage taken
on the day of 9/11."[33]

In short, like manifest destiny, the film cuts two ways, not so dar-
ingly critiquing imperialism even as it diminishes the very folk for
whom the audience is meant to feel empathy. "One should certainly
not underestimate the importance of the film's undisguised criticism of
historical colonial excesses," writes Bert Olivier. "Who can fail to recognize the theme of violently occupying the land of 'savages'...as having several historical referents?"[34] Lorenzo Veracini agrees but argues
that *Avatar* "rehearse[s] specifically...American settler colonial narratives."[35] Indeed, "The premise of the movie hinges upon the needs of a
future United States to colonize...faraway planets," write McVeigh and
Kapell.[36] Even a review that expresses deep admiration for Cameron
and the film, and one that might have said something similar about
Reagan's frontier presidency, complains that "it's unnerving that a movie
preaching peace hits its visual peak with scenes of mass destruction."[37]

Then it is back to Quaritch, who dismisses whatever genuine and
decent intent the accompanying scientists, led by Dr. Grace Augustine
(Sigourney Weaver), may have in the winning of hearts and minds
through their avatar project. And already we sense a looming moral
dilemma because Jake is attached to the science project at the same
time as he serves as a mole for the colonel to gather "good intel" for
the upcoming preemptive strike on the Na'vi.[38] "The avatar project is
a bad joke," Quaritch scoffs. "A bunch of limp-dick science majors....
Sully, I want you to learn the savages from the inside-out and gain their
trust. I need to know how to force their cooperation or hammer them
hard." Gruffly avuncular, he asks, "Can you do that for me, son?" Plus
Quaritch promises Jake his "real legs" back if he agrees to trade up new
legs for genocide.

Later Parker tells Jake, "Just find out what the blue monkeys want....
Look, killing the Indigenous looks bad, but there's one thing share-
holders hate more than bad press, and that's a bad quarterly statement."
He proclaims that "They're flea-bitten savages that live in a tree."

In short, as personified by Quaritch and Parker, those government types are grade-A bastards—dishonest, corrupt, overbearing, undemocratic, everything the frontiersman is not. And racist, an adjustment that fits changing times.

Jake, we learn quickly, is entirely unafraid. He is curious, independent, rule-avoiding. We know that nobody is the boss of him. *Avatar* cannily assumes we like that. Don't we? "We like our ideology," observes Slavoj Žižek.[39]

"IT'S MY BIRTHDAY"

As it unfolds, the film launches Jake into a kind of meet-your-new-family gambit. First, he is accidentally thrust into the frontier wilderness, where he is able to display his elemental spunk. Then, against all odds, he survives—but not, notably, without the intervention of his love interest, Neytiri (actor Zoe Zaldana),[40] and then, in a move that Dunbar could never match, by divine intercession. Jake becomes marked by the Na'vi deity Eywa as elect, "chosen," Neytiri explains when other, more hostile, Na'vi arrive on, you guessed it, horses, Pandora-style, of course (six legs, no fur). The frontier myth has seldom had it so good, suggesting that the breadth and depth of mythical sentiment remain as common and heartfelt in post-9/11 years as they ever were.

In particular, notions of rebirth, regenerative violence, and Puritan-like American exceptionalism abound.[41] In *Dances with Wolves*, director Costner also employed Christian symbols such as having Dunbar ride arms spread cross-like into certain death (sacrifice!), which he manages to escape, as a not overly subtle indirect divine thumbs-up or having him, like Jake, play the messiah role, not unlike a liberal Jesus to millions of American Christians.[42] It all made sense. But Cameron, though not precisely lazy, makes it easier for his audience and makes it really, really, obvious: God (or god?) has chosen. And she—a female, another nod to the ways in which cultural change abides—likes Jake Sully best.

And so Jake likewise is stripped and becomes, in time, fully Na'vi, literally. "Change is regenerative and sought in *Avatar*," writes Veracini. "*Avatar* replicates the classic, and equally colonial, celebratory tale of a renewed or newly acquired capacity to genuinely connect with the authentic and uncorrupted in a new place."[43] In case the visual cues aren't straightforward enough, we hear Neytiri, cast like the other females in the story as "traditional" stereotypes,[44] nagging him as he begins the process of growing up Na'vi. "You're like a baby, making noise, don't know what to do." Or "You have a strong heart. No fear. But stupid. Ignorant like a child." Or "You're like a baby." But we just know Jake is going to make it when we hear him say things such as "I have to trust my body to know what to do." And then he saves them all by leading them into a showdown they surely could never have won (or even conceived of) without him. And then he is again taken to the brink of death, similar to yet no less cheesy than Tom Cruise's character at the end of Ron Howard's frontier epic, *Far and Away*, where he dies and then, in the adoring arms of his lover, opens his eyes as if for the first time. In this way, observes Veracini, "in the context of U.S. settler discourse, the indigenisation of the settler is recurrently deployed as a way to reaffirm the settler claim against those of other colonisers and as an antidote against a variety of recurring anxieties."[45]

A variety of critics, typically less mainstream and/or somewhat more academic in approach, have interpreted the film less than favorably, despite its enormous popularity and stunning visual effects. They include, as noted, those who denounced the film for actually promoting racism and deploying timeworn gambits like the messiah complex and glorifying settler imperialism. For example, because Jake plays little more than an updated version of an otherworldly Dunbar, the messiah complex resurfaces without blush. That story was and remains arrogant, racist, and imperial. "The ecological parable is banal, politics a sop to liberalism (or an outrage to the U.S. military, per the *National Review* et al., baited into weighing in), the treatment of indigenous people paternalistic," writes Clover in *Film Quarterly*.[46]

But *Avatar* also does something more. This frontier film ultimately does what the initial *Star Wars* trilogy accomplished with some panache: it fights the American Revolution all over again. We find our hero, newly reborn, amid his American kind: a simple, Godly folk, blessed by nature, blessed by God, intuitive, clever, veritable apple pie, blue-skinned (rather than blue-coated) Yankees of the imagination.

And they have to fight a version of an evil empire that Americans have been scrapping with since they became Americans while fighting Brits. Jake leads them as ever they have imaginatively been led by various frontiersmen, garden-variety Custers and Taylors. *Sometimes there's a man.* And in *Avatar* Jake Sully is such a man.

And he and the Na'vi conquer the corrupt empire, defeat the venal standing army, with old-fashioned smarts, nerve, verve, and lesser technology. They win because their hearts are pure, pure Americana, that is. So, on one level, the movie augurs a call to arms yet nonetheless dismisses the Na'vi by centering Jake as the avatar of progress, change, the future, and righteousness, a new man for a new world he has wrestled from the empire (e.g., Great Britain stand-ins) but also from Indians (e.g., Na'vi, Indian stand-ins). "The film only reaffirms the colonial, social, and economic paradigms that it seeks to undermine by suggesting the natives' inability to liberate themselves from the forces of oppression, industry, and colonization, thereby conferring power to a privileged colonizer," conclude John James and Tom Ue.[47] In this way, Jake has gone precisely where Turner places the frontiersman, at the transformative liminal arena between two worlds, empire and Na'vi, and he has returned, as heroes must,[48] with a message: follow me. Jake frames it simply as he prepares for his final ritual of regeneration: "It's my birthday, after all." Richard Corliss, the long-running film critic at *Time*, drew particular attention to the closing shot: "In the last shot of *Avatar*, someone's closed eyes snap open."[49] Eyes wide open? Perhaps for Jake, but apparently eyes wide shut for Cameron, who ultimately chooses to resort to the oldest trick in the book, the frontier story. It worked. Many audiences reportedly applauded at the film's end.[50]

"I'M IN CHARGE"

9/11 has also rippled through television. Shortly after the film *Zombieland*, starring Woody Harrelson, was released, on April 13, 2009, *Relevant* magazine reported that the actor "attacked a paparazzo in New York on Tuesday, and claims it was because he mistook the man for a zombie. Harrelson just finished shooting a zombie movie, and says he was still in character when he was startled by the cameraman."[51] Now the dustup may well have been tongue-in-cheek and designed to sell tickets, but it points to a deeper truth about 9/11 and trauma. Somehow Harrelson's reaction oddly makes sense in a way that it wouldn't have prior to 9/11. In part, the context in which his remarks might be best assessed derives from an idea Scott Poole presents nicely:

> These creatures [zombies]...appeared as [a] pop culture phenomenon at a historical moment when the body had become of central concern in American culture as the vehicle of pleasure, of theological meaning, or of personal happiness (or all three at once). Anxiety over threats to the body became a paramount concern as evidenced by the popularity of dieting and exercise regimens, public health campaigns, and the growing acceptance of plastic surgery.[52]

Right, and just think about the growth of the horror genre, especially the unparalleled spurt in zombie flicks and television programs, since 9/11.

Traditionally, the zombie phenom in visual culture has been understood as a reaction to the trauma of real-world events ranging from the cold war to the Vietnam War to 9/11.[53] "Popular culture often provides a window into the subliminal or unstated fears of citizens, and zombies are no exception," writes Daniel W. Drezner.[54] In a dazzling little book, Drezner makes the point with deep humor and insight as he chews on the international policy ramifications for the United States of an actual zombie outbreak.

"The horror genre experienced a dramatic resurgence over the last decade," note the editors of *Horror after 9/11*, published in 2011.[55] "We have come to expect that a monster is never just a monster, but rather a metaphor that translates real anxieties into more or less palatable form," they add.[56] At one level, and necessarily, argues Terrence McSweeney, "We see ourselves in the enemy."[57] Not surprisingly, then, Laura Frost suggests we understand 9/11 as "a national wound."[58] Elsewhere, Henry A. Giroux has employed zombies to take aim at the contemporary state of American politics: "The zombie—the immoral, sub-Nietzschean, id-driven 'other' who is 'hyper-dead' but still alive as an avatar of death and cruelty—provides an apt metaphor for a new kind of authoritarianism that has a grip on contemporary politics in the United States."[59] Stephen Asma echoes Giroux in part: "An environment with too much wealth can also dehumanize. Americans appear zombie-like because their raison d'être appears to be the consumption of goods, making us seem more attached to plastic surgery, reality television, and giant SUVs than to family, honor, and integrity."[60] So it goes. The zombie phenom has become a well-established genre, a vessel from which it becomes possible to draw on a wide variety of meanings.

In any event, it seems fair to observe that, like Harrelson, Americana maintains itself "still in character" or ever ready to slip into character with respect to the frontier myth. And I am suggesting that there exists a natural affinity between the frontier myth and the zombie genre. Both are triggered by and feed on trauma. Perceived war reflexively engenders a compulsive symbolic replaying of the myth in popular culture, as we have seen with the Mexican War, Custer, and so on. And both fixate on rebirth, which makes zombies ideal vessels for frontier tales, like the ways in which the western has so capably served "over many generations," according to John Cawelti.[61] In particular, once we have taken the zombie bait and accept that some kind of apocalypse has descended upon us, what then? "Narratives about the living dead use small communities or families as their unit of social analysis," Drezner summarizes.[62] Enter the frontier myth because, in effect, zombie stories boil down to survival stories, yes, but also they therefore tend heavily toward tales of regenerating the nation.

Survival of the human race in the face of a zombie holocaust depends, ultimately, on the choices the survivors make. And who better to seize the reins at the rim of catastrophe, at the edge of the world, than the cowboy? That is what he has always done. For example, during the 1950s and 1960s, the frontier myth dominated American television in the form of the western. The western derives its semiotic power from its conflation of frontier symbology with a genre centered imaginatively on the postbellum west. But wait, given its lust for and long track record of war, doesn't the United States find itself more or less always in a postbellum state? *The Walking Dead*, the surprise zombie hit for AMC, based on the *New York Times* bestselling comic book series,[63] makes this point with real emphasis. Erin Overbey notes in the *New Yorker*

> that, at its core, it's not really a zombie show at all. While it does feature the undead, the series actually draws on the iconography and mood of the Western, complete with a reluctant sheriff, a wilderness to be explored, and "savages" to be fought. If the frontier of the old West represented a new world to be tamed, then, in "The Walking Dead," the world of the zombie apocalypse represents the latest frontier to be conquered.[64]

Writing in *Psychology Today*, Steven Schlozman asks, "Why does *The Walking Dead* enjoy such a rabid following?" In response he offers that "two concepts—the myth of the 'Wild and Free Frontier,' and the 'Rugged Individualism' that makes the freedom of this frontier possible, are both integral to the particularly American invention: the Zombie Apocalyptic Tale."[65]

Interestingly, the show pays homage to the myth by casting its two protagonists, among the ensemble cast, as a frontiersman and the frontiersman's son in training. They are imaginary cowboys, in other words. But what does such a cowboy look like? How well might he fit today with *The Walking Dead*? Fortunately, we can actually measure the results of such an inquiry.

"THE COWBOY IS A PATRIOT"

In 2004, Erik Baard, an enterprising journalist at the *Village Voice*, sought to assess George W. Bush's cowboy credentials (and found Bush wanting, as noted). As is well known, Bush endeavored to ingratiate himself in the press and with Americans as a kind of cowboy president, what with his newly purchased ranch, his folksy oratory, his relocation to Texas, his penchant for wearing cowboy hats, cowboy boots, and photo ops that showed him driving around on his ranch in a pickup. To assess Bush, Baard employed Gene Autry's ten-point cowboy code (as presented below), readily available online, which provides an almost pitch-perfect sketch of the cowboy archetype. Autry had rocketed to fame as a singing cowboy in the 1930s, on radio, movies, and later television. He performed in nearly 100 films over several decades. He even wrote some hit Christmas tunes, including "Rudolph the Red-Nosed Reindeer." Autry was beloved for the straight-arrow characters he portrayed. Adjusted to fit the times, *The Walking Dead*'s Rick, the central character and leader of a shifting band of survivors, including his immediate family (in contradistinction to Bush, at least in Baard's eyes), does Autry proud. "Wherever we find monsters, there, too, we also find heroes."[66] Shelley S. Rees comments that "*The Walking Dead* uses the tradition of the Western genre to construct Rick as a pure-hearted lawman.…[T]he established myth of the frontier, its threatening landscape steeped in potential for individual triumph, contributes to the popularity of postapocalyptic fantasy, since such texts generally offer a representative group of survivors the challenge of rebuilding a new world from the ashes."[67]

1. **"The cowboy must never shoot first, hit a smaller man, or take unfair advantage."** Given that Rick and his cohort face the constant threat of death from zombies as well as from other humans who may not be trustworthy (lots of those in the series), following a catastrophe that is neither explained nor discussed, you might expect Rick and the others to be a tad trigger-happy. But not Rick. Though he suffers and questions the nature of his suffering, his moral compass remains true on this point: he doesn't engage in preemptive violence against his kind (the undead are, well, undead and therefore don't count).[68] You might quibble and say that the undead are merely symbols of the dehumanizing effects of the trauma of 9/11, but my point is simply that, with respect to other non-undead people, Rick scores well. Even when, early on, he learns that his best friend, Shane, has had sex with his wife, Lori (they all believed for a time that Rick was dead; you know, the series is richly melodramatic too), and when Shane later appears set to kill Rick in order to have Lori for himself (yes, the gender stereotyping is blatant), Rick doesn't shoot first…until there is no doubt that Shane will fire. Now Rick acts like Bush and moves preemptively. He sidles up close and stabs Shane to death. Rick would still die, though, if not for his son, Carl, budding frontiersman, who then shoots undead/zombie Shane in the head.

2. "He must never go back on his word or a trust confided in him." This is pure Rick. He is honest and completely trustworthy. For example, in season three Rick faces the Governor, a classic incarnation of the corrupted east we are meant to understand by his pompous, self-applied title. It is as if Quaritch and Parker are conflated into one character. He is a suave, two-faced killer. Rick, though wary, keeps to his word in all their dealings. The message is clear: the government cannot be trusted, but the deeper cultural resonance upon which the government was fashioned in the United States, the frontiersman and his story, remains true to the ideal on which the nation invented itself. Rick willingly imperils the group to remain straight and true.

3. "He must always tell the truth." Rick is no liar. Sometimes it costs him popularity but never respect. He lives a truthful life also in the sense that he stays loyal to his frontiersman typecasting. Crucially, and this figures in so many westerns, in keeping with his one true path, he nurtures Carl and mentors him in the ways of the all-American boy. We get this visually as Rick's Stetson become Carl's Stetson, as Carl picks up and begins to tote the gun, as Carl, despite his tender years, also employs the gun, as Rick inadvertently teaches Carl, as Lori puts it, to become detached, "cold" to the world. But, hey, a boy's got to learn how to do what a man's got to do.

The government is the liar in this horror show. It made promises it couldn't keep—and Rick is doing something about it. "The very real sociophobia in the wake of 9/11," Kevin Wetmore argues, "is a fear of ongoing war on terror in which 'America,' by which we mean the government, the military and all authority figures, is unable to protect or solve the problems."[69] So cowboy Rick steps up.

4. "He must be gentle with children, the elderly, and animals." Rick is a good dad to Carl. He constantly puts himself in danger—and, from Lori's perspective, too often abandons them—for the greater good of the group. This is both lamentable and excusable, for Rick wears the burden of a messiah too. He bears the weight of it, and, so that we fully understand his suffering on the group's behalf, it shows, yet he manages after all is said and done and does not complain. As a father, Rick endeavors first and foremost to protect, teach, and love Carl. He hurts when Carl hurts (especially when Carl takes a bullet). And he is physically demonstrative toward his son, at least some of the time. His loyalties are divided because he must also play father to the group.

In the television series, the character of Hershel, who owns a farm where the survivors stay for a time, is an old man. Rick walks a fine line here. His first allegiance is to safeguarding and nurturing the survivors, I mean America. Yet the TV program (not the comic book) casts Hershel as an older and wiser man (though at first he is obstinate, another common enough casting—the old coot archetype). So he and Rick get on well, yet Hershel also defers to Rick, as you might expect of an older man who sees in Rick the youth and vigor needed to regain the world.

Animals do not much figure in *The Walking Dead*. Nonetheless, firmly establishing his cowboy cojones, early on in the comic series Rick is delighted to find a horse to ride for a time. The image is classic western. He's got the horse, the pistol, and the cowboy hat. And like any good hero, he is on a mission to save the world. But this is horror after all, a kind of weird inverted homage to 9/11, so creatures tend to die graphically and noisily, except frontiersmen.

5. "He must not advocate or possess racially or religiously intolerant ideas." The world has changed a lot since Autry's days. We see it in *The Walking Dead*, where people of color play in more frequent and more important roles. For example, Glenn, little more than a kid, saves Rick early on, finds love in the arms of Hershel's daughter, Maggie ("Let's fuck," she presses him several times in the print edition). Glenn is Korean American. And though he plays a key role, he also willingly subordinates himself to Rick's white leadership. So do the various, short-lived, black cast members (with the exception of the lethal, sword-wielding Michonne).

6. "He must help people in distress." At times, it seems, this is all Rick does. He leads a group of survivors, after all. The examples are simply too numerous. One case: one day, Rick and Glenn risk their lives by going to town to a long-deserted bar to rescue Hershel from himself (you know the cliché, former alcoholic doubts himself). Suddenly, two unknown survivors approach them. Ultimately, one goes for his weapon, and Rick, *qua* gunslinger, shoots and kills them both. Before they can return to Hershel's farm, however, others from the unknown group arrive and pepper the bar with fire. Eventually, Rick, Hershel, and Glenn escape, but not before Rick risks them all in order to free one of the aggressors, whose leg is impaled on a fencepost. And then he takes the kid in—but blindfolded so as not to endanger his own clan even as he seeks to aid someone who might otherwise have killed him (creating another sore point with Shane as their relationship continues to deteriorate). Before Shane eventually kills the kid by breaking his neck, the boy is shackled, black hood pulled over his head, shuttled around in vehicle trunks, held in solitary confinement, and tortured. Pure Guantanamo Bay.

7. "He must be a good worker." Again, it is mostly all work and little play in *The Walking Dead*. Organizing, gathering supplies, killing zombies, burning zombie bodies, securing more ammo, fighting other survivors who are not friendly, and so on. The program is frequently diverting, often boring, and entirely humorless.

8. "He must keep himself clean in thought, speech, action, and personal habits." Rick struggles with this because, especially as the leader, he faces unpalatable choices. For example, by the time TV Hershel is bitten in the leg by a zombie, it is clear he will not "turn" quickly, but he will turn eventually. To that point, the choices in the series are to abandon Hershel to his fate or shoot him in the head and thereby preemptively destroy a future zombie before it can menace the group. But Rick, like any good frontiersman, is clever and can think outside the box. So he cuts Hershel's leg off above the bite in order to save his life. It is a calculated gamble that pays off. It also further softens Hershel's character. One result is that, though Rick may not exactly be clean shaven, we cut him some slack. I mean, come on, it is the apocalypse.

9. "He must respect women, parents, and his nation's laws." Whether intentional or not, Autry uses the term "nation" rather than "country." The frontiersman represents the heart of the American nation. Rick is a true and faithful nationalist.

He does respect parents. He is a parent and embraces the duty and sacrifice that such a role requires. And he respects women, even if the series unevenly deals with gender stereotypes. For example, Lori is feminine in a trite, emotional way. She is pretty, a devoted mom, but given to slightly hysterical behavior. Her behavior also borders on treasonous to the family unit as she falls prey to despair. Ever the pragmatist, Rick will push on ahead without her, too, if need be, we learn. Yet other females are slightly more complicated. Andrea, as close to a sexy kitten as the series offers, discovers a predilection for marksmanship. She is good at shooting zombies in the head and enjoys doing it. Then there is Michonne, the black loner female whose weapon of choice is a sword, good for lopping off zombie noggins. She saves Andrea. Rick treats them all with respect. But, as he shouts at Lori, let there be no doubt, "I'm in charge." The burden weighs on him too. "These people look to me to keep them safe. I owe it to them to do everything in my power."

10. "The cowboy is a patriot." If a patriot loves one's country, then the series throws Rick a curveball because the country is gone. Civilization has been decimated, and the survivors are compelled to invent it all over again. Rick holds true, however, to a preapocalyptic model of behavior, adjusted to fit the horror but never abandoned or compromised. He doesn't budge from it, however much Lori or Carl or Shane might want him to. In short, insofar as the nation prefaces the country, yes, Rick is more than a mere flag-waving patriot; he embodies, he lives, he breathes the nation. He gives it life.

Consequently, while *The Walking Dead* proposes a scary new world, it is, in fact, much like the world the United States has imaginatively inhabited off and on since the coming of the Puritans. In this way, the series, despite the use of salty language (in the comics) and free and easy sexuality (in the comics) and a lot of gore, relates a deeply conservative and ultimately comforting tale not merely of survival but also of growth (Lori even gives birth…and then dies, and Carl is forced to shoot her in the head before she turns) in the face of the monstrous Other. Schlozman explains it simply. In a post-9/11 world riven with anxiety, "We revert to mythic and shared cultural *memories*" as a culturally appropriate means to assuage our fears.[70]

The series is also clever in its use of cultural markers. For example, Shane serves a narrative purpose not unlike his namesake in the 1953 classic film *Shane*, starring Alan Ladd (as Shane) and Jack Palance (as the sensual and sinewy black hat). In that film, Shane appears as if magically, thrust into the film's (and the nation's eternal mythical) conflict, a historical struggle that also figures prominently in Turner, that is, farmer-settler versus rancher.[71] Ranchers, as the film has it, tamed the west in order to make it safe for families. But the ranchers won't go quietly, and the farmers are ill equipped to fight back. So Shane does it for them even as he and the key rancher, Ryker, agree that they have outlived their historical moment.

Movie Shane's first imperative is to protect movie mother and son, Marion and little Joe. Once that is accomplished, and once his regenerative killing work is done, Shane disappears. And this is how the story of *The Walking Dead*'s Shane plays out too. Shane protects Lori and Carl, even gets Lori pregnant and aims to be a good father to Carl. In the movie, though Shane and Marion spark and her husband, Joe, acknowledges the mutual attraction as normal, it was released to a general audience, and the year was 1953—in other words, no sex. But again, once Shane of *The Walking Dead* has served his purpose, he too disappears.

But more than that, the series also conjures up the stages of development at work in the film *Shane*. It works like this. Initially, Rick and Shane are small-town cops, fighting to protect regular Americans. Then Rick gets shot and ends up in the hospital. In the meantime, the apocalypse descends. Rick wakes up in the hospital; everything has changed, and everyone, apart from zombies, is gone. Shane, assuming the worst, leaves and sets out to find Lori and Carl so he can protect them in this new wild west–like universe, where everyone is apparently on his or her own. In time Rick finds them.

Rick and Shane are fine at first. They rekindle their friendship. But problems emerge because it turns out that Shane is more linear in his thinking. In a kill-or-be-killed world, he lays aside the comfortable cloak of morality that civilization affords one. For example, a girl about Carl's age, Sophia, goes missing. Rick is willing to endanger the whole group in order to find her, whereas Shane argues that the group must prevail at all costs, even if it means leaving Sophia behind to die (it turns out she has turned, and so Rick shoots her in the head).

Shane's end comes as he slowly goes mad. But is he crazy or simply at odds with Rick's cowboy morality? Either way, by this time they find their group living on Hershel's farm. But in the new world, as in the oldest of American worlds, this is not sustainable. Stages of development beckon, and they have got to move on. Shane cannot last; the farm cannot last. But before they go it is here, as in the film, that Shane meets his end because he has outlived his usefulness. The series, as noted, frames him loosely as increasingly unstable but seems to suggest that he isn't really crazy but a postmodern incarnation of morality that reflects changing material conditions. Really, it is not unlike E. P. Thompson's Marxist argument that morality serves a function of the prevailing economic base, what Thompson termed a "moral economy."[72]

"IDEOLOGY IS"

Among others, Fredrick Pike has argued that the closing of the frontier propelled "the desire for imperialist expansion."[73] Turner argued in 1893 that America had been conditioned to expand at all costs exactly because of the effects of having done so for nearly three centuries, as the country grew inexorably westward and therefore wouldn't and couldn't stop the frontier impetus. Instead, it embraced and absorbed that impetus, made it an ethos, and wrapped it in mythological, religious drapings. And of course the expansionism has never really abated. American politicians debate, sometimes heatedly, how to go about it, but they do not seriously challenge the value of and need for expansion. And why should they? After all, America's wars, in particular those conflicts that occurred in the western hemisphere, have been cast as regenerative frontier wars in much the same way as the early and protracted struggles against Indians on the continental frontier.

But what about all the talk about expanding freedom and democracy? Anders Stephanson puts it this way: "To be free was precisely to understand this destiny and conform to the direction of divine will."[74] Divine will, as expressed by and embedded in the frontier myth, meant never having to say you're sorry; and it never meant for those subjected to American hegemony the kind of freedom and democracy that Americans have experienced and understood. Forget any ideas about winning hearts and minds. The United States has walked away from every one of its frontier wars without throwing a scrap away. The key has always been expansion, growth. "Growth is key to individual liberty and progress. The substance of growth is empire. Thus empire is benevolent. Hence the policeman who guarantees the law and order...necessary to progress is undeniably benevolent."[75] Such observations abound. In the post-9/11 world, the point is simply that Bush had a plan, he stuck to it, and it worked reasonably well until his second term, when Americans just grew sick of war, weary of lies, and then got hammered by a serious economic downturn. Americans also grew weary of Reagan's untruths and his clandestine war in Central America. The differences between these presidents are twofold. First, Reagan got lucky with the economy, whereas Bush paid the price (i.e., the great recession of 2008) for the deregulatory economic policies Reagan had initiated. Second, Reagan stuck rigorously to his mythical frontier cant, whereas Bush employed it successfully but intermittently, West and Carey show. If words mean anything, then Reagan's greater popularity derived, at least in part, from his more relentless commitment to frontier mythopoesis.

America's frontier wars have paralleled how a creationist explains the world, and you can observe this clearly by exploring the faith as it has been preached in popular culture. Now to do so, you might say, is pointless because creationists are silly, the world is more complicated, causation is more complex. But I would disagree. The signs and wonders are all around us if only we open our eyes to see them, soaked through to the bone in newspapers, erupting from movie screens, starring on television, and sermonized in presidential speeches. Too big to ignore, too important to dismiss, but so all-encompassing that it becomes mostly invisible (or pleasantly suffocating), in other words. But to dismiss creationism is to ignore the world as it exists, knowing full well that tens of millions of Americans organize their lives to fit its perceived demands—and that in itself makes creationism, or the frontier myth, the latter of which clearly has a much broader audience, worthy of study. And, unlike creationism, which is parochial and posits a kind of anti- or shadow culture, the frontier myth is mainstream all the way, from Hollywood to the White House.

Since the time of the Puritans, *the* central American cultural vision has portrayed the frontier as a special, enchanted place, a veritable cauldron of primal Americanization—in this way, the historical frontier begets the mythical frontier. "Ideology is not simply imposed on ourselves," observes Žižek. "Ideology is our spontaneous relationship to our social world."[76] In this vein, the frontier myth provides the rosiest reflection of Americana. This is where America peers into the mirror and is delighted to find some guy like Jake Sully grinning back, aw, shucks.

NOTES

CHAPTER I

1   Sigmund Freud, *Civilization and Its Discontents* (1930; reprinted, New York: Martino Publishing, 2010), 52.

2   Quoted in William Appleman Williams, *Empire as a Way of Life* (New York: Ig Publishing, 2007), 3.

3   Noam Chomsky, *9-11: Was There an Alternative?* (New York: Seven Stories Press, 2011), 12.

4   The speech is readily available on the Internet.

5   This material has been synopsized from three news sources: *New York Times, Los Angeles Times,* and *Chicago Tribune.*

6   John Mead, "9/11, Manhood, Mourning, and the American Romance," in *Reframing 9/11: Film, Popular Culture and the "War on Terror,"* ed. Jeff Birkenstein, Anna Froula, and Karen Randell (New York: Continuum, 2010), 57.

7   I use the loaded term "Indian" because it is preferred in the United States when writing about American Indigenous topics. American scholars, including those of Native background such as Vine Deloria, also employ the terms "Native," "Native American," "Aboriginal," and "Indigenous" as roughly synonymous with "Indian," a practice I have borrowed. The Canadian term "First Nations" is generally not used in the United States or when writing about American Indians. Other problematic, even offensive, terms emerge in this manuscript from a variety of primary popular culture sources. For example, the epithet "half-breed" was widely employed until well into the twentieth century in American popular culture. I have not altered quotations in any way so as to provide the most accurate representation of colonial language.

8   See Kathryn Zabelle Derounian-Stodola, *Women's Indian Captivity Narratives* (New York: Penguin, 1998).

9   See Robert F. Berkhofer, *The White Man's Indian: Images of the American Indian from Columbus to the Present* (New York: Vintage, 1979); S. Elizabeth

Bird, *Dressing in Feathers: The Construction of the Indian in American Popular Culture* (Boulder, CO: Westview, 1996); and Daniel Francis, *The Imaginary Indian: The Image of the Indian in Canadian Culture* (Vancouver: Arsenal Pulp Press, 2012).

10 "President Bush said to all of us: 'I am driven with a mission from God'. God would tell me, 'George go and fight these terrorists in Afghanistan'. And I did. And then God would tell me 'George, go and end the tyranny in Iraq'. And I did.'" Quoted in Ewen MacAskill, "God Told Me to End the Tyranny in Iraq," *Guardian*, October 7, 2005. Also see Bob Woodward, *Plan of Attack: The Definitive Account of the Decision to Invade Iraq* (New York: Simon and Schuster, 2004).

11 Anders Stephanson, *Manifest Destiny: American Expansion and the Empire of Right* (New York: Hill and Wang, 1996), 47.

12 Stacy Takacs, "The Contemporary Politics of the Western Form: Bush, *Saving Jessica Lynch*, and *Deadwood*," in Birkenstein, Froula, and Randell, *Reframing 9/11*, 153.

13 See Clifford Geertz, *The Interpretation of Cultures* (New York: Basic Books, 1977).

14 Benedict Anderson, *Imagined Communities: Reflections on the Origin and Spread of Nationalism* (New York: Verso, 2006), 102.

15 Homi Bhabha, ed., *Nation and Narration* (New York: Routledge,1990), 1.

16 Anderson, *Imagined Communities*, 6.

17 Richard Slotkin, *Gunfighter Nation: The Myth of the Frontier in Twentieth-Century America* (Norman: University of Oklahoma Press, 1998), 9.

18 Beverly J. Stoeltje, "Making the Frontier Myth in Modern Nation," *Western Folklore* 46, 4 (1987): 242.

19 Henry Nash Smith, *Virgin Land: The American West as Symbol and Myth* (1950; reprinted, Cambridge, MA: Harvard University Press, 2001); Richard Slotkin, *Regeneration through Violence: The Mythology of the American Frontier, 1600–1860* (Norman: University of Oklahoma Press, 2000).

20 Eldon Kenworthy, *America/Américas: Myth in the Making of U.S. Policy toward Latin America* (University Park: Pennsylvania State University Press, 1995), 16.

21 Jeffrey Bartholet, *Newsweek*, August 13, 2001.

22 Ray Raphael, *Founding Myths: Stories that Hide Our Patriotic Past* (New York: New Press, 2004), 4.

23 Smith, *Virgin Land*, v. Also see Slotkin, *Gunfighter Nation*, 5; Slotkin, *Regeneration*; and Earle Pomeroy, "Toward a Reorientation of Western History," *Mississippi Valley Historical Review* 41 (1955): 579–600.

24 See, for example, Joseph Campbell, *Myths to Live By* (New York: Arkana, 1993).

25 Gregory M. Pfitzer, "The Only Good Alien Is a Dead Alien: Science Fiction and the Metaphysics of Indian-Hating on the High Frontier," *Journal of American Culture* 18, 1 (1995): 51.

26 Slotkin, *Regeneration*, 6.

27 John Hellmann, *American Myth and the Legacy of Vietnam* (New York: Columbia University Press, 1991), ix.

28 Mody Boatright, "On the Nature of Myth," in *Mody Boatright, Folklorist*, ed. Ernest B. Speck (Austin: Texas Folklore Society, 1973), 109.

29 Stoeltje, "Making the Frontier Myth," 240.

30 Slotkin, *Regeneration*; also see Slotkin, *Gunfighter Nation*, 10–12.

31 See Fredrick B. Pike, *The United States and Latin America: Myths and Stereotypes of Civilization and Nature* (Austin: University of Texas Press, 1992); David Harvey, *The New Imperialism* (New York: Oxford, 2003); and Richard White, *"It's Your Misfortune and None of My Own": A New History of the American West* (Norman: University of Oklahoma Press, 1991), 613–32. Also see Slotkin, *Gunfighter Nation*; Kenworthy, *America/ Américas*; Williams, *Empire*; and Patricia Nelson Limerick, *The Legacy of Conquest: The Unbroken Past of the American West* (New York: W. W. Norton, 1987).

32 Lloyd DeMause, *The Emotional Life of Nations* (New York: Other Press, 2002).

33 Robert B. McFarlane, "Provoking War: An American Repetition Compulsion," *Journal of Psychohistory* 35, 2 (2007): 175–81. Also see DeMause, *Emotional Life*.

34 Bessel A. van der Kolk, "The Compulsion to Repetition, Re-Enactment, Revictimization, and Masochism," *Psychiatric Clinics of North America* 12, 2 (1989): 390.

35 Ibid., 396.

36 While its origins and applications lie well beyond this study, it is worth noting that the idea is central to psychoanalysis, which roots it in the unconscious, but it is also important to behavioral psychology, which locates it in formative development of a human life. See Sigmund Freud, *Beyond the Pleasure Principle*, trans. James Strachey (1920; reprinted, New York: Createspace, 2010).

37 Stephen Diamond, "Secrets of Psychotherapy: Repetitive Relationship Patterns," *Psychology Today*, September 14, 2008.

38 Mary Midgley, *The Myths We Live By* (London: Routledge, 2011), xii.

39 Richard Grossman, "The Nation Is Our Mother: Augusto Sandino and the Construction of a Peasant Nationalism in Nicaragua, 1927–1934," *Journal of Peasant Studies* 35, 1 (2008): 85.

40 David Leverenz, "The Last Real Man in America: From Natty Bumppo to Batman," *American Literary History* 3, 4 (1991): 756.

41 Pfitzer, "Only Good Alien," 51.

42 Williams, *Empire*, 21.

43 Erik H. Erikson, *Childhood and Society* (New York: W. W. Norton, 1993), 209.

44 Bhabha, *Nation*, 298.

45 William Blum, *Killing Hope: U.S. Military and CIA Interventions since World War II* (Monroe, ME: Common Courage Press, 2004), 454–62.

46 Chomsky, *9-11*, 46.

47 Williams, *Empire*.

48 *Full Metal Jacket*, dir. Stanley Kubrick, 1987.

49 Richard Henry Pratt, *Battlefield and Classroom: Four Decades with the American Indian, 1867-1904*, edited by Robert M. Utley (Norman: University of Oklahoma Press, 2003), 215. Also see Ward Churchill, *Kill the Indian, Save the Man: The Genocidal Impact of American Indian Residential Schools* (San Francisco: City Lights Publishers, 2004).

50 Gore Vidal, *Perpetual War for Perpetual Peace: How We Got to Be So Hated: Causes of Conflict in the Last Empire* (New York: Clairview Books, 2002).

51 Greg Grandin, *Empire's Workshop: Latin America, the United States, and the Rise of the New Imperialism* (New York: Holt, 2007), 3.

52 E. Bradford Burns, *At War in Nicaragua: The Reagan Doctrine and the Politics of Nostalgia* (New York: Harper and Row, 1987), 150.

53 John G. Cawelti, *The Six-Gun Mystique Sequel* (New York: Popular Press, 1999); Slotkin, *Regeneration*; Smith, *Virgin Land*.

54 Slotkin, *Gunfighter Nation*; Janet Walker, ed., *Westerns: Films through History* (New York: Routledge, 2001); Lee Clark Mitchell, *Westerns: Making the Man in Fiction and Film* (Chicago: University of Chicago Press, 1998).

55 Chad Millman and Shawn Coyne, *The Ones Who Hit the Hardest: The Steelers, the Cowboys, the '70s, and the Fight for America's Soul* (New York: Gotham Books, 2010); Varda Burstyn, *The Rites of Men: Manhood, Politics, and the Culture of Sport* (Toronto: University of Toronto Press, 1999); Allen St. John, *The Billion Dollar Game: Behind the Scenes of the Greatest Day in American Sport—Super Bowl Sunday* (New York: Doubleday, 2009).

56 Slotkin, *Gunfighter Nation*, 51–62.

57 The documents are readily available online. See, for example, http://avalon.law.yale.edu/19th_century/monroe.asp. Also see Noam Chomsky, *Hegemony or Survival: America's Quest for Global Dominance* (New York: Holt, 2004), 63–64; and Rodrigue Tremblay, *The New American Empire:*

Causes and Consequences for the United States and for the World (Concord, MA: Infinity, 2004).

58   Brian Loveman, *No Higher Law: American Foreign Policy and the Western Hemisphere since 1776* (Chapel Hill: University of North Carolina Press, 2012), 27.

59   *Red River*, dir. Howard Hawks, 1948.

60   See Gary L. Harmon, review of *John Wayne's America: The Politics of Celebrity*, by Garry Wills (New York: Simon and Schuster, 1997), https://www.h-net.org/reviews/showpdf.php?id=3149.

61   Stephen Kinzer makes a similar observation in his study of repeated American "regime-change" interventions: "By considering these operations as a continuum rather than as a series of unrelated incidents, [this] book seeks to find what they have in common." Stephen Kinzer, *Overthrow: America's Century of Regime Change from Hawaii to Iraq* (New York: Henry Holt, 2006), 2.

62   Smith, *Virgin Land*, 257, puts it this way: "The conception of civilization had been invoked to justify a number of dubious undertakings in the course of the nineteenth century, including European exploitation of native peoples all over the world."

63   See, for example, Kent Carter, *The Dawes Commission and the Allotment of the Five Civilized Tribes, 1893–1914* (New York: Ancestry Publishing, 1999); and Vine Deloria, *The Indian Reorganization Act: Congresses and Bills* (Norman: University of Oklahoma Press, 2002).

64   See Christopher M. Finan, *From the Palmer Raids to the Patriot Act: A History of the Fight for Free Speech in America* (Boston: Beacon Press, 2007); and Ann Hagedorn, *Savage Peace: Hope and Fear in America, 1919* (New York: Simon and Schuster, 2008).

65   Garry Wills, "America's Nastiest Blood Feud," *New York Review of Books*, May 24, 2012.

66   Loveman, *No Higher Law*, 9–37.

67   Loveman, ibid., explores this closely and carefully in a richly detailed study.

68   It is also worth noting that currently the U.S. is fighting in Iraq and Afghanistan and has troops at more than 700 military bases stationed around the globe, what one author identifies as clear evidence of the probable overreach of America's imperial ambitions. See Chalmers Johnson, *The Sorrows of Empire: Militarism, Secrecy, and the End of the Republic* (New York: Holt Paperbacks, 2004).

69   See Grandin, *Empire's Workshop*.

70   John J. Johnson, *Latin America in Caricature* (Austin: University of Texas Press, 1993); Lars Schoultz, *Beneath the United States: A History of U.S. Policy toward Latin America* (Cambridge, MA: Harvard University Press, 1998).

71　DeMause, *Emotional Life*, 84–85.

72　Or perhaps America has had more enemies because its successes, including freedom and wealth, have generated intense jealousy that has led to conflict. George W. Bush argued as much after 9/11. So have many presidents. But to accept such a specious line of argument is to embrace the myth of exceptionalism, for which no rational evidence exists.

73　Frederick Jackson Turner, *Frontier and Section: Selected Essays of Frederick Jackson Turner* (New York: Prentice-Hall, 1961).

74　See Stephanson, *Manifest Destiny*; and Reginald Horsman, *Race and Manifest Destiny: The Origins of American Racial Anglo-Saxonism* (Cambridge, MA: Harvard University Press, 1981).

75　Pike, *United States*, 155.

76　Quoted in Smith, *Virgin Land*, 260.

77　Turner, *Frontier and Section*, 61.

78　Limerick, *Legacy of Conquest*, 21.

79　Turner, *Frontier and Section*, 38.

80　Ibid., 43.

81　Ibid., 39.

82　Stephen Prothero draws a distinction between Christ as the "liberator long awaited by the Jewish people" and Jesus as a cultural product who belongs in a sense to all Americans. In keeping with my sources that draw no distinction, I use the names interchangeably and without the nuance Prothero employs. See Stephen Prothero, *American Jesus: How the Son of God Became a National Icon* (New York: Farrar, Straus, and Giroux, 2003), 9, 10–11.

83　Turner, *Frontier and Section*, 61. Also see 46, 57.

84　Stoeltje, "Making the Frontier Myth," 247.

85　Patricia Nelson Limerick, "Turnerians All: The Dream of a Helpful History in an Intelligible World," *American Historical Review* 100, 3 (1995): 697–715, charts the development of the historiography as it has moved away from Turner.

86　Limerick, *Legacy of Conquest*, 22.

87　See Garry Wills, *John Wayne's America: The Politics of Celebrity* (New York: Simon and Schuster, 1998).

88　Garry Wills, "John Wayne's Body," *New Yorker*, August 19, 1996.

89　For a satirical yet serious take on this image, see Erik Baard, "George Bush Ain't No Cowboy," *Village Voice*, September 21, 2004.

90　Turner, *Frontier and Section*, 56–57.

91　Fred Shannon, "A Post-Mortem on the Labor–Safety Valve Theory," *Agricultural History* 19 (1945): 31–37. Also see Susan Armitage and Elizabeth Jameson, eds., *The Women's West* (Norman: University of

Oklahoma Press, 1987); and Ray Allen Billington, ed., *The Frontier Thesis: Valid Interpretation of American History?* (New York: Holt, Reinhart and Winston, 1966).

92 Benjamin F. Wright, "American Democracy and the Frontier," *Yale Review* (December 1920): 320–65. Also see Peggy Pascoe, *Relations of Rescue: The Search for Female Moral Authority in the American West, 1874–1939* (New York: Oxford University Press, 1993); and Patricia Nelson Limerick, *The Real West* (Boulder: University Press of Colorado, 1996).

93 See Grandin, *Empire's Workshop*, 15–16; Slotkin, *Regeneration*, 36–41; and Stephanson, *Manifest Destiny*, 3–27.

94 Pfitzer, "Only Good Alien," 52.

95 Richard T. Hughes, *Myths America Lives By* (Urbana: University of Illinois Press, 2004), 30–31.

96 See Patricia Seed, "Houses, Gardens, and Fences: Signs of English Possession in the New World," in *Ceremonies of Possession in Europe's Conquest of the New World, 1492–1640* (New York: Cambridge University Press, 1995), 16–40.

97 See Carlton Smith, *Coyote Kills John Wayne: Postmodernism and Contemporary Fictions of the Transcultural Frontier* (Hanover, MA: University Press of New England, 2000), 1–3. Also see Peter C. Rollins and John E. O'Connor, eds., *Hollywood's Indian: The Portrayal of the Native American in Film* (Lexington: University of Kentucky Press, 2003).

98 Relatedly, Carter Jones Meyer and Diana Royer have observed that "Americans have always defined themselves in opposition to others. Opposing Britain, opposing Mexico, opposing American Indians, opposing the Soviet Union, opposing Iraq—the list can become quite lengthy with a few moments' thought. Employing stereotypes to characterize those we set ourselves in opposition to is the simplest way to deal with them, because reduction of a human to a symbol—especially a negative one—makes fighting them, whether physically, ideologically, or both, easier." See Carter Jones Meyer and Diana Royer, Introduction, in *Selling the Indian: Commercializing and Appropriating American Indian Cultures*, ed. Carter Jones Meyer and Diana Royer (Tucson: University of Arizona Press, 2001), xii.

99 Schoultz, *Beneath the United States*, xvi.

100 Ibid., xvii.

101 Ibid., xi.

102 Johnson, *Latin America in Caricature*, 116–56.

103 See Limerick, "Turnerians All"; and Limerick, *Legacy of Conquest*.

104 Graham Fuller, "Sending Out a Search Party for the Western," *New York Times*, March 5, 2000; Pat Dowell, "The Mythology of the Western:

Hollywood Perspectives on Race and Gender in the Nineties," *Cineaste* 21, 1–2 (1995): 6–10.

105 Richard Slotkin, "Nostalgia and Progress: Theodore Roosevelt's Myth of the Frontier," *American Quarterly* 33, 5 (1981): 613. Also see Barbara Will, "The Nervous Origins of the American Western," *American Literature* 70, 2 (1998): 295–96.

106 For a good summary and synopsis of this opinion, see Forrest McDonald, "Rugged Individualism: Frederick Jackson Turner and the Frontier Thesis," *World and I* (1990): 539–51.

107 See Slotkin, *Gunfighter Nation*.

108 Limerick, "Turnerians All."

109 Denise M. Bostdorff, *The Presidency and the Rhetoric of Foreign Crisis* (Columbus: University of South Carolina Press, 1994), 177.

110 See Slotkin's introduction in *Gunfighter Nation*.

111 The irony is delicious because Trudeau was not considered to be a friend of the United States; additionally, it points to the ubiquity and influence of American popular culture. See Michael Bliss, "Guarding a Most Famous Stream: Trudeau and the Canadian Political Tradition," in *Trudeau's Shadow: The Life and Legacy of Pierre Elliott Trudeau*, ed. Andrew Cohen and Jack L. Granatstein (Toronto: Vintage Canada, 1999), 11; and Allan Levine, *Scrum Wars: The Prime Ministers and the Media* (Toronto: Dundurn, 1996), 299–300.

112 For rich explorations of this topic, see Williams, *Empire*; and Kenworthy, *America/Américas*.

113 John L. O'Sullivan, "Annexation," *United States Democratic Review* 17, 1 (1845): 5.

114 Stephanson, *Manifest Destiny*, xii.

115 Renato Rosaldo, "Imperialist Nostalgia," *Representations* 26 (1989): 107–08.

116 Stephanson, *Manifest Destiny*, 5.

117 Hughes, *Myths*, 23.

118 Grandin, *Empire's Workshop*, 16; Bostdorff, *Presidency*, 177.

119 Smith, *Virgin Land*, 253.

120 Stephanson, *Manifest Destiny*, 14.

121 Turner, *Frontier and Section*, 61.

122 Steven Ponker, "Disasters Galore," review of *Nostradamus: The Prophecies*, trans. Richard Sieburth, *London Review of Books*, September 27, 2012.

123 Leverenz, "Last Real Man," 760.

124 David Dary, *Cowboy Culture: A Saga of Five Centuries* (Lawrence: University of Kansas Press, 1989); Vladimir Shlapentokh, Joshua Woods, and Eric Shiraev, eds., *America: Sovereign Defender or Cowboy Nation?*

(London: Ashgate, 2005). Also see two beautifully crafted coffee-table books by James P. Owen, *Cowboy Values: Recapturing What America Once Stood For* (Guilford, CT: Lyons Press, 2008) and *Cowboy Ethics* (Ketchum, ID: Stoecklein Publishing, 2005).

125 Selma H. Fraiberg, *The Magic Years: Understanding and Handling the Problems of Early Childhood* (New York: Scribner, 1996); Selma Fraiberg, S. Adelson, and E. Shapiro, "Ghosts in the Nursery: A Psychoanalytic Approach to the Problems of Impaired Infant-Mother Relationships," *Journal of the American Academy of Child and Adolescent Psychiatry* 14, 3 (1975): 387–421.

126 Historians have fallen under the cultural allure of the thesis, especially in the immediate decades after Turner's essay was published. See Limerick, "Turnerians All."

127 Iga Progoff, "Waking Dream and Living Myth," in *Myths, Dreams, and Religion*, ed. Joseph Campbell (New York: Dutton, 1970), 176–95.

CHAPTER 2

1 Mark Twain, *The Adventures of Huckleberry Finn* (New York: Knopf, Premier Classics, 2006), 337.

2 See Stephanson, *Manifest Destiny*; Horsman, *Race*; Eduardo Bonilla-Silva, *Racism without Racists: Color-Blind Racism and the Persistence of Racial Inequality in America* (New York: Rowman and Littlefield Publishers, 2009); and Charles W. Mills, *The Racial Contract* (Ithaca, NY: Cornell University Press, 1999).

3 O'Sullivan, "Annexation," reprinted in Ernesto Chávez, *The U.S. War with Mexico: A Brief History with Documents* (New York: Bedford/St. Martin's, 2008), 37–38.

4 William Appleman Williams, *The Contours of American History* (Chicago: Quadrangle Books, 1955), 270.

5 K. Jack Bauer, *The Mexican War, 1846–1848* (Lincoln: University of Nebraska Press, 1992), 2.

6 Hughes, *Myths*, 25.

7 *Detroit Democratic Free Press*, May 26, 1846. All of the newspapers considered here evinced suspicion of perceived imperial English motives and, to varying degrees, warned England to stand clear—or else. Also see, for example, *New York Herald*, May 7, 1846.

8 *New York Herald*, May 16, 1846. The charge was common in the *Herald*; also see, for example, May 17, 1846.

9 Terry Eagleton, *Holy Terror* (New York: Oxford University Press, 2005), 65.

10 Lewis Lapham, "Ignorance of Things Past," *Harper's*, May 2012.

11 Dan Rather, *Rather Outspoken: My Life in the News* (New York: Grand Central Publishing, 2012), 5.

12 Students of history can choose from a variety of terrific books on this topic, some of which include discussion of the most up-to-date kinds of citation (in the wake of the Internet and social media). See, for example, Martha C. Howell and Walter Prevenier, *From Reliable Sources: An Introduction to Historical Methods* (Ithaca, NY: Cornell University Press, 2001); Jenny S. Presnell, *The Information-Literate Historian: A Guide to Research for History Students* (New York: Oxford University Press, 2006); and Georg G. Iggers, *Historiography in the Twentieth Century: From Scientific Objectivity to the Postmodern Challenge* (Middletown, CT: Wesleyan University Press, 2005).

13 Some controversies are comparatively arcane—for example, debate about the relative importance of the Nicene Creed to Christianity—where others are almost predictable—for example, how much power the U.S. Constitution grants to the president relative to the other branches of government. For a discussion of the former, see A. Edward Siecienski, *The Filioque: History of a Doctrinal Controversy* (New York: Oxford University Press, 2010). For examples of the latter, see Steven G. Calabresi and Christopher S. Yoo, *The Unitary Executive: Presidential Power from Washington to Bush* (New Haven, CT: Yale University Press, 2008), which pitches the case for relatively stronger executive power; and Ryan Barilleaux and Christopher S. Kelley, eds., *The Unitary Executive and the Modern Presidency* (Houston: Texas A&M Press, 2010), which provides reasoned analyses that explore the expanding presidency in the context of competing arguments.

14 Devon A. Mihesuah, *Natives and Academics: Researching and Writing about American Indians* (Lincoln: University of Nebraska Press, 1998); Linda Tuhiwai Smith, *Decolonizing Methodologies: Research and Indigenous Peoples* (New York: Zed Books, 1999).

15 See, for example, Peter C. Rollins, ed., *Hollywood as Historian: American Film in a Cultural Context* (Lexington: University Press of Kentucky, 1997).

16 See Ernst Breisach, *Historiography: Ancient, Medieval, and Modern* (Chicago: University of Chicago Press, 2007).

17 In particular, see Michel de Certeau, *The Writing of History* (New York: Columbia University Press, 1992); and Simon Malpas, *The Postmodern* (New York: Routledge, 2005).

18 See, for example, Teofilo F. Ruiz, *The Terror of History: On the Uncertainties of Life in Western Civilization* (Princeton: Princeton University Press, 2011).

19 Wilson's books remain in circulation, though his role as president surely

plays the key influence in this. See, for example, *Congressional Government: A Study in American Politics* (1885; reprinted, New York: Dover Books, 2006); *The State: Elements of Historical and Practical Politics* (1889; reprinted, London: Forgotten Books, 2010); and *A History of the American People* (1902; reprinted, Ithaca, NY: Cornell University Press, 2009).

20 Eric Foner, *Reconstruction: America's Unfinished Revolution, 1863–1877* (New York: Harper Perennial Modern Classic, 2001).

21 Justin H. Smith, *The War with Mexico* (New York: Macmillan, 1919).

22 Robert W. Merry, *A Country of Vast Designs: James K. Polk, the Mexican War, and the Conquest of the American Continent* (New York: Simon and Schuster, 2009), 473–74.

23 Chávez, *The U.S. War with Mexico*, vii.

24 Timothy J. Henderson, *A Glorious Defeat: Mexico and Its War with the United States* (New York: Hill and Wang, 2008), 97–98.

25 That the vast majority of white Americans held racist views in the nineteenth century is beyond dispute. Nonetheless, see Chávez, *The U.S. War with Mexico*; John S. D. Eisenhower, *So Far from God: The U.S. War with Mexico, 1846–1848* (Norman: University of Oklahoma Press, 2000); David A. Clary, *Eagles and Empire: The United States, Mexico, and the Struggle for a Continent* (New York: Bantam, 2009); and Bauer, *Mexican War*.

26 Any good survey of Mexican history will make this point. See, for example, the sixth edition of Michael C. Meyer, William L. Sherman, and Susan M. Deeds, *The Course of Mexican History* (New York: Oxford University Press, 2006).

27 Frances Calderón de la Barca, *Life in Mexico* (1843), cited in John DiConsiglio, *Living through the Mexican-American War* (Chicago: Heinemann, 2012), 11.

28 Chávez, *The U.S. War with Mexico*, 6, 9, notes that in 1827 the ratio of Americans to Mexicans in Texas was roughly two to one (12,00 to 5,000). By 1835, Americans numbered 20,000, Mexicans still 5,000. By 1840, Americans totaled 35,000, Mexicans 4,000, and black slaves 12,000.

29 See Schoultz, *Beneath the United States*.

30 Pike, *United States*, 100.

31 Ibid., 99.

32 Paul Foos, *A Short, Offhand Killing Affair: Soldiers and Social Conflict during the Mexican-American War* (Chapel Hill: University of North Carolina Press, 2002), 3.

33 Walter Nugent, *Habits of Empire: A History of American Expansion* (New York: Alfred A. Knopf, 2008), 154.

34 White, *"It's Your Misfortune,"* 77.

35 Nugent, *Habits of Empire*, 195.

36 *Baltimore Sun*, May 14, 1846.

37 Loveman, *No Higher Law*, 52, 68.

38 Limerick, *Legacy of Conquest*, 232.

39 See Schoultz, *Beneath the United States*, 75.

40 Williams, *Contours*, 183.

41 The *New Orleans Picayune* often echoed such sentiments; see, for example, May 17, 1846.

42 Reprinted in Chávez, *The U.S. War with Mexico*, 73–75. The war message was also widely published in newspapers across the country. See, for example, *New Orleans Picayune*, May 19, 1846.

43 *Detroit Democratic Free Press*, May 23, 1846.

44 See the chapter "Atrocity: The Wages of Manifest Destiny" in Foos, *Offhand Killing Affair*, 115–37. Also see Nugent, *Habits of Empire*, 205.

45 *New York Sun*, May 20, 1846.

46 *New Orleans Picayune*, May 19, 1846.

47 Agenda-setting "theory" research was pioneered by Maxwell McCombs and Donald Shaw in the 1970s. See Maxwell McCombs, *Setting the Agenda: The News Media and Public Opinion* (Cambridge, UK: Polity Press, 2004); and Maxwell McCombs, Donald L. Shaw, and David Weaver, eds., *Communication and Democracy: Exploring the Intellectual Frontiers in Agenda-Setting Theory* (Mahwah, NJ: Lawrence Erlbaum Associates, 1997). Also see Shanto Iyengar and Richard Reeves, eds., *Do the Media Govern? Politicians, Voters, and Reporters in America* (Los Angeles: SAGE, 1997).

48 David Altheide, "Fear, Terrorism, and Popular Culture," in Birkenstein, Froula, and Randell, *Reframing 9/11*, 11.

49 The *Baltimore Sun*, May 19, 1846, for example: "We acknowledge our indebtedness to our brethren of the entire press at New Orleans."

50 *New York Sun*, May 20, 1846.

51 Distance was the crucial factor. News from Mexico arrived more quickly in New Orleans, for example, than Detroit.

52 *New York Tribune*, May 27, 1846.

53 *New Orleans Picayune*, May 3, 1846.

54 *Charleston Courier*, May 9, 1846; *Baltimore Sun*, May 12, 1846.

55 *New York Sun*, May 1, 1846; also see May 4, 1846.

56 *Detroit Democratic Free Press*, May 15, 1846.

57 Chalmers Johnson, *Blowback: The Costs and Consequences of American Empire* (New York: Holt Paperbacks, 2004).

58 *New York Sun*, May 14, 1846.

59 "All papers are liable to be hoaxed at times," the *Baltimore Sun*, May 25, 1846, opined, struggling to contain its own publishing mishap.

60 *Detroit Democratic Free Press*, May 15, 1846; May 16, 1846.

61 *New York Herald*, May 9, 1846; May 11, 1846.

62 *New York Sun*, May 4, 1846. Also see, for example, *New York Tribune*, May 1, 1846.

63 *New York Tribune*, May 6, 1846.

64 *Detroit Democratic Free Press*, May 18, 1846.

65 Ibid.

66 *Detroit Democratic Free Press*, May 21, 1846. The same report appeared in the *New York Sun*, May 16, 1846.

67 *Detroit Democratic Free Press*, May 30, 1846.

68 *New York Herald*, May 11, 1846.

69 *New Orleans Picayune*, May 3, 1846.

70 See, for example, *Baltimore Sun*, May 16, 1846.

71 The nickname was often used in the press, especially after the initial weeks of war commenced. See, for example, *New Orleans Picayune*, May 26, 1846.

72 *New Orleans Picayune*, May 3, 1846.

73 *New Orleans Picayune*, May 5, 1846.

74 *New York Herald*, May 21, 1846.

75 *New Orleans Picayune*, May 13, 1846.

76 *New Orleans Picayune*, May 19, 1846; May 20, 1846.

77 *Detroit Democratic Free Press*, May 14, 1846; also see May 26, 1846.

78 *Detroit Democratic Free Press*, May 18, 1846.

79 *New Orleans Picayune*, May 5, 1846.

80 *Detroit Democratic Free Press*, May 18, 1846.

81 *New Orleans Picayune*, May 5, 1846.

82 *New Orleans Picayune*, May 13, 1846.

83 *New Orleans Picayune*, May 16, 1846.

84 *New Orleans Picayune*, May 23, 1846.

85 *New York Herald*, May 2, 1846.

86 *New York Sun Extra*, May 9, 1846.

87 *New York Sun*, May 2, 1846; also see May 9, 1846; and May 11, 1846.

88 *Detroit Democratic Free Press*, May 2, 1846.

89 *Detroit Democratic Free Press*, May 4, 1846.

90 *Detroit Democratic Free Press*, May 19, 1846.

91 *New York Herald*, May 23, 1846.

92 *Baltimore Sun*, May 11, 1846.

93 *Detroit Democratic Free Press*, May 5, 1846.

94 *Detroit Democratic Free Press*, May 12, 1846.

95 *Detroit Democratic Free Press*, May 13, 1846.

96 *Detroit Democratic Free Press*, May 14, 1846 .

97 *Detroit Democratic Free Press*, May 15, 1846.

98 *New Orleans Picayune*, May 20, 1846. Reprinted in the *New York Sun*, May 29, 1846.

99 *New York Herald*, May 13, 1846.

100 *Detroit Democratic Free Press*, May 27, 1846.

101 *Baltimore Sun*, May 26, 1846.

102 *New York Sun*, May 8, 1846.

103 *New York Tribune*, May 8, 1846.

104 *New York Tribune*, May 9, 1846.

105 *New York Herald*, May 2, 1846.

106 Ibid.

107 *New York Herald*, May 13, 1846.

108 *New Orleans Picayune*, May 26, 1846.

109 *New Orleans Picayune*, May 2, 1846.

110 *New Orleans Picayune*, May 9, 1846; May 19, 1846.

111 *New Orleans Picayune*, May 9, 1846.

112 *Baltimore Sun*, May 28, 1846. The *New York Tribune*, May 18, 1846, also invoked God in its opposition to the war.

113 *New York Herald*, May 18, 1846.

114 *Baltimore Sun*, May 28, 1846.

115 *New York Sun*, May 11, 1846.

116 *Baltimore Sun*, May 11, 1846.

117 *New York Herald*, May 11, 1846.

118 *New Orleans Picayune*, May 12, 1846; also see May 13, 1846; and May 17, 1846. The term was widely and commonly employed by the press to refer to the actions of American troops.

119 *Detroit Democratic Free Press*, May 20, 1846.

120 *New Orleans Picayune*, May 14, 1846.

121 See *New Orleans Picayune* any day in May 1846.

122 *New Orleans Picayune*, May 23, 1846.

123 See Foos, *Offhand Killing Affair*.

124 *New York Tribune*, May 11, 1846.

125 *New York Tribune*, May 12, 1846.

126 *New York Tribune*, May 15, 1846.

127 See, for example, *New York Tribune*, May 12, 1846.

128 *New York Tribune*, May 16, 1846.

129 *New Orleans Picayune*, May 23, 1846.

130 *Detroit Democratic Free Press*, May 22, 1846.

131 *Baltimore Sun*, May 18, 1846. Also see *New York Tribune*, May 18, 1846.

132 *New York Sun*, May 14, 1846.

133 *New York Sun*, May 21, 1846.

134 *New York Herald*, May 26, 1846.

135 *New York Herald*, May 31, 1846.

136 See, for example, *New Orleans Picayune*, May 23, 1846.

137 *New Orleans Picayune*, May 24, 1846.

138 *New Orleans Picayune*, May 26, 1846.

139 Stephanson, *Manifest Destiny*, 37. Nugent, *Habits of Empire*, 205, puts deserters at 17 percent, which includes regulars and volunteers.

140 *New Orleans Picayune*, May 26, 1846.

141 *New York Herald*, May 13, 1846.

142 *New York Herald*, May 22, 1846.

143 *New Orleans Picayune*, May 17, 1846.

144 Ibid.

145 Ibid.

146 *New Orleans Picayune*, May 21, 1846.

147 The examples can be found almost daily during May 1846. See, for example, *New York Tribune*, May 15, 1846.

148 *New York Tribune*, May 14, 1846.

149 *New York Herald*, May 13, 1846.

150 *New Orleans Picayune*, February 1, 1848.

151 *New York Herald*, February 3, 1848.

152 *New York Herald*, February 6, 1848.

153 Ibid.

154 *New Orleans Picayune*, February 13, 1848.

155 *New Orleans Picayune*, February 22, 1848.

156 *New York Sun*, February 3, 1848; also see February 4, 1848.

157 *Detroit Free Press*, February 22, 1848.

158 *New York Herald*, February 6, 1848.

159 *New Orleans Picayune*, February 4, 1848.

160 Quoted in Williams, *Contours*, 277.

161 *New York Herald*, February 8, 1848.

162 *New York Herald*, February 9, 1848.

163 *New York Herald*, February 10, 1848.

164 *New York Herald*, February 14, 1848.

165 Ibid. Also see, for example, *New Orleans Picayune*, February 22, 1848; *New York Tribune*, February 16, 1848; *Baltimore Sun*, February 29, 1848; and *Detroit Democratic Free Press*, February 25, 1848.

166 *New Orleans Picayune*, February 23, 1848.

167 *Baltimore Sun*, February 22, 1848.

168 *Baltimore Sun*, February 7, 1848.

169 *New York Herald*, February 15, 1848.

170 *Detroit Democratic Free Press*, February 8, 1848.

171 *New York Herald*, February 22, 1848; also see February 23, 1848; and February 25, 1848.

172 *New York Tribune*, February 16, 1848; also see February 4, 1848; February 9, 1848; February 14, 1848; February 15, 1848; February 18, 1848; February 19, 1848; February 22, 1848; February 24, 1848; February 25, 1848; and February 26, 1848.

173 *New York Tribune*, February 26, 1848; also see February 2, 1848; and February 12, 1848.

174 *New York Herald*, February 12, 1848.

175 *New Orleans Picayune*, February 9, 1848.

176 See, for example, Roger Ebert's 1998 review of the film at rogerebert. suntimes.com.

177 Henderson, *A Glorious Defeat*, xx.

CHAPTER 3

1   *The Big Lebowski*, dir. Joel Coen, 1998.

2   Quoted in White, *"It's Your Misfortune,"* 105.

3   See Wills, *John Wayne's America*.

4   Jerry Keenan, *Encyclopedia of American Indian Wars, 1492–1890* (New York: Norton, 1999), 60.

5   See James West Davidson et al., *U.S.: A Narrative History*, 2nd ed. (New York: McGraw-Hill, 2012), 364–65.

6   James L. Roark et al., *Understanding the American Promise: A Brief History* (New York: Bedford/St. Martin's Press, 2011), 461.

7   Hugh J. Reilly dates the first printed report to the *Bozeman Times* of July 3. See his *The Frontier Newspapers and the Coverage of the Plains Indian Wars* (Denver: Praeger, 2010), 40.

8   *New York Times*, July 7, 1876.

9   The term was widely employed in the press. See Michael A. Elliott, *Custerology: The Enduring Legacy of the Indian Wars and George Armstrong Custer* (Chicago: University of Chicago Press, 2007), 66–67.

10   For example, "Some doubt was at first expressed in regards to the truth of the report." *Chicago Tribune*, July 6, 1876.

11   Keenan, *Encyclopedia*, 61–62.

12   *9/11: The Filmmaker's Commemorative Edition*, dir. Jules Naudet, 2002.

13 *San Francisco Daily Bulletin*, June 21, 1876.

14 *San Francisco Daily Bulletin*, June 2, 1876.

15 See, for example, Horatio Alger, *Ragged Dick: Or, Street Life in New York with the Boot-Blacks* (1868; reprinted, New York: Createspace, 2012).

16 See Hughes, *Myths*.

17 Godfrey Hodgson, *The Myth of American Exceptionalism* (New Haven, CT: Yale University Press, 2010).

18 Bauer, *Mexican War*, 1.

19 Vine Deloria Jr., *Custer Died for Your Sins: An Indian Manifesto* (Norman: University of Oklahoma Press, 1988).

20 *Chicago Tribune*, July 7, 1876.

21 Prothero, *American Jesus*, 294.

22 See Dee Brown, *Bury My Heart at Wounded Knee* (New York: Henry Holt, 1993).

23 The phrasing is still popular. See, for example, Custer's Last Stand Reenactment website at http://www.custerslaststand.org/.

24 See Elliott, *Custerology*.

25 *Rocky Mountain News*, June 1, 1876. Also see *San Francisco Daily Bulletin*, June 12, 1876.

26 See, for example, *Chicago Tribune*, June 14, 1876.

27 *Rocky Mountain News*, June 6, 1876.

28 *Chicago Tribune*, June 1, 1876.

29 *Chicago Tribune*, July 8, 1876.

30 *New York Times*, June 7, 1876.

31 *New York Times*, June 9, 1876.

32 *Rocky Mountain News*, June 6, 1876.

33 Reilly, *Frontier Newspapers*, 130.

34 *Rocky Mountain News*, June 6, 1876.

35 *Rocky Mountain News*, June 27, 1876.

36 *Rocky Mountain News*, June 11, 1876.

37 The phrase was used in two newspapers: *San Francisco Daily Bulletin*, June 23, 1848; and *Rocky Mountain News*, June 24, 1876. Also see *Rocky Mountain News*, July 4, 1876.

38 *Rocky Mountain News*, July 4, 1876.

39 *New York Times*, June 29, 1876.

40 *Rocky Mountain News*, June 6, 1876.

41 *Rocky Mountain News*, June 30, 1876.

42 *Rocky Mountain News*, June 10, 1876.

43 *Rocky Mountain News*, June 6, 1876.

44 *Rocky Mountain News*, June 18, 1876.

45   *New York Times*, June 10, 1876.

46   *New York Tribune*, June 10, 1876.

47   *Chicago Tribune*, June 28, 1876.

48   *Chicago Tribune*, June 22, 1876.

49   *Chicago Tribune*, June 5, 1876.

50   *Chicago Tribune*, June 4, 1876.

51   Ibid.

52   *Chicago Tribune*, June 5, 1876.

53   *San Francisco Daily Bulletin*, June 3, 1848; June 5, 1848; June 8, 1848; *Rocky Mountain News*, June 14, 1876; *New York Times*, June 17, 1876.

54   *Rocky Mountain News*, June 14, 1876.

55   *New York Times*, June 4, 1876.

56   *Chicago Tribune*, June 5, 1876.

57   *New York Tribune*, June 2, 1876.

58   Ibid.; also see June 8, 1876.

59   *Rocky Mountain News*, July 4, 1876.

60   *Chicago Tribune*, June 5, 1876.

61   *Chicago Tribune*, June 21, 1876.

62   *Rocky Mountain News*, July 4, 1876.

63   Ibid.

64   *Rocky Mountain News*, June 8, 1876.

65   *Chicago Tribune*, June 19, 1876.

66   *San Francisco Daily Bulletin*, June 2, 1876; *Rocky Mountain News*, June 10, 1876; *New York Times*, June 11, 1876; *San Francisco Daily Bulletin*, June 13, 1876; *New York Times*, June 13, 1876; *Rocky Mountain News*, June 16, 1876; *Rocky Mountain News*, June 23, 1876; *San Francisco Daily Bulletin*, June 26, 1876; *Rocky Mountain News*, June 30, 1876; *Chicago Tribune*, July 5, 1876.

67   *New York Tribune*, June 3, 1876. The same story appeared in the *Chicago Tribune*, June 3, 1876.

68   *San Francisco Daily Bulletin* June 10, 1876.

69   *New York Times*, June 24, 1876.

70   *New York Times*, June 26, 1876.

71   Elliott, *Custerology*, 59.

72   *Rocky Mountain News*, July 4, 1876.

73   *New York Times*, June 4, 1876.

74   Seed, *Ceremonies of Possession*,16–40.

75   *New York Times*, June 10, 1876; also see June 25, 1876.

76   *New York Times*, July 7, 1876.

77   *San Francisco Daily Bulletin*, June 9, 1848.

78   Reilly, *Frontier Newspapers*, xvii–xxiv, 47.

79 Although some of the headlines were printed after Custer's death, the news had yet to break in the east.

80 *Chicago Tribune*, June 1, 1876.

81 *New York Tribune*, June 2, 1876.

82 *New York Times*, June 2, 1876.

83 *New York Tribune*, June 2, 1876.

84 *Chicago Tribune*, June 3, 1876.

85 *Chicago Tribune*, June 5, 1876.

86 *Rocky Mountain News*, June 8, 1876.

87 *New York Times*, June 8, 1876.

88 *Rocky Mountain News*, June 8, 1876.

89 *New York Times*, June 9, 1876.

90 *Rocky Mountain News*, June 9, 1876.

91 Ibid.

92 *New York Tribune*, June 10, 1876.

93 *Rocky Mountain News*, June 11, 1876.

94 *New York Times*, June 11, 1876.

95 *Chicago Tribune*, June 11, 1876.

96 *New York Times*, June 13, 1876.

97 *New York Times*, June 17, 1876.

98 *Chicago Tribune*, June 19, 1876.

99 *San Francisco Daily Bulletin*, June 20, 1848.

100 *Rocky Mountain News*, June 21, 1876.

101 *New York Times*, June 21, 1876. This headline was a repeat of June 13, 1876.

102 *Rocky Mountain News*, June 24, 1876. Crook, in fact, was forced to retreat at the Battle of the Rosebud, the paper reported just a day later; see June 25, 1876; and June 27, 1876.

103 *New York Times*, June 24, 1876.

104 *New York Times*, June 25, 1876.

105 *Chicago Tribune*, June 27, 1876.

106 *New York Times*, June 27, 1876.

107 *New York Times*, July 1, 1876.

108 *Chicago Tribune*, July 5, 1876.

109 *New York Times*, June 25, 1876; also see June 26, 1876.

110 *New York Tribune*, June 16, 1876.

111 Ibid.

112 *Rocky Mountain News*, June 3, 1876.

113 *Shane*, dir. George Stevens, 1953.

114 Kevin Adams, *Class and Race in the Frontier Army: Military Life in the West, 1870–1890* (Norman: University of Oklahoma Press, 2009), 125.

115 Stephen T. Asma, *On Monsters: An Unnatural History of Our Worst Fears* (New York: Oxford University Press, 2009), 99.

116 Roland Barthes, *Mythologies* (New York: Farrar, Straus, and Giroux, 1972).

117 *Rocky Mountain News*, June 10, 1876.

118 *New York Times*, June 29, 1876.

119 Ibid.

120 *New York Tribune*, June 24, 1876.

121 *New York Tribune*, July 7, 1876.

122 *Chicago Tribune*, July 6, 1876.

123 The same phrase, reprinted from the *Helena Montana Herald*, appeared in the *New York Tribune*, June 6, 1876, and *New York Times*, July 6, 1876. It appeared in the *San Francisco Daily Bulletin*, identified as a "SPECIAL TO THE BULLETIN," July 6, 1876.

124 On June 6, 1876, the *New York Tribune*, *New York Times*, and *Rocky Mountain News* printed nearly the identical copy and identified its source as the *Helena Montana Herald*.

125 See Jerome A. Greene, *Washita: The U.S. Army and the Southern Cheyennes,1867–1869* (Norman: University of Oklahoma Press, 2008); and Brown, *Bury My Heart*.

126 See, for example, *Chicago Tribune*, July 7, 1876; and *New York Times*, July 7, 1876.

127 See John Coward, *The Newspaper Indian: Native American Identity in the Press, 1820–90* (Urbana: University of Illinois Press, 1999). Also see Mary Ann Weston, *Native Americans in the News: Images of Indians in the Twentieth Century Press* (Westport, CT: Greenwood Press, 1996).

128 *Chicago Tribune*, July 7, 1876.

129 Ibid. Parts of this passage also appeared in the *New York Tribune*, July 7, 1876.

130 *Chicago Tribune*, July 9, 1876.

131 Also see, for example, *Chicago Tribune*, July 8, 1876. The paper ramped up its rhetorical attacks on Sitting Bull and filled columns in the days after Custer's death. For example, on July 15, under the headline "THE SAVAGES," a story heaped the principal blame on Sitting Bull and claimed he and his "band" had stolen "$15,000 or $20,000 in money and jewelry"; it then went on to describe in explicit and maudlin terms how scalps were effected in "Injun country." *Chicago Tribune*, July 15, 1876.

132 *New York Tribune*, July 19, 1876.

133 *San Francisco Daily Bulletin*, July 6, 1876.

134 *Rocky Mountain News*, July 7, 1876.

135 Ibid.

136 *Chicago Tribune*, July 7, 1876.

137 *New York Times*, July 7, 1876. The same report appeared in the *San Francisco Daily Bulletin*, July 8, 1876, and *Rocky Mountain News*, July 8, 1876.

138 *Chicago Tribune*, July 7, 1876.

139 Ibid.

140 See David Cowart, "The Tarzan Myth and Jung's Genesis of the Self," *Journal of American Culture* 2, 2 (1979): 220–30; and Eric Cheyfitz, *The Poetics of Imperialism: Translation and Colonization from* The Tempest *to* Tarzan (New York: Oxford University Press, 1991).

141 Edgar Rice Burroughs, *Tarzan of the Apes* (1912; reprinted, New York: Oxford University Press, 2010), 96.

142 Harold E. Hinds, "Mexican and Mexican-American Images in the Western Novels of Louis L'Amour," *Latin American Literary Review* 5, 10 (1977): 129–41.

143 Louis L'Amour, *Hondo* (1953; reprinted, New York: Bantam Books, 1983), 1.

144 Pfitzer, "Only Good Alien."

145 See John W. Davis, *Wyoming Range War: The Infamous Invasion of Johnson County* (Norman: University of Oklahoma Press, 2012).

146 Colin A. Clarke, "Like a Mirror Reflecting Itself: Natty Bumppo, *The Virginian*, and the Fate of the American Frontier," paper presented at the Eleventh Cooper Seminar, State University of New York College at Oneonta, July 1997; Stoeltje, "Making."

147 Owen Wister, *The Virginian* (1902; reprinted, New York: Oxford University Press, 1998), 11–13.

148 George A. Custer, *My Life on the Plains: Or, Personal Experiences with Indians* (1874; reprinted, n.p.: Leonaur, 2009).

149 *Rocky Mountain News*, July 9, 1876. Also see *Chicago Tribune*, July 8, 1876.

150 *Chicago Tribune*, July 8, 1876.

151 *New York Tribune*, July 7, 1876. Also see *Chicago Tribune*, July 7, 1876; and July 8, 1876.

152 *New York Times*, July 7, 1876.

153 *Chicago Tribune*, July 7, 1876.

154 Ibid.

155 *Rocky Mountain News*, July 7, 1876.

156 *Chicago Tribune*, July 7, 1876.

157 *Chicago Tribune*, July 9, 1876.

158 *Chicago Tribune*, July 14, 1876. Also see *New York Tribune*, July 7, 1876; *San Francisco Daily Bulletin*, July 7, 1876; and *Rocky Mountain News*, July 8, 1876.

159 *Chicago Tribune*, July 12, 1876.

160 Even today the correspondence between Custer and his wife perhaps strikes one as surprisingly intimate and touching. See Marguerite Merington, *The Custer Story: The Life and Intimate Letters of General George A. Custer and His Wife Elizabeth* (Lincoln: University of Nebraska Press, 1987).

161 Stoeltje, "Making," 239.

162 *New York Times*, July 8, 1876.

163 *San Francisco Daily Bulletin*, July 10, 1876.

164 *San Francisco Daily Bulletin*, July 8, 1876.

165 See Thomas Powers, *The Killing of Crazy Horse* (New York: Knopf, 2010), 68.

CHAPTER 4

1 Quoted in Grandin, *Empire's Workshop*, 1.

2 Williams, *Empire*, 20.

3 Horsman, *Race*.

4 Schoultz, *Beneath the United States*.

5 See Mark Cronlund Anderson, "The Mythical Frontier, the Mexican Revolution, and the Press: An Imperial Subplot," *Canadian Review of American Studies* 37, 1 (2007): 1–22.

6 Enrique Krauze, *Biografía del poder, 2: Francisco I. Madero, místico de la libertad* (Mexico City: Fondo de Cultura Económica, 1987). Also see Enrique Krauze, *Mexico: Biography of Power* (New York: Harper Perennial, 1998), 245–73. To put Madero in the context of his times, see Alan Knight, *The Mexican Revolution*, 2 vols. (New York: Oxford University Press, 1990).

7 See Douglas W. Richmond, *Venustiano Carranza's Nationalist Struggle, 1893–1920* (Lincoln: University of Nebraska Press, 1984); and Enrique Krauze, *Biografía del poder, 5: Venustiano Carranza, puente entre siglos* (Mexico City: Fondo de Cultura Económica, 1987).

8 The literature on Villa is vast. The most comprehensive study remains Friedrich Katz, *The Life and Times of Pancho Villa* (Stanford: Stanford University Press, 1998).

9 A second reason that the main thrust of the propaganda war was waged in the United States was that the vast majority of Americans were literate enough to digest press reports, whereas Mexicans generally were not. Hence, the propaganda wars were fought mostly, though not exclusively, in the United States.

10 See Mark Cronlund Anderson, *Pancho Villa's Revolution by Headlines* (Norman: University of Oklahoma Press, 2001).

·11   See Robert W. Johannsen, *To the Halls of the Montezumas: The Mexican War in the American Imagination* (New York: Oxford University Press, 1988); and John A. Britton, *Revolution and Ideology: Images of the Mexican Revolution in the United States* (Lexington: University of Kentucky Press, 1995).

12   See Bird, *Dressing in Feathers*; Berkhofer, *White Man's Indian*; Johnson, *Latin America*; Coward, *Newspaper Indian*; and Weston, *Native Americans*.

13   Anderson, *Pancho Villa's Revolution*, 45–79.

14   *New York Times*, March 26, 1916.

15   See David Spurr, *The Rhetoric of Empire: Colonial Discourse in Journalism, Travel Writing, and Imperial Administration* (Durham: Duke University Press, 1993); Stuart Hall, ed., *Representation: Cultural Representations and Signifying Practices* (Thousand Oaks, CA: SAGE, 1997); Edward W. Said, *Covering Islam: How the Media and the Experts Determine How We See the Rest of the World* (New York: Vintage, 1997); and Edward W. Said, *Culture and Imperialism* (New York: Vintage, 1994).

16   See Margarita de Orellana, *Filming Pancho Villa: How Hollywood Shaped the Mexican Revolution* (New York: Verso, 2004).

17   Larry A. Harris, *Pancho Villa and the Columbus Raid* (Whitefish, MT: Kessinger Publishing, 2010).

18   Turner, *Frontier and Section*, 61.

19   *Collier's*, June 13, 1914.

20   *Forum*, January 1914.

21   Ibid.

22   Ibid.

23   See Carroll Smith-Rosenberg, *Disorderly Conduct: Visions of Gender in Victorian America* (New York: Oxford University Press, 1986); Nancy F. Cott, *The Bonds of Womanhood: "Woman's Sphere" in New England, 1780–1835* (New Haven, CT: Yale University Press, 1977); and Johnson, *Latin America*, 72–115.

24   *Chicago Tribune*, January 11, 1914.

25   *Chicago Tribune*, July 7, 1914.

26   *Los Angeles Times*, October 21, 1913.

27   *North American Review*, July 1914.

28   *Everybody's*, June 1914.

29   *Nation*, December 25, 1914.

30   During the fall of 2010 and early winter of 2011, the Museo de Arte Carillo Gil in Mexico City staged a show, curated by art historian Juan Manuel Aurrecoechea, that explored hundreds of American editorial cartoons published during the Mexican Revolution. See www.museocarillogil.com.

31 The press was well aware of Villa's propaganda acumen. See, for example, *Chicago Tribune*, July 21, 1914; and *Nation*, March 18, 1915. Also see Anderson, *Pancho Villa's Revolution*, 45–79.

32 See Anderson, *Pancho Villa's Revolution*, 196–200.

33 *New York Times*, February 21, 1914.

34 *Everybody's*, June 1914.

35 *Chicago Tribune*, April 20, 1914.

36 Clarence Clendenen noted that Villa "understood well the part that newspapers could play in forming public opinion in the United States." See his *The United States and Pancho Villa: A Study in Unconventional Diplomacy* (Ithaca, NY: Cornell University Press, 1961), 75. Also see Manuel A. Machado, *Centaur of the North: Francisco Villa, the Mexican Revolution, and Northern Mexico* (Austin: Eakin Press, 1988), 46; John Reed, *Insurgent Mexico* (1914; reprinted, New York: International Publishers, 1965), 10; Louis Stevens, *Here Comes Pancho Villa: The Anecdotal History of a Genial Killer* (New York: Frederick A. Stokes, 1930), 11, 28, 125–26; and Timothy Turner, *Bullets, Bottles, and Gardenias* (Dallas: South-West Press, 1935), 175.

37 Anderson, *Pancho Villa's Revolution*, 4–5, 49, 81.

38 *Nation*, March 18, 1915.

39 *New York Times*, April 24, 1914.

40 *San Francisco Examiner*, March 29, 1914.

41 *San Francisco Examiner*, May 17, 1914.

42 *Literary Digest*, April 18, 1914.

43 *San Francisco Examiner*, May 27, 1914.

44 *San Francisco Examiner*, June 11, 1914.

45 *San Francisco Examiner*, September 26, 1914.

46 Ibid.

47 *Chicago Tribune*, July 21, 1914.

48 *New York Times*, September 29, 1914.

49 *New York Times*, October 15, 1914.

50 *Nation*, September 17, 1914.

51 See Friedrich Katz, "Pancho Villa and the Attack on Columbus, New Mexico," *American Historical Review* 83, 1 (1978): 101–30.

52 See Joseph A. Stout Jr., *Border Conflict: Villistas, Carrancistas, and the Punitive Expedition, 1915–1920* (Houston: Texas Christian University Press, 1999); and John S. D. Eisenhower, *Intervention! The United States and the Mexican Revolution, 1913–1917* (New York: W. W. Norton, 1995), 217–300.

53 *Chicago Tribune*, March 5, 1916.

54 *Los Angeles Times*, March 3, 1916.

55 *Los Angeles Times*, March 5, 1916.

56 *Los Angeles Times*, March 6, 1916.

57 *New York Times*, March 9, 1916.

58 *New York Times*, March 10, 1916.

59 Ibid.

60 *New York Times*, March 19, 1916. Also see the *New York Times Magazine* article on the capture of Geronimo, March 19, 1916.

61 *New York Times*, March 31, 1916.

62 *Los Angeles Times*, March 10, 1916.

63 Ibid.

64 *Los Angeles Times*, March 11, 1916.

65 Ibid.

66 Also see *Los Angeles Times*, March 13, 1916, where Villa is referred to as being as "cunning as a fox" and as "deadly as a rattlesnake."

67 See Stout, *Border Conflict*.

68 *Chicago Tribune*, March 13, 1916.

69 *Chicago Tribune*, March 11, 1916.

70 *Chicago Tribune*, March 12, 1916.

71 *Chicago Tribune*, March 12, 1916.

72 *Chicago Tribune*, March 13, 1916.

73 Meredith Mason Brown, *Frontiersman: Daniel Boone and the Making of America* (Baton Rouge: Louisiana State University Press, 2008).

CHAPTER 5

1 Gayatri Chakravorty Spivak, *Nationalism and the Imagination* (New York: Seagull Books, 2010), 40.

2 W. Scott Poole, *Monsters in America: Our Historical Obsession with the Hideous and the Haunting* (Waco, TX: Baylor University Press, 2011), 5.

3 Information comparing textbook sales is difficult to find because publishers are reluctant to release sales figures. I have relied on a study that tabulated results from 792 course syllabi. See Daniel J. Cohen, "By the Book: Assessing the Place of Textbooks in U.S. Survey Courses." *Journal of American History* 91, 4 (2005): 1405–15.

4 Gary B. Nash et al., *The American People: Creating a Nation and a Society*, 7th ed. (New York: Prentice Hall, 2011), 504–05.

5 Davidson et al., *U.S.*, 366–67.

6 John Mack Faragher et al., *Out of Many: A History of the American People*, 6th ed. (New York: Prentice Hall, 2011), 467–68.

7 Roark et al., *Understanding the American Promise*, 462–64.

8 Ibid., 464.

9   *Los Angeles Times*, April 26, 1928.

10   See William M. LeoGrande, *Our Own Backyard: The United States in Central America, 1977–1992* (Chapel Hill: University of North Carolina Press, 1998).

11   *Time*, January 7, 1935.

12   *Time*, May 14, 1936.

13   *Los Angeles Times*, July 21, 1927.

14   *Los Angeles Times*, January 26, 1928.

15   *Harper's*, June 1931.

16   *Harper's*, January 1936.

17   Stephanson, *Manifest Destiny*, 90; also see Grandin, *Empire's Workshop*, 2.

18   Michel Gobat, *Confronting the American Dream: Nicaragua under U.S. Imperial Rule* (Durham: Duke University Press, 2007), 1.

19   Jeffery M. Paige, *Coffee and Power: Revolution and the Rise of Democracy in Central America* (Cambridge, MA: Harvard University Press, 1997), 162. Also see Lester D. Langley and Thomas Schoonover, *The Banana Men: American Mercenaries and Entrepreneurs in Central America, 1880–1930* (Lexington: University Press of Kentucky, 1995).

20   See David W. Dent, *The Legacy of the Monroe Doctrine: A Reference Guide to U.S. Involvement in Latin America and the Caribbean* (Westport: Greenwood Press, 1999), 279–296.

21   *Los Angeles Times*, July 21, 1927.

22   See Steven C. Topik and Allen Wells, *The Second Conquest of Latin America: Coffee, Henequen, and Oil during the Export Boom, 1850–1930* (Austin: University of Texas Press, 1998).

23   Loveman, *No Higher Law*, 194.

24   See, for example, a website that students love: http://en.wikipedia.org/wiki/United_States_non-interventionism.

25   LeoGrande, *Our Own Backyard*, 11.

26   Grandin, *Empire's Workshop*, 39–40.

27   Thomas W. Walker and Christine J. Wade, *Nicaragua: Living in the Shadow of the Eagle* (Boulder, CO: Westview Press, 2011), 12.

28   John A. Booth and Thomas W. Walker, *Understanding Central America* (Boulder, CO: Westview Press, 1993), 23–24. Also see William Walker, *The War in Nicaragua* (1860; reprinted, Tucson: University of Arizona Press, 1985).

29   Kinzer, *Overthrow*, 3.

30   Gobat, *Confronting*, 69.

31   Ibid., 3. Also see LeoGrande, *Our Own Backyard*, 12.

32   See Cyrus Veeser, *A World Safe for Capitalism: Dollar Diplomacy and*

America's Rise to Global Power (New York: Columbia University Press, 2007); Russell Crandall, *Gunboat Democracy: U.S. Interventions in the Dominican Republic, Grenada, and Panama* (New York: Rowman and Littlefield, 2006); and Andrew Graham-Yooll, *Imperial Skirmishes: War and Gunboat Diplomacy in Latin America* (Northampton, MA: Olive Branch Press, 2002).

33 *Time*, February 13, 1933.

34 *Time*, September 9, 1929.

35 David F. Schmitz, *The United States and Right-Wing Dictatorships* (New York: Cambridge University Press, 2006), 182.

36 Blum, *Killing Hope*, 290.

37 *Time*, July 6, 1936. Also see *Los Angeles Times*, February 13, 1928.

38 *Los Angeles Times*, June 24, 1928.

39 *New York Times*, July 17, 1927.

40 *Harper's*, June 1926.

41 *Los Angeles Times*, March 17, 1928.

42 *Los Angeles Times*, May 10, 1928.

43 *Los Angeles Times*, December 25, 1928. The same story, including identical quotations, was printed the next day in the *New York Times*.

44 *New York Times*, February 15, 1931.

45 See, for example, *Los Angeles Times*, July 30, 1927; *New York Times*, January 16, 1929; and *Los Angeles Times*, January 16, 1929.

46 *Los Angeles Times*, May 10, 1928.

47 *New York Times*, July 9, 1932. Also see *Los Angeles Times*, April 23, 1928.

48 *Time*, May 28, 1928.

49 *New York Times*, July 19, 1927.

50 *New York Times*, February 25, 1928.

51 *Los Angeles Times*, July 19, 1927; also see December 26, 1929.

52 *Los Angeles Times*, August 25, 1927; also see February 15, 1928, and April 13, 1928.

53 *New York Times*, July 18, 1927. Also see *Los Angeles Times*, January 26, 1928; January 3, 1931; and April 14, 1931.

54 *Time*, January 16, 1928; *New York Times*, January 21, 1928.

55 *New York Times*, July 1, 1928. Also see *Los Angeles Times*, January 26, 1928.

56 *Los Angeles Times*, March 25, 1934.

57 See Schoultz, *Beneath the United States*; and Johnson, *Latin America*.

58 *Time*, May 28, 1928. Also see *Los Angeles Times*, February 12, 1928.

59 *Los Angeles Times*, May 21, 1928.

60 *Time*, March 5, 1934; also see April 16, 1934.

61 *New York Times*, July 18, 1927.

62 See, for example, *New York Times*, January 16, 1929, and May 18, 1930.

63 *New York Times*, July 19, 1927. Also see *Los Angeles Times*, July 21, 1927; July 30, 1927; January 18, 1928; and January 16, 1929. Also see *New York Times*, October 22, 1927; October 25, 1927; January 2, 1928; January 16, 1928; April 15, 1928; and June 24, 1930.

64 *Time*, May 4, 1931.

65 *Los Angeles Times*, January 14, 1931.

66 *Harper's*, December 1926.

67 *Time*, August 27, 1928.

68 *Harper's*, December 1926.

69 *New York Times*, April 22, 1931. Also see *Los Angeles Times*, April 23, 1928, and January 1, 1929.

70 *New York Times*, April 22, 1931.

71 *Los Angeles Times*, January 1, 1929.

72 See Crandall, *Gunboat Democracy*; Graham-Yooll, *Imperial Skirmishes*; and Veeser, *A World Safe for Capitalism*.

73 *Time*, March 7, 1927.

74 See Elizabeth Furniss, *The Burden of History: Colonialism and the Frontier Myth in a Rural Canadian Community* (Vancouver: UBC Press, 2000).

75 *Time*, January 30, 1928. The *Los Angeles Times* and *Harper's* made similar claims regarding the power of the printed press to shape public opinion. See *Los Angeles Times*, July 10, 1929; and *Harper's*, December 1930 and June 1931.

76 *Time*, February 6, 1928. Also see *Los Angeles Times*, January 26, 1928.

77 *Los Angeles Times*, February 7, 1928.

78 *Time*, April 13, 1931.

79 Schmitz, *United States*, 181.

80 *Time*, November 5, 1928.

81 See Amy Louise Wood, *Lynching and Spectacle: Witnessing Racial Violence in America, 1890–1940* (Chapel Hill: University of North Carolina Press, 2011); and Leon F. Litwack, *Trouble in Mind: Black Southerners in the Age of Jim Crow* (New York: Vintage, 1999).

82 *New York Times*, October 22, 1927; also see April 24, 1928.

83 *New York Times*, October 22, 1927. Also see *Los Angeles Times*, March 25, 1934.

84 *New York Times*, April 29, 1931.

85 *New York Times*, February 4, 1933.

86 *Los Angeles Times*, July 5, 1928; also see July 23, 1928.

87 *Los Angeles Times*, January 1, 1929; also see December 26, 1929.

88 *Los Angeles Times*, December 25, 1928.

89 *New York Times*, October 25, 1927. Also see *Los Angeles Times*, August 25, 1927; and *New York Times*, April 15, 1928.

90   *Los Angeles Times*, July 27, 1930.

91   *New York Times*, January 6, 1928. The Villa connection resurfaced two days after Sandino was assassinated. See *New York Times*, February 23, 1934.

92   *Los Angeles Times*, July 30, 1927.

93   *New York Times*, March 4, 1928.

94   *New York Times*, July 1, 1928.

95   See Stout, *Border Conflict*.

96   *Time*, January 16, 1928.

97   *Los Angeles Times*, July 21, 1927; also see April 14, 1928.

98   *Time*, February 13, 1933.

99   *New York Times*, July 28, 1928.

100 *New York Times*, January 6, 1928.

101 *Time*, April 20, 1931.

102 *New York Times*, February 17, 1928.

103 *New York Times*, January 21, 1928.

104 *New York Times*, February 11, 1928.

105 *Time*, December 31, 1928.

106 *Time*, February 18, 1929.

107 *New York Times*, February 11, 1929.

108 *Time*, September 9, 1929.

109 *New York Times*, August 29, 1928.

110 *Los Angeles Times*, July 21, 1927.

111 *Los Angeles Times*, February 19, 1928.

112 Also see *Los Angeles Times*, April 13, 1932.

113 *Time*, April 27, 1931.

114 *New York Times*, February 3, 1933; also see March 3, 1933.

115 *New York Times*, February 4, 1933.

116 *New York Times*, February 23, 1934.

117 *Los Angeles Times*, February 23, 1934.

118 *Los Angeles Times*, February 24, 1934.

119 See, for example, *Los Angeles Times*, July 20, 1927; July 21, 1927; and July 22, 1927.

120 *Los Angeles Times*, January 18, 1928; also see February 12, 1928.

121 *Los Angeles Times*, February 19, 1928. Also see *Time*, December 10, 1928; and *Los Angeles Times*, January 4, 1929.

122 Booth and Walker, *Understanding Central America*, 130.

123 See Slotkin, "Nostalgia and Progress."

124 *Los Angeles Times*, June 24, 1928.

125 *Harper's*, June 1930.

CHAPTER 6

1   Philip Caputo, *A Rumor of War* (New York: Henry Holt, 1996), xx.

2   Paul Chaat Smith, *Everything You Know about Indians Is Wrong* (Minneapolis: University of Minnesota Press, 2009), 175, 179.

3   Also see Grandin, *Empire's Workshop*, 21.

4   William W. Cobb, *The American Foundation Myth in Vietnam: Reigning Paradigms and Raining Bombs* (New York: University Press of America, 1998), 4.

5   Ibid., 13.

6   See an interview with McNamara, available on Youtube at https://www.youtube.com/watch?v=5AaGVAipGpo.

7   See, for example, Geoff Simons, *Vietnam Syndrome: Impact on U.S. Foreign Policy* (New York: Palgrave Macmillan, 1998), 3–24.

8   Gail E. S. Yoshitani, *Reagan on War: A Reappraisal of the Weinberger Doctrine, 1980–1984* (Houston: Texas A&M Press, 2012), 140–41.

9   Andrew J. Bacevich, *The New American Militarism: How Americans Are Seduced by War* (New York: Oxford University Press, 2013), 112.

10 Linda Dittmar and Gene Michaud, eds., *From Hanoi to Hollywood: The Vietnam War in American Film* (New Brunswick, NJ: Rutgers University Press, 1990).

11 Slotkin, *Regeneration*, 57–145.

12 John Tirman, *The Deaths of Others: The Fate of Civilians in America's Wars* (New York: Oxford University Press, 2011),184.

13 Cobb, *American Foundation Myth*, 11.

14 See Custer, *My Life on the Plains*, passim.

15 S. C. Gwynne, *Empire of the Summer Moon: Quanah Parker and the Rise and Fall of the Comanches, the Most Powerful Indian Tribe in American History* (New York: Scribner, 2011). Also see John Demos, *The Unredeemed Captive: A Family Story from Early America* (New York: Vintage, 1995).

16 *New York Times*, November 9, 2003.

17 Gaylyn Studlar and David Desser, "Never Having to Say You're Sorry: *Rambo's* Rewriting the Vietnam War," in Dittmar and Michaud, *From Hanoi to Hollywood*, 107–08.

18 *Rambo, First Blood*, dir. Ted Kotcheff, 1982.

19 Studlar and Desser, "Never Having to Say You're Sorry," 109.

20 Cowart, "Tarzan Myth," 222.

21 Barbara Mortimer, *Hollywood's Frontier Captives: Cultural Anxiety and the Captivity Plot in American Film* (New York: Routledge, 1999), 155. Also see Studlar and Desser, "Never Having to Say You're Sorry."

22 Bacevich, *New American Militarism*, 99.

23 Barry Langford, *Film Genre: Hollywood and Beyond* (Edinburgh: Edinburgh University Press, 2006), 125.

24 To arrive at these figures, I Googled "Rambo body count." Flowingdata.com registered fifty-eight kills, Moviebodycounts.com and Geekstir.com espied sixty-seven kills, and Darkhorizons.com counted sixty-nine kills.

25 See, for example, Ronald Reagan, "Remarks Honoring the Vietnam War's Unknown Soldier," May 28, 1984.

26 See http://www.thedailybeast.com/newsweek, January 15, 2008.

27 Bill Hendon and Elizabeth A. Stewart, *An Enormous Crime: The Definitive Account of American POWs Abandoned in Southeast Asia* (New York: St. Martin's, 2008).

28 Frank Anton and Tommy Denton, *Why Didn't You Get Me Out? A POW's Nightmare in Vietnam* (New York: St. Martin's, 2000).

29 Studlar and Desser, "Never Having to Say You're Sorry," 109.

30 Harold Schechter and Jonna G. Semeiks, "Leatherstocking in 'Nam: Rambo, *Platoon*, and the American Frontier Myth," *Journal of Popular Culture* 24, 4 (1991): 18.

31 Ronald H. Carpenter, "America's Tragic Metaphor: Our Twentieth-Century Combatants as Frontiersmen," *Quarterly Journal of Speech* 76, 1 (1990): 1–22.

32 Schechter and Semeiks, "Leatherstocking," 23.

33 Frank Graziano, *Wounds of Love: The Mystical Marriage of Saint Rose of Lima* (New York: Oxford University Press, 2004).

34 *Rambo III*, dir. Peter MacDonald, 1988.

35 Loveman, *No Higher Law*, 6, 83.

36 Studlar and Desser, "Never Having to Say You're Sorry," 111.

37 Smith, *Virgin Land*, 253.

CHAPTER 7

1 Abigail A. Kohn, *Shooters: Myths and Realities of America's Gun Cultures* (New York: Oxford University Press, 2004), 83.

2 Mary Rowlandson, "A Narrative of the Captivity and Restoration of Mrs. Mary Rowlandson" (1682), in Derounian-Stodola, *Women's Captivity Narratives*, 45.

3 See LeoGrande, *Our Own Backyard*, 5–6.

4 Michael Grow, *U.S. Presidents and Latin American Interventions: Pursuing Regime Change in the Cold War* (Lawrence: University Press of Kansas, 2008), 114–36; Don M. Coerver and Linda B. Hall, *Tangled Destinies: Latin*

America and the United States (Albuquerque: University of New Mexico Press, 1999), 150; Kenworthy, America/Américas, 73.

5 Dent, *Legacy*, 295.

6 Grandin, *Empire's Workshop*, 115.

7 Gallup News Service, June 7, 2004. For example, a comparison of public approval ratings for presidents from Truman through Obama's first term shows that Reagan was middle of the pack, though his second-term ratings were much stronger than his first term's. Also see "Presidential Approval Ratings History," *Wall Street Journal*, http://online.wsj.com/public/resources/documents/info-presapp0605-31.html.

8 Richard Sobel, "The Polls—A Report: Public Opinion about United States Intervention in El Salvador and Nicaragua," *Public Opinion Quarterly* 53, 1 (1989): 115.

9 See Grandin, *Empire's Workshop*, 126–36; Loveman, *No Higher Law*, 321; Kenworthy, *America/Américas*, 115–21; and Christian Smith, *Resisting Reagan: The U.S. Central America Peace Movement* (Chicago: University of Chicago Press, 1996), 45–56.

10 Ronald Reagan, Address on Central America, April 27, 1983.

11 Loveman, *No Higher Law*, 329.

12 Ronald Reagan, State of the Union Address, January 26, 1982.

13 Ronald Reagan, State of the Union Address, February 6, 1985.

14 Ronald Reagan, Speech to the Republican National Convention, July 17, 1980.

15 Ibid.

16 Ronald Reagan, Speech to the United Nations General Assembly, June 17, 1982.

17 Ronald Reagan, Address to the Nation on National Security, March 23, 1983.

18 Loveman, *No Higher Law*, 202–05.

19 Ronald Reagan, Speech to the Republican National Convention, August 23, 1984.

20 Ronald Reagan, Speech on Foreign Policy, December 16, 1988.

21 Ibid.

22 See Slotkin, *Regeneration*.

23 See Reagan, Address to the Republican National Convention, July 17, 1980; and Reagan, State of the Union Address, January 26, 1982.

24 Also see Ronald Reagan, Remarks Honoring the Vietnam War's Unknown Soldier, May 28, 1984.

25 Also see his famous "Evil Empire" speech; Ronald Reagan, Speech to the National Association of Evangelicals, March 8, 1983; Ronald Reagan, Remarks on U.S. Casualties in Lebanon and Grenada, November 4, 1983;

and Reagan, Remarks Honoring the Vietnam War's Unknown Soldier, May 28, 1984. He also praised the mujahideen and "freedom fighters" in his final State of the Union Address, January 25, 1988.

26 Reagan, State of the Union Address, January 25, 1988. Also see Ronald Reagan, Farewell Address at the Republican National Convention, August 15, 1988.

27 Ronald Reagan, State of the Union Address, January 25, 1984.

28 Ronald Reagan, Second Inaugural Address, January 21, 1985.

29 Reagan, Address on Central America, April 27, 1983.

30 Reagan, Address to British Parliament, June 8, 1982.

31 Ronald Reagan, Speech to the Conservative Political Action Conference, February 18, 1983. Also see Ronald Reagan, Remarks on U.S. Casualties in Lebanon and Grenada, April 27, 1983.

32 Ronald Reagan, Speech to the National Association of Evangelicals, November 4, 1983.

33 Ronald Reagan, State of the Union Address, February 4, 1986.

34 Grandin, *Empire's Workshop*, 90.

35 Reagan, Address to the Nation on National Security, March 23, 1983. Also see Ronald Reagan, Speech to the Nation on Lebanon and Grenada, October 27, 1983; and Reagan, Remarks on U.S. Casualties in Lebanon and Grenada, November 4, 1983.

36 Quoted in Grandin, *Empire's Workshop*, 68.

37 Reagan, State of the Union Address, February 6, 1985.

38 Ronald Reagan, State of the Union Address, January 27, 1987.

39 Reagan, Address on Central America, April 27, 1983.

40 Ibid.

41 See, for example, Reagan, State of the Union Address, January 26, 1982.

42 Reagan, Address to Congress, April 27, 1983.

43 Ibid.

44 See Joseph A. McCartin, "The Strike that Busted Unions," *New York Times*, August 2, 2011; and Stacey Hirsch, "Reagan Presidency Pivotal for Unions, Workers: Organized Labor's Situation Worsened under His Administration," *Baltimore Sun*, June 8, 2004.

45 Reagan, Speech to the Republican National Convention, August 23, 1984.

46 See Schmitz, *United States*, 200.

47 Reagan, Speech to the Republican National Convention, August 23, 1984.

48 See Schoultz, *Beneath the United States*; and Johnson, *Latin America*.

49 Reagan, Speech to the Republican National Convention, August 23, 1984.

50 See, for example, Grandin, *Empire's Workshop*; Schoultz, *Beneath the United States*; LeoGrande, *Our Own Backyard*; and Loveman, *No Higher Law*.

51 Reagan, Address on Central America, April 27, 1983.

52 Reagan, State of the Union Address, February 6, 1985.

53 Reagan, State of the Union Address, January 27, 1987.

54 See Loveman, *No Higher Law*, 282–83.

55 Stoeltje, "Making," 241. This topic has been widely mined; see, for example, Pfitzer, "Only Good Alien," 61–64.

56 Reagan, State of the Union Address, January 25, 1984.

57 See Teresa Whitfield, *Paying the Price: Ignacio Ellacuria and the Murdered Jesuits of El Salvador* (Philadelphia: Temple University Press, 1994).

58 Hughes, *Myths*, 122. See, in general, the chapter "The Myth of the Millennial Nation," 91–125.

59 See Stephanson, *Manifest Destiny*, 127.

60 Reagan, Address to the Republican National Convention, July 17, 1980.

61 Reagan, Remarks on the Fortieth Anniversary on D-Day, June 6, 1984.

62 This phrasing is common enough to appear in most of the twenty-five speeches I have considered in this chapter. See, for example, Reagan, State of the Union Address, January 26, 1982.

63 These phrases were widely used and spanned the breadth of Reagan's eight years in office. See, for example, Reagan, Address to the Republican National Convention, July 17, 1980; Reagan, First Inaugural Address, January 20, 1981; and Reagan, State of the Union Address, January 26, 1982.

64 See Slotkin, "Nostalgia."

65 Reagan, First Inaugural Address, January 20, 1981.

66 Reagan, Remarks on U.S. Casualties in Lebanon and Grenada, November 4, 1983. Also see Reagan, Address Announcing His Candidacy for Reelection, January 29, 1984; and Reagan, Second Inaugural Address, January 21, 1985.

67 Reagan, State of the Union Address, January 27, 1987.

68 Reagan, Speech to the National Association of Evangelicals, March 8, 1983.

69 Reagan, State of the Union Address, February 6, 1985. Also see Reagan, State of the Union Address, January 27, 1987.

70 Reagan, First Inaugural Address, January 20, 1981.

71 Reagan, State of the Union Address, January 25, 1984.

72 See LeoGrande, *Our Own Backyard*, 311–14, 320–22; and Coerver and Hall, *Tangled Destinies*,166–68.

73 Blum, *Killing Hope*, 292–93.

74 Reagan, Second Inaugural Address, January 21, 1985. Reagan also characterized his presidency as "a second American Revolution…pushing back frontiers." See Reagan, State of the Union Address, February 6, 1985.

75 Reagan, Address to British Parliament, June 8, 1982.

76 LeoGrande, *Our Own Backyard*, 4.

77 Reagan, Address to British Parliament, June 8, 1982.

78 Also see Reagan, Speech to the United Nations General Assembly, June 17, 1982.

79 Reagan, Address to British Parliament, June 8, 1982.

80 Reagan, Speech to the United Nations General Assembly, June 17, 1982.

81 Reagan, State of the Union Address, January 25, 1984.

82 Loveman, *No Higher Law*, 325–27.

83 Reagan, State of the Union Address, January 25, 1984.

84 Reagan, Speech to the National Association of Evangelicals, March 8, 1983.

85 Reagan, Speech to the Conservative Political Action Conference, February 18, 1983.

86 Reagan, State of the Union Address, February 6, 1985.

87 Schmitz, *United States*, 3, 241.

88 Reagan, Speech to the Conservative Political Action Conference, February 18, 1983. Also see Reagan, Remarks on U.S. Casualties in Lebanon and Grenada, November 4, 1983.

89 Reagan, Speech to the National Association of Evangelicals, March 8, 1983.

90 See Schmitz, *United States*, 4.

91 Reagan, State of the Union Address, January 27, 1987.

92 S. O. Lilienfeld et al., "Fearless Dominance and the U.S. Presidency: Implications of Psychopathic Personality Traits for Successful and Unsuccessful Political Leadership," *Journal of Personal Social Psychology* 103, 3 (2012): 489–505. Also see "Psychopathic Traits: What Successful Presidents Have in Common," *Time*, September 11, 2012; and "The Psychopathic Trait Successful Presidents Have in Common," CNN.com, September 13, 2013.

93 Reagan, Farewell Address at the Republican National Convention, August 15, 1988.

94 Reagan, Speech on Foreign Policy, December 16, 1988.

95 Ronald Reagan, Farewell Address, January 11, 1989.

96 Nash et al., *American People*, 914–15.

97 Faragher et al., *Out of Many*, 816.

98 Roark et al., *Understanding*, 844.

99 Davidson et al., *U.S.*, 666.

100 Reagan, State of the Union Address, January 27, 1987.

101 Grandin, *Empire's Workshop*, 5.

102 Reagan, State of the Union Address, January 27, 1987.

103 Reagan, Speech to the National Association of Evangelicals, March 8, 1983.

104 Pfitzer, "Only Good Alien," 51.

105 See Williams, *Empire*.

CHAPTER 8

1 Cited in MacAskill, "God Told Me," *Guardian*, October 7, 2005. The attribution has generated some discussion about the frequency with which Bush made this and similar statements as well as questions about the accuracy of the reporter's notes. See Al Kalem's column in the *Washington Post*, October 13, 2005.

2 Linden MacIntyre, *The Bishop's Man* (Toronto: Vintage Canada, 2010), 382.

3 Eric Hobsbawm, *Nations and Nationalism since 1780* (New York: Cambridge University Press, 1990), 12.

4 The phrase continues to sell novels, as a quick perusal on Amazon.com will demonstrate.

5 Ruiz, *Terror of History*, 61.

6 See ibid., passim.

7 John C. Lyden, *Film as Religion: Myths, Morals, and Rituals* (New York: New York University Press, 2003), 3.

8 Hughes, *Myths*, 87–88.

9 See Williams, *Contours*, 270.

10 Burns, for example, writing pre-9/11, makes a similar case for U.S. behavior in Nicaragua during the 1980s. See Burns, *At War in Nicaragua*, 149. Also see Chomsky, *9-11*.

11 Quoted in Kohn, *Shooters*, 147.

12 Grandin, *Empire's Workshop*, 149.

13 David Crockett, *A Narrative of the Life of David Crockett of the State of Tennessee* (1834; reprinted, Norman: Bison Books, 1987).

14 Mark West and Chris Carey, "(Re)Enacting Frontier Justice: The Bush Administration's Tactical Narration of the Old West Fantasy after September 11," *Quarterly Journal of Speech* 92, 4 (2006): 379.

15 Ibid., 381–86.

16 Mead, "9/11."

17 *Avatar*, dir. James Cameron, 2009.

18 Stephen McVeigh and Matthew Wilhelm Kapell, "Surveying James Cameron's Reluctant Political Commentaries: 1984–2009," in *The Films of James Cameron: Critical Essays*, ed. Matthew Wilhelm Kapell and Stephen McVeigh (Jefferson, NC: McFarland and Company, 2011), 19.

19 Lorenzo Veracini, "*District 9* and *Avatar*: Science Fiction and Settler Colonialism," *Journal of Intercultural Studies* 32, 4 (2011): 364.

20 *Avatar* grossed nearly $2.8 billion; see http://www.boxofficemojo.com.

21 David Denby, "Going Native: *Avatar* and *Sherlock Holmes*," *New Yorker*, January 4, 2010. Also see J. Hoberman, "*Avatar*'s Sticker Shock and Awe,"

Village Voice, December 15, 2009; and Ethan Alter, "Film Review: *Avatar*," *Film Journal*, December 15, 2009.

22 Roger Ebert, "*Avatar*," December 11, 2009, Roger.Ebert.com.

23 Craig Detweiler, "James Cameron's Cathedral: *Avatar* Revives the Religious Spectacle," *Journal of Religion and Film* 14, 1 (2010), https://www.unomaha.edu/jrf/Vol14no1/Reviews/Detweiler_Avatar.html.

24 Carol Linnit, "Film Review: *Avatar*," *Journal of Religion and Film* 14, 1 (2010): https://www.unomaha.edu/jrf/Vol14no1/Reviews/Linnitt_Avatar.html. Also see Joshua M. Moritz, "Science Fiction, *ET*, and the Theological Cosmology of *Avatar*," *Theology and Science* 8, 2 (2010): 131.

25 C. Scott Littleton dates the "goes Native" narrative archetype in *Avatar* to as early as sixteenth-century Yucatán, Mexico. See his "Gonzalo Guerrero and the Maya Resistance to the Spanish Conquistadors: A Sixteenth Century 'Avatar' of *Avatar*," in Kapell and McVeigh, *Films of James Cameron*, 200–15.

26 Cited in Ace G. Pilkington, "Fighting the History Wars on the Big Screen: From *The Terminator* to *Avatar*," in Kapell and McVeigh, *Films of James Cameron*, 63.

27 Mark Cronlund Anderson, *Cowboy Imperialism and Hollywood Film* (New York: Peter Lang, 2007).

28 David Brooks, "The Messiah Complex," *New York Times*, January 7, 2010.

29 See Bruce Baum, "Hollywood on Race in the Age of Obama: *Invictus*, *Precious*, and *Avatar*," *New Political Science* 32, 4 (2010): 630–32.

30 Roger Ebert, "*Dances with Wolves*," November 9, 1990, Roger.Ebert.com.

31 See Kimberly Rosenfeld, "*Terminator* to *Avatar*: A Postmodern Shift," *Jump Cut: A Review of Contemporary Media* 52 (2010), http://www.ejumpcut.org/archive/jc52.2010/RosenfeldAvatar/.

32 Joshua Clover, "The Struggle for Space," *Film Quarterly* 63, 2 (2010): 6.

33 McVeigh and Kapell, "Surveying," 38.

34 Bert Olivier, "*Avatar*: Ecopolitics, Technology, Science, Art, and Myth," *South African Journal of Art History* 25, 3 (2010): 1.

35 Veracini, "*District 9*," 355.

36 McVeigh and Kapell, "Surveying," 37.

37 Peter Travers, "*Avatar*," *Rolling Stone*, December 2009.

38 See McVeigh and Kapell, "Surveying," 18.

39 Slavoj Žižek, in *The Pervert's Guide to Ideology*, dir. Sophie Fiennes, 2013.

40 Richard Corliss simply called this hackneyed plot contrivance "a grunt falls in love with a princess." See his "*Avatar*, a World of Wonder," *Time*, December 14, 2009.

41 Veracini, "*District 9*," 362.

42 Prothero, *American Jesus*, 3–16.

43 Veracini, "*District 9*," 357.

44 Melissa R. Plaufcan, "*Avatar*," *Journal of Feminist Family Therapy* 22, 4 (2010): 317.

45 Veracini, "*District 9*," 361.

46 Clover, "Struggle," 6.

47 John James and Tom Ue, "'I See You': Colonial Narrative and the Act of Seeing in *Avatar*" in Kapell and McVeigh, *Films of James Cameron*, 191.

48 See Lyden, *Film*, 60–63.

49 Corliss, "*Avatar*."

50 Ken Hillis, "From Capital to Karma: James Cameron's *Avatar*," *Postmodern Culture* 19, 3 (2009), http://muse.jhu.edu/login?auth=0&type=summary&url=/journals/postmodern_culture/v019/19.3.hillis.html.

51 "Natural Born Killer Zombie," *Relevant*, April 13, 2009.

52 Poole, *Monsters in America*, 196.

53 Mathias Nilges, "The Aesthetics of Destruction: Contemporary U.S. Cinema and TV Culture," in Birkenstein, Froula, and Randell, *Reframing 9/11*, 24; Anna Froula, "Prolepsis and the 'War on Terror': Zombie Pathology and the Culture of Fear in *28 Days Later…*," in Birkenstein, Froula, and Randell, *Reframing 9/11*, 195.

54 Daniel W. Drezner, *Theories of International Politics and Zombies* (Princeton: Princeton University Press, 2011), 4. Also see Shawn McIntosh and Marc Leverette, eds., *Zombie Culture: Autopsies of the Living Dead* (Lanham, MD: Scarecrow Press); Kevin J. Wetmore, *Post-9/11 Horror in American Cinema* (New York: Continuum, 2012); and Birkenstein, Froula, and Randell, *Reframing 9/11*.

55 Aviva Briefel and Sam J. Miller, eds., *Horror after 9/11: World of Fear, Cinema of Terror* (Austin: University of Texas Press, 2011), 1.

56 Ibid., 4.

57 Terence McSweeney, "The *Land of the Dead* and the Home of the Brave: Romero's Vision of a Post-9/11 America," in Birkenstein, Froula, and Randell, *Reframing 9/11*, 115.

58 Laura Frost, "Black Screens, Lost Bodies: The Cinematic Apparatus of 9/11 Horror," in Briefel and Miller, *Horror after 9/11*, 34.

59 Henry A. Giroux, *Zombie Politics and Culture in the Age of Casino Capitalism* (New York: Peter Lang, 2011), 2.

60 Asma, *On Monsters*, 241.

61 Cawelti, *Six-Gun Mystique*, 9.

62 Drezner, *Theories*, 14.

63 Robert Kirkman et al., *The Walking Dead: Compendium One* (Berkeley: Image Comics, 2013).

64 Erin Overbey, "*The Walking Dead* Returns," *New Yorker*, October 12, 2012, http://www.newyorker.com/books/double-take/the-walking-dead-returns.

65 Steven Schlozman, "Zombies on the Great Frontier," *Psychology Today*, April 9, 2012, https://www.psychologytoday.com/blog/grand-rounds/201204/zombies-the-great-frontier.

66 Asma, *On Monsters*, 23.

67 Shelley S. Rees, "Frontier Values Meet Big-City Zombies: The Old West in AMC's *The Walking Dead*," in *Undead in the West: Vampires, Zombies, Mummies, and Ghosts on the Cinematic* Frontier, ed. Cynthia J. Miller and A. Bowdoin Van Riper (Lanham, MD: Scarecrow Press, 2012), 80–81.

68 If you interpret the zombies as so many Indian stand-ins, then Rick's violence may be seen as adhering to the Bush Doctrine, that is, preemptive.

69 Wetmore, *Post-9/11 Horror*, 163.

70 Schlozman, "Zombies."

71 It is not a one-way street. Other films, demonstrating the wide-ranging ideological utility of the frontier myth, such as Kevin Costner's 2003 *Open Range*, reverse this equation.

72 E. P. Thompson, *The Making of the English Working Class* (New York: Vintage, 1966).

73 Pike, *United States and Latin America*, 157.

74 Stephanson, *Manifest Destiny*, 8.

75 Williams, *Empire*, 109.

76 Žižek, in *Pervert's Guide*.

REFERENCES

Adams, Kevin. *Class and Race in the Frontier Army: Military Life in the West, 1870–1890*. Norman: University of Oklahoma Press, 2009.

Alger, Horatio. *Ragged Dick: Or, Street Life in New York with the Boot-Blacks.* 1868; reprinted, New York: Createspace Independent Publishing, 2012.

Alter, Ethan. "Film Review: *Avatar.*" *Film Journal*, December 15, 2009.

Altheide, David. "Fear, Terrorism, and Popular Culture." In Birkenstein, Froula, and Randell, *Reframing 9/11*, 11–22.

Anderson, Benedict. *Imagined Communities: Reflections on the Origin and Spread of Nationalism*. New York: Verso, 2006.

Anderson, Mark Cronlund. *Cowboy Imperialism and Hollywood Film*. New York: Peter Lang, 2007.

——. "The Mythical Frontier, the Mexican Revolution, and the Press: An Imperial Subplot." *Canadian Review of American Studies* 37, 1 (2007): 1–22.

——. *Pancho Villa's Revolution by Headlines*. Norman: University of Oklahoma Press, 2001.

Anton, Frank, and Tommy Denton. *Why Didn't You Get Me Out? A POW's Nightmare in Vietnam*. New York: St. Martin's Press, 2000.

Armitage, Susan, and Elizabeth Jameson, eds. *The Women's West*. Norman: University of Oklahoma Press, 1987.

Asma, Stephen T. *On Monsters: An Unnatural History of Our Worst Fears*. New York: Oxford University Press, 2009.

Baard, Erik. "George Bush Ain't No Cowboy." *Village Voice*, September 21, 2004.

Bacevich, Andrew J. *The New American Militarism: How Americans Are Seduced by War*. New York: Oxford University Press, 2013.

Barilleaux, Ryan, and Christopher S. Kelley, eds. *The Unitary Executive and the Modern Presidency*. Houston: Texas A&M Press, 2010.

Barthes, Roland. *Mythologies*. New York: Farrar, Straus, and Giroux, 1972.

Bartholet, Jeffrey. "Alaska: Oil's Ground Zero." *Newsweek*, August 13, 2001.

Bauer, K. Jack. *The Mexican War, 1846–1848*. Lincoln: University of Nebraska Press, 1992.

Baum, Bruce. "Hollywood on Race in the Age of Obama: *Invictus, Precious,* and *Avatar.*" *New Political Science* 32, 4 (2010): 627–36.

Berkhofer, Robert F. *The White Man's Indian: Images of the American Indian from Columbus to the Present*. New York: Vintage, 1979.

Bhabha, Homi, ed. *Nation and Narration*. New York: Routledge, 1990.

Billington, Ray Allen, ed. *The Frontier Thesis: Valid Interpretation of American History?* New York: Holt, Rinehart, and Winston, 1966.

Bird, S. Elizabeth, ed. *Dressing in Feathers: The Construction of the Indian in American Popular Culture*. Boulder, CO: Westview Press, 1996.

Birkenstein, Jeff, Anna Froula, and Karen Randell, eds. *Reframing 9/11: Film, Popular Culture and the "War on Terror."* New York: Continuum, 2010.

Bliss, Michael. "Guarding a Most Famous Stream: Trudeau and the Canadian Political Tradition." In *Trudeau's Shadow: The Life and Legacy of Pierre Elliott Trudeau*, edited by Andrew Cohen and Jack L. Granatstein, 9–19. Toronto: Vintage Canada, 1999.

Blum, William. *Killing Hope: U.S. Military and CIA Interventions since World War II*. Monroe, ME: Common Courage Press, 2004.

Boatright, Mody. "On the Nature of Myth." In *Mody Boatright: Folklorist*, edited by Ernest B. Speck, 108–14. Austin: Texas Folklore Society, 1973.

Bonilla-Silva, Eduardo. *Racism without Racists: Color-Blind Racism and the Persistence of Racial Inequality in America*. New York: Rowman and Littlefield, 2009.

Booth, John A., and Thomas W. Walker, *Understanding Central America*. Boulder, CO: Westview Press, 1993.

Bostdorff, Denise M. *The Presidency and the Rhetoric of Foreign Crisis*. Columbus: University of South Carolina Press, 1994.

Breisach, Ernst. *Historiography: Ancient, Medieval, and Modern*. Chicago: University of Chicago Press, 2007.

Briefel, Aviva, and Sam J. Miller, eds. *Horror after 9/11: World of Fear, Cinema of Terror*. Austin: University of Texas Press, 2011.

Britton, John A. *Revolution and Ideology: Images of the Mexican Revolution in the United States*. Lexington: University of Kentucky Press, 1995.

Brooks, David. "The Messiah Complex." *New York Times*, January 7, 2010.

Brown, Dee. *Bury My Heart at Wounded Knee*. New York: Henry Holt, 1993.

Brown, Meredith Mason. *Frontiersman: Daniel Boone and the Making of America*. Baton Rouge: Louisiana State University Press, 2008.

Burns, E. Bradford. *At War in Nicaragua: The Reagan Doctrine and the Politics of Nostalgia*. New York: Harper and Row, 1987.

Burroughs, Edgar Rice. *Tarzan of the Apes*. 1912; reprinted, New York: Oxford University Press, 2010.

Burstyn, Varda. *The Rites of Men: Manhood, Politics, and the Culture of Sport*. Toronto: University of Toronto Press, 1999.

Calabresi, Steven G., and Christopher S. Yoo. *The Unitary Executive: Presidential Power from Washington to Bush*. New Haven, CT: Yale University Press, 2008.

Campbell, Joseph. *Myths to Live By*. New York: Arkana, 1993.

Caputo, Philip. *A Rumor of War*. New York: Henry Holt, 1996.

Carpenter, Ronald H. "America's Tragic Metaphor: Our Twentieth-Century Combatants as Frontiersmen." *Quarterly Journal of Speech* 76, 1 (1990): 1–22.

Carter, Kent. *The Dawes Commission and the Allotment of the Five Civilized Tribes, 1893–1914*. New York: Ancestry Publishing, 1999.

Cawelti, John G. *The Six-Gun Mystique Sequel*. New York: Popular Press, 1999.

Certeau, Michel de. *The Writing of History*. New York: Columbia University Press, 1992.

Chávez, Ernesto. *The U.S. War with Mexico: A Brief History with Documents*. New York: Bedford/St. Martin's Press, 2008.

Cheyfitz, Eric. *The Poetics of Imperialism: Translation and Colonization from The Tempest to Tarzan*. New York: Oxford University Press, 1991.

Chomsky, Noam. *Hegemony or Survival: America's Quest for Global Dominance*. New York: Henry Holt, 2004.

———. *9-11: Was There an Alternative*. New York: Seven Stories Press, 2011.

Churchill, Ward. *Kill the Indian, Save the Man: The Genocidal Impact of American Indian Residential Schools*. San Francisco: City Lights Publishers, 2004.

Clarke, Colin A. "Like a Mirror Reflecting Itself: Natty Bumppo, *The Virginian*, and the Fate of the American Frontier." Paper presented at the Eleventh Cooper Seminar, State University of New York College at Oneonta, July 1997.

Clary, David A. *Eagles and Empire: The United States, Mexico, and the Struggle for a Continent*. New York: Bantam, 2009.

Clendenen, Clarence. *The United States and Pancho Villa: A Study in Unconventional Diplomacy*. Ithaca, NY: Cornell University Press, 1961.

Clover, Joshua. "The Struggle for Space." *Film Quarterly* 63, 2 (2010): 6–7.

Cobb, William W. *The American Foundation Myth in Vietnam: Reigning Paradigms and Raining Bombs*. Lanham, MD: University Press of America, 1998.

Coerver, Don M., and Linda B. Hall. *Tangled Destinies: Latin America and the United States*. Albuquerque: University of New Mexico Press, 1999.

Cohen, Daniel J. "By the Book: Assessing the Place of Textbooks in U.S. Survey Courses." *Journal of American History* 91, 4 (2005): 1405–15.

Corliss, Richard. "*Avatar*, a World of Wonder." *Time*, December 14, 2009.

Cott, Nancy F. *The Bonds of Womanhood: "Woman's Sphere" in New England, 1780–1835*. New Haven, CT: Yale University Press, 1977.

Coward, John. *The Newspaper Indian: Native American Identity in the Press, 1820–90*. Urbana: University of Illinois Press, 1999.

Cowart, David. "The Tarzan Myth and Jung's Genesis of the Self." *Journal of American Culture* 2, 2 (1979): 220–30.

Crandall, Russell. *Gunboat Democracy: U.S. Interventions in the Dominican Republic, Grenada, and Panama*. New York: Rowman and Littlefield, 2006.

Crockett, David. *A Narrative of the Life of David Crockett of the State of Tennessee*. 1834; reprinted, Norman: Bison Books, 1987.

Custer, George A. *My Life on the Plains: Or, Personal Experiences with Indians*. 1874; reprinted, n.p.: Leonaur, 2009.

Dary, David. *Cowboy Culture: A Saga of Five Centuries*. Lawrence: University of Kansas Press, 1989.

Davidson, James West, Brian DeLay, Christine Leigh Heyrman, Mark H. Lytle, and Michael B. Stoff. *U.S.: A Narrative History*. 2nd ed. New York: McGraw Hill, 2012.

Davis, John W. *Wyoming Range War: The Infamous Invasion of Johnson County*. Norman: University of Oklahoma Press, 2012.

Deloria, Vine, Jr. *Custer Died for Your Sins: An Indian Manifesto*. Norman: University of Oklahoma Press, 1988.

———. *The Indian Reorganization Act: Congresses and Bills*. Norman: University of Oklahoma Press, 2002.

DeMause, Lloyd. *The Emotional Life of Nations*. New York: Other Press, 2002.

Demos, John. *The Unredeemed Captive: A Family Story from Early America*. New York: Vintage, 1995.

Denby, David. "Going Native: *Avatar* and *Sherlock Holmes*." *New Yorker*, January 4, 2010.

Dent, David W. *The Legacy of the Monroe Doctrine: A Reference Guide to U.S. Involvement in Latin America and the Caribbean*. Westport, CT: Greenwood Press, 1999.

de Orellana, Margarita. *Filming Pancho Villa: How Hollywood Shaped the Mexican Revolution*. New York: Verso, 2004.

Derounian-Stodola, Kathryn Zabelle. *Women's Indian Captivity Narratives*. New York: Penguin, 1998.

Detweiler, Craig. "James Cameron's Cathedral: *Avatar* Revives the Religious Spectacle." *Journal of Religion and Film* 14, 1 (2010), https://www.unomaha.edu/jrf/Vol14no1/Reviews/Detweiler_Avatar.html.

Diamond, Stephen. "Secrets of Psychotherapy: Repetitive Relationship Patterns." *Psychology Today*, September 14, 2008.

DiConsiglio, John. *Living through the Mexican-American War*. Chicago: Heinemann, 2012.

Dittmar, Linda, and Gene Michaud, eds. *From Hanoi to Hollywood: The Vietnam War in American Film*. New Brunswick, NJ: Rutgers University Press, 1990.

Dowell, Pat. "The Mythology of the Western: Hollywood Perspectives on Race and Gender in the Nineties." *Cineaste* 21, 1–2 (1995): 6–10.

Drezner, Daniel W. *Theories of International Politics and Zombies*. Princeton, NJ: Princeton University Press, 2011.

Eagleton, Terry. *Holy Terror*. New York: Oxford University Press, 2005.

Ebert, Roger. "*Avatar*." December 11, 2009. Roger.Ebert.com.

———. "*Dances with Wolves*." November 9, 1990. Roger.Ebert.com.

———. "*Red River*." March 1, 1998. rogerebert.suntimes.com.

Eisenhower, John S. D. *Intervention! The United States and the Mexican Revolution, 1913–1917*. New York: W. W. Norton, 1995.

———. *So Far from God: The U.S. War with Mexico, 1846–1848*. Norman: University of Oklahoma Press, 2000.

Elliott, Michael A. *Custerology: The Enduring Legacy of the Indian Wars and George Armstrong Custer*. Chicago: University of Chicago Press, 2007.

Erikson, Erik H. *Childhood and Society*. New York: W. W. Norton, 1993.

Faragher, John Mack, Mari Jo Buhle, Daniel Czitrom, and Susan H. Armitage. *Out of Many: A History of the American People*. 6th ed. New York: Prentice-Hall, 2011.

Finan, Christopher M. *From the Palmer Raids to the Patriot Act: A History of the Fight for Free Speech in America*. Boston: Beacon Press, 2007.

Foner, Eric. *Reconstruction: America's Unfinished Revolution, 1863–1877*. New York: Harper Perennial Modern Classic, 2001.

Foos, Paul. *A Short, Offhand Killing Affair: Soldiers and Social Conflict during the Mexican-American War*. Chapel Hill: University of North Carolina Press, 2002.

Fraiberg, Selma H. *The Magic Years: Understanding and Handling the Problems of Early Childhood*. New York: Scribner, 1996.

Fraiberg, Selma, S. Adelson, and E. Shapiro. "Ghosts in the Nursery: A Psychoanalytic Approach to the Problems of Impaired Infant-Mother Relationships." *Journal of the American Academy of Child and Adolescent Psychiatry* 14, 3 (1975): 387–421.

Francis, Daniel. *The Imaginary Indian: The Image of the Indian in Canadian Culture*. Vancouver: Arsenal Pulp Press, 2012.

Freud, Sigmund. *Beyond the Pleasure Principle*. Translated by James Strachey. 1920; reprinted, New York: Createspace Independent Publishing, 2010.

———. *Civilization and Its Discontents*. 1930; reprinted, New York: Martino Publishing, 2010.

Frost, Laura. "Black Screens, Lost Bodies: The Cinematic Apparatus of 9/11 Horror." In Briefel and Miller, *Horror after 9/11*, 13–39.

Froula, Anna. "Prolepsis and the 'War on Terror': Zombie Pathology and the Culture of Fear in *28 Days Later…*." In Birkenstein, Froula, and Randell, *Reframing 9/11*, 195–208.

Fuller, Graham. "Sending Out a Search Party for the Western." *New York Times*, March 5, 2000.

Furniss, Elizabeth. *The Burden of History: Colonialism and the Frontier Myth in a Rural Canadian Community*. Vancouver: UBC Press, 2000.

Geertz, Clifford. *The Interpretation of Cultures*. New York: Basic Books, 1977.

Giroux, Henry A. *Zombie Politics and Culture in the Age of Casino Capitalism*. New York: Peter Lang, 2011.

Gobat, Michel. *Confronting the American Dream: Nicaragua under U.S. Imperial Rule*. Durham: Duke University Press, 2005.

Graham-Yooll, Andrew. *Imperial Skirmishes: War and Gunboat Diplomacy in Latin America*. Northampton, MA: Olive Branch Press, 2002.

Grandin, Greg. *Empire's Workshop: Latin America, the United States, and the Rise of the New Imperialism*. New York: Henry Holt, 2007.

Graziano, Frank. *Wounds of Love: The Mystical Marriage of Saint Rose of Lima*. New York: Oxford University Press, 2004.

Greene, Jerome A. *Washita: The U.S. Army and the Southern Cheyennes, 1867–1869*. Norman: University of Oklahoma Press, 2008.

Grossman, Richard. "The Nation Is Our Mother: Augusto Sandino and the Construction of a Peasant Nationalism in Nicaragua, 1927–1934." *Journal of Peasant Studies* 35, 1 (2008): 80–89.

Grow, Michael. *U.S. Presidents and Latin American Interventions: Pursuing Regime Change in the Cold War*. Lawrence: University of Kansas Press, 2008.

Gwynne, S. C. *Empire of the Summer Moon: Quanah Parker and the Rise and Fall of the Comanches, the Most Powerful Indian Tribe in American History*. New York: Scribner, 2011.

Hagedorn, Ann. *Savage Peace: Hope and Fear in America, 1919*. New York: Simon and Schuster, 2008.

Hall, Stuart, ed. *Representation: Cultural Representations and Signifying Practices*. Thousand Oaks, CA: SAGE, 1997.

Harmon, Gary L. Review of *John Wayne's America: The Politics of Celebrity*, by Garry Wills. H-Net Reviews in the Humanities and Social Sciences, https://www.h-net.org/reviews/showpdf.php?id=3149.

Harris, Larry A. *Pancho Villa and the Columbus Raid*. Whitefish, MT: Kessinger Publishing, 2010.

Harvey, David. *The New Imperialism*. New York: Oxford University Press, 2003.

Hellmann, John. *American Myth and the Legacy of Vietnam*. New York: Columbia University Press, 1991.

Henderson, Timothy J. *A Glorious Defeat: Mexico and Its War with the United States.* New York: Farrar, Straus, and Giroux, 2007.

Hendon, Bill, and Elizabeth A. Stewart. *An Enormous Crime: The Definitive Account of American POWs Abandoned in Southeast Asia.* New York: St. Martin's Press, 2008.

Hillis, Ken. "From Capital to Karma: James Cameron's *Avatar.*" *Postmodern Culture* 19, 3 (2009), http://muse.jhu.edu/login?auth=0&type= summary&url=/journals/postmodern_culture/v019/19.3.hillis.html.

Hinds, Harold E. "Mexican and Mexican-American Images in the Western Novels of Louis L'Amour." *Latin American Literary Review* 5, 10 (1977): 129–41.

Hirsch, Stacey. "Reagan Presidency Pivotal for Unions, Workers: Organized Labor's Situation Worsened under His Administration." *Baltimore Sun*, June 8, 2004.

Hoberman, J. "*Avatar*'s Sticker Shock and Awe." *Village Voice*, December 15, 2010.

Hobsbawm, Eric. *Nations and Nationalism since 1780.* New York: Cambridge University Press, 1990.

Hodgson, Godfrey. *The Myth of American Exceptionalism.* New Haven, CT: Yale University Press, 2010.

Horsman, Reginald. *Race and Manifest Destiny: The Origins of American Racial Anglo-Saxonism.* Cambridge, MA: Harvard University Press, 1986.

Howell, Martha C., and Walter Prevenier. *From Reliable Sources: An Introduction to Historical Methods.* Ithaca, NY: Cornell University Press, 2001.

Hughes, Richard T. *Myths America Lives By.* Urbana: University of Illinois Press, 2004.

Iggers, Georg G. *Historiography in the Twentieth Century: From Scientific Objectivity to the Postmodern Challenge.* Middletown, CT: Wesleyan University Press, 2005.

Iyengar, Shanto, and Richard Reeves, eds. *Do the Media Govern? Politicians, Voters, and Reporters in America.* Los Angeles: SAGE, 1997.

James, John, and Tom Ue. "'I See You': Colonial Narrative and the Act of Seeing in *Avatar.*" In Kapell and McVeigh, *Films of James Cameron*, 186–99.

Johannsen, Robert W. *To the Halls of the Montezumas: The Mexican War in the American Imagination.* New York: Oxford University Press, 1988.

Johnson, Chalmers. *Blowback: The Costs and Consequences of American Empire.* New York: Holt Paperbacks, 2007.

———. *The Sorrows of Empire: Militarism, Secrecy, and the End of the Republic.* New York: Holt Paperbacks, 2004.

Johnson, John J. *Latin America in Caricature.* Austin: University of Texas Press, 1993.

Kapell, Matthew Wilhelm, and Stephen McVeigh, eds. *The Films of James Cameron: Critical Essays*. Jefferson, NC: McFarland and Company, 2011.

Katz, Friedrich. *The Life and Times of Pancho Villa*. Stanford: Stanford University Press, 1998.

———. "Pancho Villa and the Attack on Columbus, New Mexico." *American Historical Review* 83, 1 (1978): 101–30.

Keenan, Jerry. *Encyclopedia of American Indian Wars, 1492–1890*. New York: Norton, 1999.

Kenworthy, Eldon. *America/Américas: Myth in the Making of U.S. Policy toward Latin America*. University Park: Pennsylvania State University Press, 1995.

Kinzer, Stephen. *Overthrow: America's Century of Regime Change from Hawaii to Iraq*. New York: Henry Holt, 2006.

Kirkman, Robert, Charlie Adlard, Tony Moore, and Cliff Rathburn. *The Walking Dead: Compendium One*. Berkeley: Image Comics, 2013.

Knight, Alan. *The Mexican Revolution*. 2 vols. New York: Oxford University Press, 1990.

Kohn, Abigail A. *Shooters: Myths and Realities of America's Gun Cultures*. New York: Oxford University Press, 2004.

Krauze, Enrique. *Biografía del poder, 2: Francisco I. Madero, místico de la libertad*. Mexico City: Fondo de Cultura Económica, 1987.

———. *Biografía del poder, 5: Venustiano Carranza, puente entre siglos*. Mexico City: Fondo de Cultura Económica, 1987.

———. *Mexico: Biography of Power*. New York: Harper Perennial, 1998.

L'Amour, Louis. *Hondo*. 1953; reprinted, New York: Bantam Books, 1983.

Langford, Barry. *Film Genre: Hollywood and Beyond*. Edinburgh: Edinburgh University Press, 2006.

Langley, Lester D., and Thomas Schoonover. *The Banana Men: American Mercenaries and Entrepreneurs in Central America, 1880–1930*. Lexington: University of Kentucky Press, 1995.

Lapham, Lewis. "Ignorance of Things Past." *Harper's*, May 2012.

LeoGrande, William M. *Our Own Backyard: The United States in Central America, 1977–1992*. Chapel Hill: University of North Carolina Press, 1998.

Leverenz, David. "The Last Real Man in America: From Natty Bumppo to Batman." *American Literary History* 3, 4 (1991): 753–81.

Levine, Allan. *Scrum Wars: The Prime Ministers and the Media*. Toronto: Dundurn, 1996.

Lilienfeld, S. O., I. D. Waldman, K. Landfield, A. L. Watts, S. Rubenzer, and T. R. Faschingbauer. "Fearless Dominance and the U.S. Presidency: Implications of Psychopathic Personality Traits for Successful and Unsuccessful Political Leadership." *Journal of Personal Social Psychology* 103, 3 (2012): 489–505.

Limerick, Patricia Nelson. *The Legacy of Conquest: The Unbroken Past of the American West*. New York: W. W. Norton, 1987.

——. *The Real West*. Boulder: University of Colorado Press, 1996.

——. "Turnerians All: The Dream of a Helpful History in an Intelligible World." *American Historical Review* 100, 3 (1995): 697–715.

Linnit, Carol. "Film Review: *Avatar*." *Journal of Religion and Film* 14, 1 (2010), https://www.unomaha.edu/jrf/Vol14no1/Reviews/Linnitt_Avatar.html.

Littleton, C. Scott. "Gonzalo Guerrero and the Maya Resistance to the Spanish Conquistadors: A Sixteenth Century 'Avatar' of *Avatar*." In Kapell and McVeigh, *Films of James Cameron*, 200–15.

Litwack, Leon F. *Trouble in Mind: Black Southerners in the Age of Jim Crow*. New York: Vintage, 1999.

Loveman, Brian. *No Higher Law: American Foreign Policy and the Western Hemisphere since 1776*. Chapel Hill: University of North Carolina Press, 2012.

Lyden, John C. *Film as Religion: Myths, Morals, and Rituals*. New York: New York University Press, 2003.

MacAskill, Ewen. "God Told Me to End the Tyranny in Iraq." *Guardian*, October 7, 2005.

Machado, Manuel A. *Centaur of the North: Francisco Villa, the Mexican Revolution, and Northern Mexico*. Austin: Eakin Press, 1988.

MacIntyre, Linden. *The Bishop's Man*. Toronto: Vintage Canada, 2010.

Malpas, Simon. *The Postmodern*. New York: Routledge, 2005.

McCartin, Joseph A. "The Strike that Busted Unions." *New York Times*, August 2, 2011.

McCombs, Maxwell. *Setting the Agenda: The News Media and Public Opinion*. Cambridge, UK: Polity Press, 2004.

McCombs, Maxwell, Donald L. Shaw, and David Weaver, eds. *Communication and Democracy: Exploring the Intellectual Frontiers in Agenda-Setting Theory*. Mahwah, NJ: Lawrence Erlbaum Associates, 1997.

McDonald, Forrest. "Rugged Individualism: Frederick Jackson Turner, and the Frontier Thesis." *The World and I* (May 1990): 539–51.

McFarlane, Robert B. "Provoking War: An American Repetition Compulsion." *Journal of Psychohistory* 35, 2 (2007): 175–81.

McIntosh, Shawn, and Marc Leverette, eds. *Zombie Culture: Autopsies of the Living Dead*. Lanham, MD: Scarecrow Press, 2008.

McSweeney, Terence. "The *Land of the Dead* and the Home of the Brave: Romero's Vision of a Post-9/11 America." In Birkenstein, Froula, and Randell, *Reframing 9/11*, 107–16.

McVeigh, Stephen, and Matthew Wilhelm Kapell. "Surveying James Cameron's Reluctant Political Commentaries: 1984–2009." In Kapell and McVeigh, *The Films of James Cameron*, 15–43.

Mead, John. "9/11, Manhood, Mourning, and the American Romance." In Birkenstein, Froula, and Randell, *Reframing 9/11*, 57–68.

Merington, Marguerite, ed. *The Custer Story: The Life and Intimate Letters of General George A. Custer and His Wife Elizabeth*. Lincoln: University of Nebraska Press, 1987.

Merry, Robert W. *A Country of Vast Designs: James K. Polk, the Mexican War, and the Conquest of the American Continent*. New York: Simon and Schuster, 2009.

Meyer, Carter Jones, and Diana Royer, eds. *Selling the Indian: Commercializing and Appropriating American Indian Cultures*. Tucson: University of Arizona Press, 2001.

Meyer, Michael C., William L. Sherman, and Susan M. Deeds. *The Course of Mexican History*. New York: Oxford University Press, 2006.

Midgley, Mary. *The Myths We Live By*. London: Routledge, 2011.

Mihesuah, Devon A. *Natives and Academics: Researching and Writing about American Indians*. Lincoln: University of Nebraska Press, 1998.

Millman, Chad, and Shawn Coyne. *The Ones Who Hit the Hardest: The Steelers, the Cowboys, the '70s, and the Fight for America's Soul*. New York: Gotham Books, 2010.

Mills, Charles W. *The Racial Contract*. Ithaca, NY: Cornell University Press, 1999.

Mitchell, Lee Clark. *Westerns: Making the Man in Fiction and Film*. Chicago: University of Chicago Press, 1998.

Moritz, Joshua M. "Science Fiction, *ET*, and the Theological Cosmology of *Avatar*." *Theology and Science* 8, 2 (2010): 127–31.

Mortimer, Barbara. *Hollywood's Frontier Captives: Cultural Anxiety and the Captivity Plot in American Film*. New York: Routledge, 1999.

Nash, Gary B., Julie Roy Jeffrey, John R. Howe, Allan M. Winkler, Allen F. Davis, Charlene Mires, Peter J. Frederick, and Carla Gardina Pestana. *The American People: Creating a Nation and a Society*. Concise 7th ed. New York: Prentice-Hall, 2011.

Nilges, Mathias. "The Aesthetics of Destruction: Contemporary U.S. Cinema and TV Culture." In Birkenstein, Froula, and Randell, *Reframing 9/11*, 23–34.

Nugent, Walter. *Habits of Empire: A History of American Expansion*. New York: Alfred A. Knopf, 2008.

Olivier, Bert. "*Avatar*: Ecopolitics, Technology, Science, Art, and Myth." *South African Journal of Art History* 25, 3 (2010): 1–16.

O'Sullivan, John L. "Annexation." *United States Democratic Review* 17, 1 (1845): 5–10.

Overbey, Erin. "*The Walking Dead* Returns." *New Yorker*, October 12, 2012. http://www.newyorker.com/books/double-take/the-walking-dead-returns.

Owen, James P. *Cowboy Ethics*. Ketchum, ID: Stoecklein Publishing, 2005.

———. *Cowboy Values: Recapturing What America Once Stood For*. Guilford, CT: Lyons Press, 2008.

Paige, Jeffery M. *Coffee and Power: Revolution and the Rise of Democracy in Central America*. Cambridge, MA: Harvard University Press, 1997.

Pascoe, Peggy. *Relations of Rescue: The Search for Female Moral Authority in the American West, 1874–1939*. New York: Oxford University Press, 1993.

Pfitzer, Gregory M. "The Only Good Alien Is a Dead Alien: Science Fiction and the Metaphysics of Indian-Hating on the High Frontier." *Journal of American Culture* 18, 1 (1995): 51–67.

Pike, Fredrick B. *The United States and Latin America: Myths and Stereotypes of Civilization and Nature*. Austin: University of Texas Press, 1992.

Pilkington, Ace G. "Fighting the History Wars on the Big Screen: From *The Terminator* to *Avatar*." In Kapell and McVeigh, *Films of James Cameron*, 44–71.

Plaufcan, Melissa R. "*Avatar*." *Journal of Feminist Family Therapy* 22, 4 (2010): 314–17.

Pomeroy, Earle. "Toward a Reorientation of Western History." *Mississippi Valley Historical Review* 41 (1955): 579–600.

Ponker, Steven. "Disasters Galore." Review of *Nostradamus: The Prophecies*, translated by Richard Sieburth. *London Review of Books*, September 27, 2012.

Poole, W. Scott. *Monsters in America: Our Historical Obsession with the Hideous and the Haunting*. Waco, TX: Baylor University Press, 2011.

Powers, Thomas. *The Killing of Crazy Horse*. New York: Knopf, 2010.

Pratt, Richard Henry. *Battlefield and Classroom: Four Decades with the American Indian, 1867–1904*. Edited by Robert M. Utley. Norman: University of Oklahoma Press, 2003.

"Presidential Approval Ratings History." *Wall Street Journal*, http://online.wsj.com/public/resources/documents/info-presapp0605-31.html.

Presnell, Jenny S. *The Information-Literate Historian: A Guide to Research for History Students*. New York: Oxford University Press, 2006.

Progoff, Iga. "Waking Dream and Living Myth." In *Myths, Dreams, and Religion*, edited by Joseph Campbell, 176–95. New York: Dutton, 1970.

Prothero, Stephen. *American Jesus: How the Son of God Became a National Icon*. New York: Farrar, Straus, and Giroux, 2003.

"The Psychopathic Trait Successful Presidents Have in Common." CNN.com, September 13, 2013.

"Psychopathic Traits: What Successful Presidents Have in Common." *Time*, September 11, 2012.

Raphael, Ray. *Founding Myths: Stories that Hide Our Patriotic Past*. New York: New Press, 2004.

Rather, Dan. *Rather Outspoken: My Life in the News.* New York: Grand Central Publishing, 2012.

Reed, John. *Insurgent Mexico.* 1914; reprinted, New York: International Publishers, 1965.

Rees, Shelley S. "Frontier Values Meet Big-City Zombies: The Old West in AMC's *The Walking Dead.*" In *Undead in the West: Vampires, Zombies, Mummies, and Ghosts on the Cinematic* Frontier, edited by Cynthia J. Miller and A. Bowdoin Van Riper, 80–94. Lanham, MD: Scarecrow Press, 2012.

Reilly, Hugh J. *The Frontier Newspapers and the Coverage of the Plains Indian Wars.* Denver: Praeger, 2010.

Richmond, Douglas W. *Venustiano Carranza's Nationalist Struggle, 1893–1920.* Lincoln: University of Nebraska Press, 1984.

Roark, James L., Michael P. Johnson, Patricia Cline Cohen, Sarah Stage, Alan Lawson, and Susan M. Hartmann. *Understanding the American Promise: A Brief History.* New York: Bedford/St. Martin's Press, 2011.

Rollins, Peter C., ed. *Hollywood as Historian: American Film in a Cultural Context.* Lexington: University of Kentucky Press, 1997.

Rollins, Peter C., and John E. O'Connor, eds. *Hollywood's Indian: The Portrayal of the Native American in Film.* Lexington: University of Kentucky Press, 2003.

Rosaldo, Renato. "Imperialist Nostalgia." *Representations* 26 (1989): 107–22.

Rosenfeld, Kimberly. "*Terminator* to *Avatar*: A Postmodern Shift." *Jump Cut: A Review of Contemporary Media* 52 (2010), http://www.ejumpcut.org/archive/jc52.2010/RosenfeldAvatar/.

Ruiz, Teofilo F. *The Terror of History: On the Uncertainties of Life in Western Civilization.* Princeton, NJ: Princeton University Press, 2011.

Said, Edward W. *Covering Islam: How the Media and the Experts Determine How We See the Rest of the World.* New York: Vintage, 1997.

———. *Culture and Imperialism.* New York: Vintage, 1994.

Schechter, Harold, and Jonna G. Semeiks. "Leatherstocking in 'Nam: Rambo, *Platoon*, and the American Frontier Myth." *Journal of Popular Culture* 24, 4 (1991): 17–25.

Schlozman, Steven. "Zombies on the Great Frontier." *Psychology Today*, April 9, 2012. https://www.psychologytoday.com/blog/grand-rounds/201204/zombies-the-great- frontier.

Schmitz, David F. *The United States and Right-Wing Dictatorships.* New York: Cambridge University Press, 2006.

Schoultz, Lars. *Beneath the United States: A History of U.S. Policy toward Latin America.* Cambridge, MA: Harvard University Press, 1998.

Seed, Patricia. *Ceremonies of Possession in Europe's Conquest of the New World, 1492–1640.* New York: Cambridge University Press, 1995.

Shannon, Fred. "A Post-Mortem on the Labor–Safety Valve Theory." *Agricultural History* 19 (1945): 31–37.

Shlapentokh, Vladimir, Joshua Woods, and Eric Shiraev, eds. *America: Sovereign Defender or Cowboy Nation?* London: Ashgate, 2005.

Siecienski, A. Edward. *The Filioque: History of a Doctrinal Controversy.* New York: Oxford University Press, 2010.

Simons, Geoff. *Vietnam Syndrome: Impact on U.S. Foreign Policy.* New York: Palgrave Macmillan, 1998.

Slotkin, Richard. *Gunfighter Nation: The Myth of the Frontier in Twentieth-Century America.* Norman: University of Oklahoma Press, 1998.

———. "Nostalgia and Progress: Theodore Roosevelt's Myth of the Frontier." *American Quarterly* 33, 5 (1981): 608–37.

———. *Regeneration through Violence: The Mythology of the American Frontier, 1600–1860.* Norman: University of Oklahoma Press, 2000.

Smith, Paul Chaat. *Everything You Know about Indians Is Wrong.* Minneapolis: University of Minnesota Press, 2009.

Smith, Carlton. *Coyote Kills John Wayne: Postmodernism and Contemporary Fictions of the Transcultural Frontier.* Hanover, MA: University of New England Press, 2000.

Smith, Christian. *Resisting Reagan: The U.S. Central America Peace Movement.* Chicago: University of Chicago Press, 1996.

Smith, Henry Nash. *Virgin Land: The American West as Symbol and Myth.* 1950; reprinted, Cambridge, MA: Harvard University Press, 2007.

Smith, Justin H. *The War with Mexico.* New York: Macmillan, 1919.

Smith, Linda Tuhiwai. *Decolonizing Methodologies: Research and Indigenous Peoples.* New York: Zed Books, 1999.

Smith-Rosenberg, Carroll. *Disorderly Conduct: Visions of Gender in Victorian America.* New York: Oxford University Press, 1986.

Sobel, Richard. "The Polls—A Report: Public Opinion about United States Intervention in El Salvador and Nicaragua." *Public Opinion Quarterly* 53, 1 (1989): 114–28.

Speck, Ernest B., ed. *Mody Boatright, Folklorist.* Austin: Texas Folklore Society, 1973.

Spivak, Gayatri Chakravorty. *Nationalism and the Imagination.* New York: Seagull Books, 2010.

Spurr, David. *The Rhetoric of Empire: Colonial Discourse in Journalism, Travel Writing, and Imperial Administration.* Durham: Duke University Press, 1993.

Stephanson, Anders. *Manifest Destiny: American Expansion and the Empire of Right.* New York: Hill and Wang, 1996.

Stevens, Louis. *Here Comes Pancho Villa: The Anecdotal History of a Genial Killer.* New York: Frederick A. Stokes, 1930.

St. John, Allen. *The Billion Dollar Game: Behind the Scenes of the Greatest Day in American Sport—Super Bowl Sunday.* New York: Doubleday, 2009.

Stoeltje, Beverly J. "Making the Frontier Myth in Modern Nation." *Western Folklore* 46, 4 (1987): 235–53.

Stout, Joseph A., Jr. *Border Conflict: Villistas, Carrancistas, and the Punitive Expedition, 1915–1920.* Houston: Texas Christian University Press, 1999.

Studlar, Gaylyn, and David Desser. "Never Having to Say You're Sorry: *Rambo's* Rewriting the Vietnam War." In Dittmar and Michaud, *From Hanoi to Hollywood,* 101–12.

Takacs, Stacy. "The Contemporary Politics of the Western Form: Bush, *Saving Jessica Lynch,* and *Deadwood.*" In Birkenstein, Froula, and Randell, *Reframing 9/11,* 153–63.

Thompson, E. P. *The Making of the English Working Class.* New York: Vintage, 1966.

Tirman, John. *The Deaths of Others: The Fate of Civilians in America's Wars.* New York: Oxford University Press, 2011.

Topik, Steven C., and Allen Wells. *The Second Conquest of Latin America: Coffee, Henequen, and Oil during the Export Boom, 1850–1930.* Austin: University of Texas Press, 1998.

Travers, Peter. "*Avatar.*" *Rolling Stone,* December 14, 2009.

Tremblay, Rodrigue. *The New American Empire: Causes and Consequences for the United States and for the World.* Concord, MA: Infinity, 2004.

Turner, Frederick Jackson. *Frontier and Section: Selected Essays of Frederick Jackson Turner.* New York: Prentice-Hall, 1961.

Turner, Timothy. *Bullets, Bottles, and Gardenias.* Dallas: South-West Press, 1935.

Twain, Mark. *The Adventures of Huckleberry Finn.* 1885; reprinted, New York: Knopf, Premier Classics, 2006.

van der Kolk, Bessel A. "The Compulsion to Repetition, Re-Enactment, Revictimization, and Masochism." *Psychiatric Clinics of North America* 12, 2 (1989): 389–411.

Veeser, Cyrus. *A World Safe for Capitalism: Dollar Diplomacy and America's Rise to Global Power.* New York: Columbia University Press, 2007.

Veracini, Lorenzo. "*District 9* and *Avatar*: Science Fiction and Settler Colonialism." *Journal of Intercultural Studies* 32, 4 (2011): 355–67.

Vidal, Gore. *Perpetual War for Perpetual Peace: How We Got to Be So Hated, Causes of Conflict in the Last Empire.* New York: Clairview Books, 2002.

Walker, Janet, ed. *Westerns: Films through History.* New York: Routledge, 2001.

Walker, Thomas W., and Christine J. Wade. *Nicaragua: Living in the Shadow of the Eagle.* Boulder, CO: Westview Press, 2011.

Walker, William. *The War in Nicaragua*. 1860; reprinted, Tucson: University of Arizona Press, 1985.

West, Mark, and Chris Carey. "(Re)Enacting Frontier Justice: The Bush Administration's Tactical Narration of the Old West Fantasy after September 11." *Quarterly Journal of Speech* 92, 4 (2006): 379–412.

Weston, Mary Ann. *Native Americans in the News: Images of Indians in the Twentieth Century Press*. Westport, CT: Greenwood Press, 1996.

Wetmore, Kevin J. *Post-9/11 Horror in American Cinema*. New York: Continuum, 2012.

White, Richard. *"It's Your Misfortune and None of My Own": A New History of the American West*. Norman: University of Oklahoma Press, 1991.

Whitfield, Teresa. *Paying the Price: Ignacio Ellacuria and the Murdered Jesuits of El Salvador*. Philadelphia: Temple University Press, 1994.

Will, Barbara. "The Nervous Origins of the American Western." *American Literature* 70, 2 (1998): 293–316.

Williams, William Appleman. *The Contours of American History*. Chicago: Quadrangle Books, 1955.

———. *Empire as a Way of Life*. New York: Ig Publishing, 2007.

Wills, Garry. "America's Nastiest Blood Feud." *New York Review of Books*, May 24, 2012.

———. *John Wayne's America: The Politics of Celebrity*. New York: Simon and Schuster, 1998.

———. "John Wayne's Body." *New Yorker*, August 19, 1995.

Wilson, Woodrow. *Congressional Government: A Study in American Politics*. 1885; reprinted, New York: Dover Books, 2006.

———. *A History of the American People*. 1902; reprinted, Ithaca, NY: Cornell University Press, 2009.

———. *The State: Elements of Historical and Practical Politics*. 1889; reprinted, London: Forgotten Books, 2010.

Wister, Owen. *The Virginian*. 1902; reprinted, New York: Oxford University Press, 1998.

Wood, Amy Louise. *Lynching and Spectacle: Witnessing Racial Violence in America, 1890–1940*. Chapel Hill: University of North Carolina Press, 2011.

Woodward, Bob. *Plan of Attack: The Definitive Account of the Decision to Invade Iraq*. New York: Simon and Schuster, 2004.

Wright, Benjamin F. "American Democracy and the Frontier." *Yale Review* (December 1920): 320–65.

Yoshitani, Gail E. S. *Reagan on War: A Reappraisal of the Weinberger Doctrine, 1980–1984*. Houston: Texas A&M Press, 2012.

VISUAL RESOURCES

9/11: The Filmmaker's Commemorative Edition. Directed by Jules Naudet, 2002.

Avatar. Directed by James Cameron, 2009.

The Big Lebowski. Directed by Joel Coen, 1998.

Dances with Wolves. Directed by Kevin Costner, 1990.

Far and Away. Directed by Ron Howard, 1992.

Full Metal Jacket. Directed by Stanley Kubrick, 1987.

The Green Berets. Directed by John Wayne, 1968.

The Man Who Shot Liberty Valance. Directed by John Ford, 1962.

The Pervert's Guide to Ideology. Directed by Sophie Fiennes, 2013.

Rambo, First Blood. Directed by Ted Kotcheff, 1982.

Rambo: First Blood, Part Two. Directed by George Cosmatos, 1985.

Rambo III. Directed by Peter MacDonald, 1988.

Red River. Directed by Howard Hawks, 1948.

Shane. Directed by George Stevens, 1953.

The Walking Dead. Television series created by Frank Darabont, 2010.

INDEX

Adams, Kevin, 79

Afghanistan war, 2, 11, 32, 166–68, 170, 194, 199, 206

agenda-setting, by American press, 42, 44, 97, 140, 176

Alger, Horatio, 67

Alien, 19

Allen, L.L., 52

Altheide, David, 42

America: as chosen people, 2–3, 23, 25, 31, 45, 67, 127, 181, 187, 191–92, 203; as cowboy nation, 26–27, 147, 151; creation story of, 2, 12, 18, 27, 54, 67, 87, 89, 166, 172, 178–79, 184, 197, 200; frontier myth of, 5, 12, 18, 24–25, 28, 198, 200, 203. *See also* frontier myth; frontier war; manifest destiny; Monroe Doctrine

American exceptionalism, 3–4, 22–25, 67, 75, 178, 187–88, 190, 198, 211. *See also* manifest destiny; Puritan religious views

American expansionism, 10, 21, 31–33, 69, 81, 94, 147, 223

American Foundation Myth in Vietnam, The, 151

American imperialism, 9–10, 21, 31–32, 38–39, 69, 86–87, 98, 127–28, 132, 135, 140, 147; and manifest destiny, 22, 32, 38, 94, 97, 119, 126, 127, 185, 192, 195, 210

American isolationism, 10, 14, 95, 130

American press: coverage of U.S. in Nicaragua, 126–27, 129, 133–147; coverage on Indians, 52, 67, 71–73, 75–77, 80–81, 83, 89, 125–26, 129, 134; on Mexican Revolution, 94–119; on Mexican War, 40–58, 60, 65, 71, 80, 97, 99, 120, 146; portrayal of Augusto Sandino, 132, 134–36, 138, 141–46; portrayal of Francisco Villa, 96–98, 107–15, 117, 119–20; portrayal of George Custer, 32, 65–66, 78–79, 84, 86, 99; portrayal of Mexicans, 57, 98–101, 104, 107, 113–14, 117. *See also* agenda-setting

American Revolution, 9, 11, 13, 39, 180, 190, 212

Anderson, Benedict, 4–5, 8, 28

Anton, Frank, 162

Apache Indians, 3, 113

Apocalypse Now, 153

Arapaho Indians, 70, 72, 199

Argo, 154

Asma, Stephen T., 79, 215

Associated Press, 8, 43

Autry, Gene, 217, 219–20; cowboy code of, 216

Avatar, 7, 19, 26, 155, 163, 203, 205, 207–9, 211; as frontier film, 210, 212

44, 47–48; in Nicaragua, 126, 198; in Vietnam, 151. *See also* frontier myth; manifest destiny; myth; western genre

Frost, Laura, 214

Full Metal Jacket, 10, 151, 153

Ghost Dance, 121–25

Giroux, Henry A., 214–15

Gobat, Michel, 132

Goldwater, Barry, 178

Good Neighbor Policy, 10, 146. *See also* Roosevelt, President Franklin D.

Goodman, John, 63

Grandin, Greg, 10, 14, 130, 197, 203

Grant, President Ulysses S., 70

Greeley, Horace, 44, 54

Green Berets, The, 150, 153

Grossman, Richard, 8

Gulf of Tonkin. *See* Tonkin, Gulf of

Gulf Wars, 11, 14, 27

gunboat diplomacy, 10, 132

Haig, Alexander, 183

Harper's magazine, 134; coverage of U.S. in Nicaragua, 127; portrayal of Central American countries, 137; portrayal of Latin America, 147

Harrelson, Woody, 213–15

Hawks, Howard, 58

Hearst, William Randolph, 101, 110

Hellman, John, 6

Henderson, Timothy J., 37, 61

Hendon, Bill, 162

High Noon, 157

Hitler, Adolf, 155, 184

Hobsbawm, Eric, 200

homosocialism: and George Custer, 79; and *Rambo* movies, 155, 161, 167, 170

Hoover, President Herbert, 138, 145–46

Horror after 9/11, 214

Houston, Sam, 37

Howard, Ron, 212

Huddleston, David, 64

Huerta, Victoriano, 96, 101, 107, 109, 111

Hughes, Richard T., 23, 31, 201

Hussein, Saddam, 3, 201

Indian wars, 3, 10, 66–68, 89, 125, 147, 151, 180; as against "cowboys," 26–27; as defensive, 26, 50–53, 70, 76, 80, 82; end of, 121–22; long history of, 4, 9, 13; as portrayed in press, 77, 89, 123–24, 134, 142; role in America's creation story, 2, 4, 7, 9, 12, 32, 69, 197, 200

Indians: as averse to civilization, 16, 26, 37, 50, 57, 67, 70, 107–8, 137, 143–44; portrayed as devils, 25, 72, 74, 81, 88–89; portrayed as in league with Satan, 20–21, 75, 182, 203–4; portrayed as savage, 2, 55, 59–60, 81–83, 90, 104, 117, 122, 125–26, 134, 154, 163, 175, 207; portrayed as scalpers, 71–76. *See also* Apache Indians; Arapaho Indians; Cheyenne Indians; Comanche Indians; Crow Indians; Indian wars; Lakota Sioux Indians; Mandan Indians; Pawnee Indians; Rees Indians; Shoshone Indians

Iran hostage crisis, 154, 175, 196

Iran-Contra affair, 175–76, 186, 196

Iraq wars, 2, 11, 14, 61, 151, 153, 201, 204, 206

Jackson, President Andrew, 16, 30, 42, 44

Shoshone Indians, 83

Sioux Indians. *See* Lakota Sioux Indians

Sitting Bull, Chief, 71–72, 80, 82, 83, 98

Slotkin, Richard, 5–7, 22, 203

Smith, Henry Nash, 5–6, 16, 24, 172

Smith, Justin H., 35

Smith, Paul Chaat, 149

Somoza Debayle, Anastasio, 133

Somoza Debayle, Luis, 133

Somoza family dynasty, 133, 140, 177

Somoza García, Anastasio, 133, 147

Spencer, Herbert, 131

Spivak, Gayatri Chakravorty, 121

Stallone, Sylvester, 154–55, 158, 161–62, 164, 167, 169, 171. *See also* *Rambo* movies

Star Wars initiative, 186

Star Wars trilogy, 19, 212

Stephanson, Anders, 3, 23, 127, 223

Stewart, Elizabeth A., 162

Stockdale, Admiral James, 162

Stoeltje, Beverly J., 5, 90, 186

Studlar, Gaylyn, 171

Taft, President William Howard, 21, 129, 131, 139

Takacs, Stacy, 4

Taken and *Taken 2*, 154

Taliban, 166, 176, 194

Tarzan of the Apes, 17, 79, 84–85, 88, 154, 204. *See also* Burroughs, Edgar Rice

Taylor, General Zachary, 44, 46, 54, 83, 213; portrayal of, 50–52, 57

Texan war of independence, 30, 38–40

Thatcher, Margaret, 190

Thompson, E.P., 223

Thoreau, Henry David, 41

Time magazine: on *Avatar*, 213; on Central America, 137; on manifest destiny, 127, 139; portrayal of Augusto Sandino, 132, 136, 144–45; portrayal of Nicaraguans, 145; portrayal of Ronald Reagan, 194; on U.S. occupation of Nicaragua, 133, 140–41, 143

Tirman, John, 154

Tonkin, Gulf of, 26; confrontation in, 151–52, 161, 165. *See also* Tonkin Resolution

Tonkin Resolution, 151–52, 165

trauma: and repetition, 7–10, 15, 23, 167–68, 202–3

Treaty of Guadalupe Hidalgo, 54

Tropic Thunder, 159

Trudeau, Prime Minister Pierre, 22

True Grit, 169

Turner, Frederick Jackson, 55, 58, 60, 180–81; and American exceptionalism, 22, 178, 187; and democracy, 16, 19–20, 22, 45, 223; as endorsing manifest destiny, American expansion, 21–24, 42, 80, 94, 119, 126, 147, 187, 204, 223; and the frontiersman, 17–18, 24, 58, 60, 79, 119, 154, 156, 213; and regeneration, 23, 66, 172; thesis of, 16–27, 36, 88, 94, 98, 104, 107, 119, 201, 204, 222

Ue, Tom, 213

United States of America. *See* America

U.S. Seventh Cavalry, 81, 84, 122, 124, 167. *See also* Custer, Colonel George Armstrong

Veracini, Lorenzo, 210, 211–212

Vietnam Syndrome, 152–53, 155, 157

Vietnam War, 4, 11, 14, 26, 61,
87, 153, 160, 179, 189, 193; and
captivity narratives, 162–63, 171,
181; as depicted in movies, 10, 19,
63, 151, 155, 209, 214; as frontier
conflict, 26–27, 32, 94, 147, 149–51,
161, 163; as similar to Mexican
War, 151–52; winning of in *Rambo*
movies, 149–73
Villa, Francisco "Pancho," 93, 147,
199; and Augusto Sandino, 142–43;
as modified frontiersman, 96–98,
108, 110, 112–13, 119; as portrayed
in press, 96–97, 107–15, 117,
119–20
Village Voice, 205, 216
*Virgin Land: The American West as
Symbol and Myth*, 5. *See also* Smith,
Henry Nash
Virginian, The, 17, 85, 109. *See also*
Wister, Owen

Walker, William, 130, 133–34
Walking Dead, The, 7, 19, 26–27, 171,
203–4, 215–23; Shane character in,
217, 220–21, 223. *See also* frontier
myth; zombie genre
war on terror, 3, 204, 206, 218
Washington, President George, 12, 14,
55, 95, 182, 189
Washington Star, 106
Wayne, John, 12, 19, 25, 58–60, 63, 78,
150, 153, 169, 204
weapons of mass destruction (WMD),
26, 200–201
Weaver, Sigourney, 210
West, Mark, 203, 224
western genre, 11, 85, 205, 215, 217;
and frontier myth, 2, 11, 19, 23, 47,
84, 144, 169, 205, 215, 223; and the

frontiersman, 18, 26, 63, 85, 112,
216–19. *See also* frontier myth;
manifest destiny; myth
Whig Party, 30, 36, 43, 54
White, Richard, 22
*Why Didn't You Get Me Out? A POW's
Nightmare in Vietnam*, 162
Williams, William Appleman, 9, 31,
41, 54, 93, 198, 202
Wills, Garry, 14, 19
Wilson, President Woodrow, 21–22,
34–35, 95, 97, 187; and Mexican
Revolution, 96, 104, 106–7, 109,
112–13, 129
Winthrop, John, 181, 195
Wister, Owen, 17, 85, 147
Worthington, Sam, 209
Wounded Knee, South Dakota, 13;
massacre at, 66, 68, 121–25. *See also*
Lakota Sioux Indians

Zaldana, Zoe, 211
Zelaya, José Santos, 130–32
Žižek, Slavoj, 211, 225
zombie genre, 7, 214–17, 220–22. *See
also* frontier myth; *Walking Dead, The*
Zombieland, 213

ABOUT THE AUTHOR

Dr. Mark Cronlund Anderson was born in Minneapolis, raised in Kenora, Ontario, and earned a Ph.D. in Latin American History from the University of California in 1995. His previous publications include: *Pancho Villa's Revolution by Headlines* (2001); *Cowboy Imperialism and Hollywood Film* (2007), which won the 2010 John G. Cawelti Award for the best book in American culture awarded by the Popular Culture Association and American Culture Association; and *Seeing Red: A History of Natives in Canadian Newspapers* (co-authored with Dr. Carmen Robertson), which won three 2011 Saskatchewan Book Awards, including best scholarly work. He currently teaches at Luther College, University of Regina, in Regina, Saskatchewan.